Taste of Home

BEST*LOVED
COOKIES
&BARS

Taste of Home
B O O K S

REIMAN MEDIA GROUP, INC. • GREENDALE, WISCONSIN

Taste of Home.

A TASTE OF HOME/READER'S DIGEST BOOK

Editor:	Faithann Stoner
Art Director:	Nicholas Mork
Project Art Director:	Jessie Sharon
Layout Designer:	Kathy Crawford
Proofreaders:	Vicki Jensen, Jean Duerst
Editorial Assistant:	Barb Czysz
Food Director:	Diane Werner RD
Recipe Testing and Editing:	Taste of Home Test Kitchen
Food Photography:	Reiman Photo Studio
Vice President, Executive Editor/Books:	Heidi Reuter Lloyd
Senior Editor, Retail/Direct Marketing Books:	Mark Hagen
Creative Director:	Ardyth Cope
Chief Marketing Officer:	Lisa Karpinski
Senior Vice President, Editor in Chief:	Catherine Cassidy
President, Consumer Marketing:	Dawn Zier
President, Food & Entertaining:	Suzanne M. Grimes
President and Chief Executive Officer:	Mary G. Berner

Pictured on front cover: Buttery Spritz Cookies (p. 79),
Vanilla Butter Rollouts (p. 117), Cherry Snowballs (p. 57) and Calypso Cups (p. 57).

International Standard Book Number (10): 0-89821-609-5
International Standard Book Number (13): 978-0-89821-609-7
Library of Congress Control Number: 2008925125

For other Taste of Home books and products, visit www.tasteofhome.com.
For more Reader's Digest products and information, visit
www.rd.com (in the United States)
www.rd.ca (in Canada)

Printed in China
1 3 5 7 9 10 8 6 4 2

You can create scrumptious memories at holiday time and any time you like with the 349 tempting recipes in this *Taste of Home Best-Loved Cookies & Bars* cookbook.

Sincere compliments will be coming your way from family and friends after you put them in a festive frame of mind by baking the cookies, bars and brownies you find here. Put the tasty creations on your holiday treat trays, in your bake-sale packages, on your potluck buffets and take them to all other occasions that require something sweet and special.

You can bake with confidence since these recipes all come from *Taste of Home*—America's #1 cooking magazine—and are best-loved treats shared by home cooks who rely on easy recipes that produce delicious results every time.

Find new favorites here that are sure to garner satisfied smiles as folks savor every mouth-watering morsel!

DROP
cookies

SALTED PEANUT COOKIES
PAGE 11

CHOCOLATE MINT DREAMS
PAGE 21

TRIPLE-CHOCOLATE
BROWNIE COOKIES
PAGE 23

CHRISTMAS COOKIES IN A JAR

LORI DANIELS, BEVERLY, WEST VIRGINIA
With layers of vanilla chips, oats and dried cranberries, this cookie mix looks as good as it tastes! For a special gift, tuck a jar in a pretty basket with a wooden spoon, cookie sheet, kitchen timer and instructions.

- ⅓ **cup sugar**
- ⅓ **cup packed brown sugar**
- ¾ **cup all-purpose flour**
- ½ **teaspoon baking powder**
- ⅛ **teaspoon baking soda**
- ⅛ **teaspoon salt**
- 1 **cup quick-cooking oats**
- 1 **cup orange-flavored dried cranberries**
- 1 **cup vanilla *or* white chips**

ADDITIONAL INGREDIENTS
- ½ **cup butter, melted**
- 1 **egg**
- 1 **teaspoon vanilla extract**

- ❄ In a 1-qt. glass jar, layer the sugar a brown sugar, packing well between ea layer. Combine the flour, baking powd baking soda and salt; spoon into jar. T with oats, cranberries and chips. Cov and store in a cool dry place for up to months.

- ❄ **TO PREPARE COOKIES:** Pour cookie mix to a large mixing bowl; stir to combin Beat in butter, egg and vanilla. Cov and refrigerate for 30 minutes.

- ❄ Drop by tablespoonfuls 2 in. apart on ungreased baking sheets. Bake at 375° 8-10 minutes or until browned. Remove wire racks to cool. YIELD: 3 dozen.

FULL-OF-CHIPS COOKIES

DOLORES HARTFORD, TROY, PENNSYLVANIA
My mom created this recipe with my daughter. Mom would have these cookies ready for Karissa whenever sh came home from college.

- 1 **cup butter-flavored shortening**
- ¾ **cup sugar**
- ¾ **cup packed brown sugar**
- 2 **eggs**
- 1 **teaspoon vanilla extract**
- 2¼ **cups all-purpose flour**
- 1 **teaspoon baking soda**
- ¾ **teaspoon salt**
- ⅓ **cup *each* semisweet chocolate chips, peanut butter chips, butterscotch chips and vanilla *or* white chips**
- ⅓ **cup milk chocolate M&M's**
- ⅓ **cup Reese's pieces candy**

- ❄ In a large mixing bowl, cream shortenir and sugars. Add eggs, one at a tim beating well after each addition. Beat vanilla. Combine the flour, baking sod and salt; gradually add to creamed mi ture. Stir in chips and candy.

- ❄ Drop by rounded tablespoonfuls 2 i apart onto ungreased baking sheets. Ba at 375° for 7-9 minutes or until light browned around edges. Remove to wi racks to cool. YIELD: about 4 dozen.

CHRISTMAS COOKIES IN A JAR

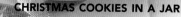

FROSTED GINGER CREAMS

ROSTED
INGER CREAMS

RLEY CLARK, COLUMBIA, MISSOURI

ave many recipes featuring ginger,
t these soft cookies are real gems.
e hint of lemon in the cream cheese
sting is a nice complement.

/4 **cup shortening**

/2 **cup sugar**

1 **egg**

/3 **cup molasses**

2 **cups all-purpose flour**

1 **teaspoon ground ginger**

/2 **teaspoon baking soda**

/2 **teaspoon salt**

/2 **teaspoon ground cinnamon**

/2 **teaspoon ground cloves**

/3 **cup water**

OSTING

/2 **ounces cream cheese, softened**

3 **tablespoons butter, softened**

1 **cup plus 3 tablespoons
   confectioners' sugar**

1/2 **teaspoon vanilla extract**

1 **to 2 teaspoons lemon juice**

✲ In a large mixing bowl, cream shortening
and sugar. Beat in egg and molasses.
Combine the flour, ginger, baking soda,
salt, cinnamon and cloves; gradually add
to creamed mixture alternately with water
(dough will be soft).

✲ Drop by heaping teaspoonfuls 2 in. apart
onto greased baking sheets. Bake at 400°
for 7-8 minutes or until tops are cracked.
Remove to wire racks to cool.

✲ In a small mixing bowl, beat the cream
cheese, butter and confectioners' sugar
until light and fluffy. Beat in vanilla and
enough lemon juice to achieve spreading consistency. Frost cookies. Store in the
refrigerator. YIELD: about 4 dozen.

MINTY MERINGUE DROPS

MINTY MERINGUE DROPS

KAREN WISSING, VASHON, WASHINGTON
These pretty mint green drops are dotted with chocolate chips. My kids don't consider it the Christmas season until I make them.

- 2 **egg whites**
- ¼ **teaspoon cream of tartar**
- ¾ **cup sugar**
- ⅛ **teaspoon vanilla extract**
- 2 **to 6 drops green food coloring, optional**
- 1 **package (10 ounces) mint chocolate chips**

❈ Lightly grease baking sheets or line with parchment paper; set aside.

❈ In a large mixing bowl, beat egg whites until foamy. Add cream of tartar, beating until soft peaks form. Gradually beat in sugar, 1 tablespoon at a time, until stiff peaks form. Beat in vanilla and food coloring if desired. Fold in the chocolate chips.

❈ Drop by rounded tablespoonfuls 2 in. apart onto prepared baking sheets. Bake at 250° for 30-35 minutes or until dry to the touch. Remove to wire racks to cool. Store in an airtight container. YIELD: about 2½ dozen.

EDITOR'S NOTE: If mint chocolate chips are not available, place 2 cups (12 ounces) semi-sweet chocolate chips and ¼ teaspoon peppermint extract in a plastic bag; seal and toss to coat. Allow chips to stand for 24-48 hours.

TOFFEE ALMOND SANDIES

VICKI CROWLEY, MONTICELLO, IOWA
I knew after sampling these cookies from a friend that I had to add the recipe to my bulging files!

- 1 **cup butter, softened**
- 1 **cup vegetable oil**
- 1 **cup sugar**
- 1 **cup confectioners' sugar**
- 2 **eggs**
- 1 **teaspoon almond extract**
- 4½ **cups all-purpose flour**
- 1 **teaspoon baking soda**
- 1 **teaspoon cream of tartar**
- 1 **teaspoon salt**
- 2 **cups sliced almonds**
- 1 **package English toffee bits (10 ounces) or almond brickle chip (7½ ounces)**

❈ In a mixing bowl, cream butter, oil a sugars. Add eggs, one at a time, beati well after each addition. Beat in extra Combine flour, baking soda, cream of t tar and salt; gradually add to the cream mixture. Stir in almonds and toffee bit:

❈ Drop by teaspoonfuls 2 in. apart on ungreased baking sheets. Bake at 350° 10-12 minutes or until golden brow Remove to wire racks to cool. YIELD dozen.

TOFFEE ALMOND SANDIES

RANBERRY MACAROONS

NE GUILBEAU, MELBOURNE, FLORIDA

doily-lined tray piled high with
ese cookies never fails to draw
clamations of admiration from all
o see them. Crunchy on the outside
d chewy on the inside, the cookies
ve a wonderful taste and texture.

- 4 **egg whites**
- 4 **teaspoon cream of tartar**
- 1 **teaspoon almond extract**
- 3 **cups sugar**
- 2 **drops red food coloring, optional**
- 1 **cup sliced almonds, chopped**
- 4 **cup flaked coconut**
- 2 **cup finely chopped dried cranberries**
- 3 **cups cornflakes, finely crushed**

In a large mixing bowl, beat the egg
whites, cream of tartar and almond extract on medium speed until soft peaks
form. Gradually beat in sugar, 2 tablespoons at a time, on high until stiff glossy
peaks form. Add food coloring if desired.
Fold in the almonds, coconut, cranberries
and cornflakes.

Drop by rounded teaspoonfuls 2 in. apart
onto well-greased baking sheets. Bake
at 325° for 20-22 minutes. Remove to wire
racks to cool. YIELD: about 4½ dozen.

EPPERMINT COOKIES

NNA LOCK, FORT COLLINS, COLORADO

ese drop cookies have a touch of
ppermint candy in every bite.
ey're so easy to make and taste so
od, that you should plan on making
re than one batch for the holidays.

- 3 **cup butter-flavored shortening**
- 4 **cup sugar**
- 1 **egg**
- 2 **cups all-purpose flour**
- 2 **teaspoon baking powder**
- 2 **teaspoon salt**
- 2 **cup crushed peppermint candies**

In a mixing bowl, cream shortening and
sugar; beat in egg. Combine flour, baking
powder and salt; stir into the creamed
mixture. Fold in the candy.

LACE COOKIES

❊ Drop by teaspoonfuls onto a greased baking sheet. Bake at 350° for 10-12 minutes or until cookie edges just begin to
brown. Remove to wire racks to cool.
YIELD: 3½ dozen.

LACE COOKIES

BONNIE THOMPSON, CAVE CITY, KENTUCKY

These delicate treats have big pecan
flavor. They're a terrific addition to any
holiday cookie tray or as a hostess gift.

- 1 **cup chopped pecans**
- 1 **cup sugar**
- ¼ **cup all-purpose flour**
- ¼ **teaspoon baking powder**
- ⅛ **teaspoon salt**
- 1 **egg**
- ½ **cup butter, melted**
- 1 **teaspoon vanilla extract**

Pecan halves

❊ Grind the pecans and sugar in a food
processor. Place in a bowl; add flour,
baking powder and salt. In another bowl,
beat egg; add butter and vanilla. Stir into flour mixture.

❊ Drop by teaspoonfuls about 3 in. apart
onto lightly greased foil-lined baking
sheets. Place a pecan half in the center
of each cookie.

❊ Bake at 325° for 8-10 minutes or until
golden brown and lacy. Allow cookies to
cool completely before carefully removing
from foil. YIELD: about 4½ dozen.

BEST✶LOVED
cookies
&BARS

don't overmix!

Avoid overmixing the dough. If it's handled too much, the cookies will be tough.

MOM'S SOFT RAISIN COOKIES

PEARL COCHENOUR, WILLIAMSPORT, OHIO

With four sons in service during World War II, my mother sent these favorite cookies as a taste from home to "her boys" in different parts of the world. These days, my grandchildren are enjoying them as we did.

- 1 cup water
- 2 cups raisins
- 1 cup shortening
- 1¾ cups sugar
- 2 eggs, lightly beaten
- 1 teaspoon vanilla extract
- 3½ cups all-purpose flour
- 1 teaspoon baking powder
- 1 teaspoon baking soda
- 1 teaspoon salt
- ½ teaspoon ground cinnamon
- ½ teaspoon ground nutmeg
- ½ cup chopped walnuts

❋ Combine raisins and water in a small saucepan; bring to a boil. Cook for 3 minutes; remove from the heat and let cool (do not drain).

❋ In a mixing bowl, cream shortening; gradually add sugar. Add eggs and vanilla. Combine dry ingredients; gradually add to creamed mixture and blend thoroughly. Stir in nuts and raisins.

❋ Drop by teaspoonfuls 2 in. apart onto greased baking sheets. Bake at 350° for 12-14 minutes. Remove to wire racks to cool. YIELD: 6 dozen.

MOM'S SOFT RAISIN COOKIES

PISTACHIO CRANBERRY COOKIES

ARLENE KROLL, VERO BEACH, FLORIDA

I came up with this recipe one year when looking for a cookie that had a little red and green in it. The combination of cranberries and pistachios is delicious.

- ½ cup butter, softened
- ½ cup vegetable oil
- ½ cup sugar
- ½ cup packed brown sugar
- 1 egg
- 1 teaspoon vanilla extract
- 1¾ cups all-purpose flour
- ½ teaspoon salt
- ½ teaspoon baking powder
- ½ teaspoon baking soda
- 1 cup crisp rice cereal
- ½ cup old-fashioned oats
- ½ cup dried cranberries
- ½ cup chopped pistachios

❋ In a large mixing bowl, cream the butter, oil and sugars. Beat in egg and vanilla. Combine the flour, salt, baking powder and baking soda; gradually add to the creamed mixture. Stir in the cereal, oats, cranberries and pistachios.

❋ Drop by tablespoonfuls 2 in. apart on ungreased baking sheets. Bake at 350° 10-12 minutes or until lightly browned. Remove to wire racks to cool. YIELD: dozen.

ROSEMARY HONEY COOKIES

AUDREY THIBODEAU, MESA, ARIZONA

You'll be delighted with this unusual cookie's wonderful flavor.

- ½ cup shortening
- ¼ cup butter, softened
- ¾ cup sugar
- 1 egg
- ¼ cup honey
- 1 tablespoon lemon juice
- 2 cups all-purpose flour

BEST LOVED
cookies & BARS

2 teaspoons dried rosemary, crushed
1 teaspoon baking soda
½ teaspoon salt
½ teaspoon ground cinnamon
¼ teaspoon ground nutmeg

In a mixing bowl, cream shortening, butter and sugar. Beat in egg, honey and lemon juice. Combine dry ingredients; add to creamed mixture.

Drop by teaspoonfuls 2 in. apart onto greased baking sheets. Bake at 325° for 12-14 minutes or until lightly browned. Remove to wire racks to cool. YIELD: about 4 dozen.

BLACK FOREST OATMEAL CRISPS

PAULA SMITH, NAPERVILLE, ILLINOIS

Although the recipe for my hearty chocolate-cherry novelties is sized right for a bake sale or cookie exchange, it can be cut in half for smaller gatherings.

1 cup butter-flavored shortening
1 cup sugar
1 cup packed brown sugar
2 eggs
2 tablespoons milk
1 teaspoon almond extract
3 cups all-purpose flour
1 teaspoon baking soda
¼ teaspoon salt
½ teaspoon baking powder
2 cups quick-cooking oats
6 squares (1 ounce *each*) white baking chocolate, chopped *or* 1 cup vanilla *or* white chips
½ cups chopped red candied cherries
1 cup (6 ounces) semisweet chocolate chips
¼ cup slivered almonds

In a mixing bowl, cream shortening and sugars. Add the eggs, one at a time, beating well after each addition. Beat in milk and extract. Combine flour, baking soda, salt and baking powder; gradually add to the creamed mixture. Stir in the remaining ingredients.

SALTED PEANUT COOKIES

❊ Drop by heaping teaspoonfuls 2 in. apart onto ungreased baking sheets. Bake at 375° for 8-10 minutes or until golden brown. Remove to wire racks to cool. YIELD: about 14 dozen.

SALTED PEANUT COOKIES

CHARLEEN BLOCK, HUTCHINSON, MINNESOTA
Instead of walnuts or pecans, this chocolate chip cookie recipe calls for salted peanuts. Whenever I bake these, friends and family come running!

1½ cups shortening
1 cup sugar
1 cup packed brown sugar
3 eggs
1 teaspoon vanilla extract
3¾ cups all-purpose flour
2 teaspoons baking soda
1 teaspoon salt
1½ cups semisweet chocolate chips
1½ cups salted peanuts

❊ In a large mixing bowl, cream shortening and sugars. Add eggs, one at a time, beating well after each addition. Beat in vanilla. Combine the flour, baking soda and salt; gradually add to creamed mixture. Stir in chocolate chips and peanuts.

❊ Drop by tablespoonfuls 2 in. apart onto greased baking sheets. Bake at 350° for 10-12 minutes or until lightly browned. Remove to wire racks to cool. YIELD: 10 dozen.

HOLIDAY GUMDROP COOKIES

LETAH CHILSTON, RIVERTON, WYOMING
Making these cookies, I feel I'm keeping my mother's Christmas spirit alive. They were her special treat each year at holiday time. These cookies are great for keeping children busy—they can cut up the gumdrops and eat all the black ones (they turn the dough gray).

1½ **cups spice gumdrops**
¾ **cup coarsely chopped walnuts**
½ **cup golden raisins**
1¾ **cups all-purpose flour,** *divided*
½ **cup shortening**
1 **cup packed brown sugar**
1 **egg**
¼ **cup buttermilk**
½ **teaspoon baking soda**
½ **teaspoon salt**

❉ Cut gumdrops into small pieces, reserv
black ones for another use. Place gu
drops in a bowl. Add walnuts, raisins a
¼ cup flour; toss to coat. Set aside.

❉ In a mixing bowl, cream shortening a
brown sugar. Add egg; beat in butterm
Combine baking soda, salt and remain
flour; stir into creamed mixture. Add gu
drop mixture and mix well. Chill fo
hour.

❉ Drop by rounded teaspoonfuls 2 in. ap
onto ungreased baking sheets. Bake
400° for 8-10 minutes. Cool for 2 m
utes before removing to a wire rack. YIE
about 3 dozen.

PUMPKIN DROP COOKIES

PRISCILLA ANDERSON, SALT LAKE CITY, UTAH

Packed with the flavors of Christmases past, these pumpkin drop cookies with creamy caramel frosting are simply scrumptious and as much a part of our holiday as mistletoe and carols! They are a great way to use our home-canned pumpkin.

- 1 **cup butter, softened**
- 1/2 **cup sugar**
- 1/2 **cup packed brown sugar**
- 1 **egg**
- 1 **cup canned pumpkin**
- 2 **teaspoons vanilla extract**
- 2 **cups all-purpose flour**
- 1 **teaspoon baking powder**
- 1 **teaspoon baking soda**
- 1 **teaspoon ground cinnamon**
- 1/2 **teaspoon salt**
- 3/4 **cup chopped pecans**

PENUCHE FROSTING

- 3 **tablespoons brown sugar**
- 2 **tablespoons butter**
- 3 **tablespoons milk**
- 3/4 **to 2 cups confectioners' sugar**

In a large mixing bowl, cream butter and sugars. Beat in egg. Add pumpkin and vanilla. Combine the flour, baking powder, baking soda, cinnamon and salt; gradually add to the creamed mixture. Stir in pecans.

Drop by rounded teaspoonfuls 2 in. apart onto ungreased baking sheets. Bake at 350° for 11-13 minutes or until edges are lightly browned. Remove to wire racks to cool.

For frosting, in a small saucepan, bring brown sugar and butter to a boil. Cook and stir over medium heat for 1 minute. Remove from the heat; cool for 10 minutes. Transfer to a large mixing bowl; beat in milk. Beat in enough confectioners' sugar to achieve spreading consistency. Frost cookies. YIELD: about 5 dozen.

SOFT LEMON-GINGER COOKIES

SHARON BRETZ, HAVRE DE GRACE, MARYLAND

You can't beat the tangy combination of lemon and ginger in these distinctive cookies. I often get requests for this recipe.

- 1/2 **cup butter, softened**
- 1 **cup packed brown sugar**
- 1 **egg**
- 3 **tablespoons sour cream**
- 1/2 **teaspoon lemon extract**
- 1/2 **teaspoon vanilla extract**
- 1 3/4 **cups all-purpose flour**
- 1 **teaspoon baking soda**
- 1 **teaspoon cream of tartar**
- 1 **teaspoon ground ginger**
- 1/4 **teaspoon salt**

❄ In a small mixing bowl, cream butter and brown sugar. Beat in the egg, sour cream and extracts. Combine the flour, baking soda, cream of tartar, ginger and salt; gradually beat into creamed mixture.

❄ Drop by rounded teaspoonfuls 2 in. apart onto ungreased baking sheets. Bake at 350° for 10-12 minutes or until lightly browned. Immediately remove from pans to wire racks. YIELD: 2 dozen.

SOFT LEMON-GINGER COOKIES

best pans for baking

Use heavy-gauge dull aluminum baking sheets with one or two low sides. When a recipe calls for greased baking sheets, use shortening or nonstick cooking spray. Dark finishes may cause the cookies to become overly browned.

BEST☀LOVED
cookies
&BARS

make cookies uniform size

For even baking, make cookies the same size and thickness unless the recipe states otherwise. Place cookie dough 2 to 3 in. apart on a cool baking sheet.

FROSTED CASHEW COOKIES

FROSTED CASHEW COOKIES

SHEILA WYUM, RUTLAND, NORTH DAKOTA
It was my sister's sister-in-law who discovered this recipe. We enjoy the cookies at Christmas, but they're rich and elegant for a special coffee and can be tucked in a lunch box besides. Years ago, I entered them at our country fair. They won a blue ribbon and were named grand champion.

  ½ **cup butter, softened**
  1 **cup packed brown sugar**
  1 **egg**
  ⅓ **cup sour cream**
  ½ **teaspoon vanilla extract**
  2 **cups all-purpose flour**
  ¾ **teaspoon** *each* **baking powder, baking soda and salt**
1¾ **cups salted cashew halves**

BROWNED BUTTER FROSTING
  ½ **cup butter**
  3 **tablespoons half-and-half cream**
  ¼ **teaspoon vanilla extract**
  2 **cups confectioners' sugar**
Additional cashew halves, optional

❋ In a mixing bowl, cream the butter and brown sugar. Beat in egg, sour cream and vanilla; mix well. Combine dry ingredients;

add to creamed mixture and mix w● Fold in the cashews.

❋ Drop by rounded teaspoonfuls or greased baking sheets. Bake at 375° 8-10 minutes or until lightly browne Remove to wire racks to cool.

❋ For the frosting, lightly brown butter i● small saucepan. Remove from the he● add cream and vanilla. Beat in confectio● ers' sugar until smooth and thick. Fr● cookies. Top each with a cashew half if ● sired. YIELD: about 3 dozen.

COOKIES IN A JIFFY

CLARA HIELKEMA, WYOMING, MICHIGAN
You'll be amazed and delighted with how quickly you can whip up a batch these homemade cookies.

  1 **package (9 ounces) yellow cake m●**
  ⅔ **cup quick-cooking oats**
  ½ **cup butter, melted**
  1 **egg**
  ½ **cup red and green Holiday M&M's** *or* **butterscotch chips**

❋ In a mixing bowl, beat the first four i● gredients. Stir in the M&M's or chip● Drop by tablespoonfuls 2 in. apart on● ungreased baking sheets.

❋ Bake at 375° for 10-12 minutes or un● lightly browned. Immediately remove wire racks to cool. YIELD: 2 dozen.

COOKIES IN A JIFFY

BEST♦LOVED
cookies
& BARS

MAPLE MACADAMIA NUT COOKIES

NDA POZZANGHERA
OCHESTER, NEW YORK

My son, Jason, and I had fun coming up with this cookie recipe. Every bite is packed with maple flavor, vanilla chips, milk chocolate chips and chopped macadamia nuts.

- ¼ cups butter, softened
- ½ cups confectioners' sugar
- 1 egg
- 2 tablespoons maple flavoring
- 1 teaspoon vanilla extract
- 2 cups all-purpose flour
- 1 teaspoon baking soda
- 1 teaspoon cream of tartar
- 2 cups quick-cooking oats
- ¾ cup vanilla chips or white chips
- ¾ cup milk chocolate chips
- ¾ cup chopped macadamia nuts

APLE ICING

- ½ cups confectioners' sugar
- ¼ cup heavy whipping cream
- 3 teaspoons maple flavoring
- 1 teaspoon vanilla extract
- ⅛ teaspoon salt

In a large mixing bowl, cream butter and confectioners' sugar. Beat in the egg, maple flavoring and vanilla. Combine the flour, baking soda and cream of tartar; gradually add to the creamed mixture. Stir in the oats, chips and nuts.

Drop by heaping teaspoonfuls 2 in. apart onto greased baking sheets. Bake at 350° for 10-12 minutes or until lightly browned. Remove to wire racks to cool.

In a bowl, combine icing ingredients until smooth; drizzle over cookies. Store in the refrigerator. YIELD: about 4½ dozen.

CHEWY GINGER DROP COOKIES

CHEWY GINGER DROP COOKIES

LOIS FURCRON, COUDERSPORT, PENNSYLVANIA
This recipe originated with my grandmother. My mom, an excellent baker, also made these cookies. Then I baked them for my family...my daughters made them...and now my granddaughters are making them—a true legacy I'm happy to share.

- ½ cup shortening
- ½ cup sugar
- 2 cups all-purpose flour
- ½ teaspoon baking soda
- ½ teaspoon ground ginger
- ¼ teaspoon salt
- ½ cup molasses
- ¼ cup water

Additional sugar

❈ In a mixing bowl, cream shortening and sugar. Combine flour, baking soda, ginger and salt. Combine molasses and water. Add dry ingredients to the creamed mixture alternately with molasses mixture.

❈ Drop by rounded teaspoonfuls 2 in. apart onto greased baking sheets. Sprinkle with sugar. Bake at 350° for 13-15 minutes or until edges are set. Remove to wire racks to cool. YIELD: 2½ dozen.

stir it by hand!

If your mixer begins to strain because the cookie dough is too thick, use a wooden spoon to stir in the last of the flour or ingredients such as nuts, chips or dried fruit.

SOFT MINCEMEAT COOKIES

EVELYN WADEY, BLACKFALDS, ALBERTA

We call these "Santa's cookies" because they're what we put out for Santa instead of the usual decorated Christmas cutouts. These cookies remain a traditional part of my holiday baking. Besides a plate for Santa, they fill gift plates for family and friends.

- ¼ cup butter, softened
- ¾ cup packed brown sugar
- 2 eggs
- ¾ cup mincemeat
- 1½ cups all-purpose flour
- 1½ teaspoons baking soda
- ½ teaspoon ground cinnamon
- ¼ teaspoon ground nutmeg
- ¼ teaspoon salt
- 1½ cups (9 ounces) semisweet chocolate chips
- ½ cup chopped walnuts, optional

❊ In a mixing bowl, cream the butter and brown sugar. Add eggs and mincemeat; mix well. Combine flour, baking soda, cinnamon, nutmeg and salt; add to the creamed mixture and mix well. Fold in chocolate chips and walnuts if desired.

❊ Drop by tablespoonfuls 2 in. apart onto greased baking sheets. Bake at 350° for 10-12 minutes or until golden brown. Remove to wire racks to cool. YIELD: about 4 dozen.

SOFT MINCEMEAT COOKIES

BUTTER WAFERS

EVELYN STARR, RAYMOND, WASHINGTON

These crisp drop cookies are great for folks who don't like their treats too sweet and who don't want to fuss with rolling out the dough.

- 1 cup butter, softened
- ⅓ cup confectioners' sugar
- 1 cup all-purpose flour
- ⅔ cup cornstarch

Colored sugar, optional

❊ In a mixing bowl, cream butter and confectioners' sugar. Combine flour and cornstarch; add to creamed mixture and mix well.

❊ Drop by rounded tablespoonfuls 3 in. apart onto ungreased baking sheet (cookies will spread). Sprinkle with colored sugar if desired.

❊ Bake at 325° for 12-15 minutes or until edges are lightly browned and tops are set. Cool for 2 minutes before carefully removing to wire racks. YIELD: about 2 dozen.

ALMOND CHOCOLATE COOKIES

SHARON KNIPE, FORT MADISON, IOWA

With crisp outsides and brownie-like insides, these cookies were a big hit when my 5-year-old son took a batch to share at preschool. In fact, kids of all ages love them.

- 1 cup butter, softened
- ¾ cup packed brown sugar
- ⅔ cup sugar
- ½ cup baking cocoa
- 2 to 3 teaspoons almond extract
- 1 teaspoon vanilla extract
- 2 eggs
- 2¼ cups all-purpose flour
- 1 teaspoon baking soda

❊ In a mixing bowl, beat the butter, sugar, cocoa and extracts until creamy. Add eggs, one at a time, beating well after each addition. Combine the flour and baking soda; gradually add to the sugar mixture.

BEST LOVED
cookies
& BARS

Drop by rounded teaspoonfuls 2 in. apart onto ungreased baking sheets. Bake at 375° for 7-9 minutes or until edges are firm. Remove to wire racks to cool. YIELD: 6½ dozen.

ANDIED FRUIT COOKIES

ORENCE MONSON, DENVER, COLORADO

nese no-fuss drop cookies are both utty and fruity, so they're always a hit holiday time.

- ½ cup butter, softened
- ¾ cup sugar
- 1 egg
- ¼ cups all-purpose flour
- ½ teaspoon baking soda
- ½ teaspoon salt
- ½ teaspoon ground cinnamon
- ½ cups pitted dates, chopped
- ½ cup *each* chopped candied cherries and pineapple
- ¾ cup coarsely chopped Brazil nuts, toasted
- ¾ cup chopped almonds, toasted

In a mixing bowl, cream butter and sugar. Add egg; mix well. Combine flour, baking soda, salt and cinnamon; gradually add to the creamed mixture and mix well. Fold in fruits and nuts.

Drop by teaspoonfuls 2 in. apart onto greased baking sheets. Bake at 375° for 8-10 minutes or until lightly browned. Remove to wire racks to cool. YIELD: 7 dozen.

ANILLA CHIP MAPLE COOKIES

EBRA HOGENSON, BREWSTER, MINNESOTA

ince my husband farms, I try to have mple meals and snacks available, as I ever know when he and his father will ome in from the fields. These cookies ave a distinct maple flavor and stay noist and soft, although they're never my cookie jar for long!

- 1 cup shortening
- ½ cup butter, softened
- 2 cups packed brown sugar

VANILLA CHIP MAPLE COOKIES

- 2 eggs
- 1 teaspoon vanilla extract
- 1 teaspoon maple flavoring
- 3 cups all-purpose flour
- 2 teaspoons baking soda
- 2 cups vanilla *or* white chips
- ½ cup chopped pecans

FROSTING

- ¼ cup butter, softened
- 4 cups confectioners' sugar
- 1 teaspoon maple flavoring
- 4 to 6 tablespoons milk
- 3½ cups pecan halves

✳ In a mixing bowl, cream the shortening, butter and brown sugar. Add eggs, one at a time, beating well after each addition. Beat in vanilla and maple flavoring. Combine the flour and baking soda; gradually add to creamed mixture. Stir in vanilla chips and pecans.

✳ Drop by rounded tablespoonfuls 2 in. apart onto ungreased baking sheets. Bake at 350° for 8-10 minutes or until golden brown. Cool for 2 minutes before removing to wire racks.

✳ In a mixing bowl, cream butter and confectioners' sugar. Beat in maple flavoring and enough milk to achieve spreading consistency. Frost cooled cookies. Top each with a pecan half. YIELD: 7 dozen.

baking cookies

Leave at least 2 in. around the baking sheet and the oven walls for good heat circulation. For best results, bake only one sheet of cookies at a time. If you need to bake two sheets at once, switch the position of the baking sheets about halfway through the baking time.

BEST✳LOVED
cookies
&BARS

check cookies for doneness

Check the cookies when the minimum baking time has been reached, baking longer if needed. Follow the doneness tests given in the individual recipe.

ITALIAN CHRISTMAS COOKIES

DORIS MARSHALL, STRASBURG, PENNSYLVANIA

A single batch of these mouth-watering cookies is never enough. I usually make one to give away and two more to keep at home. Adding ricotta cheese to the batter makes the morsels extra moist.

- 1 cup butter, softened
- 2 cups sugar
- 3 eggs
- 1 carton (15 ounces) ricotta cheese
- 2 teaspoons vanilla extract
- 4 cups all-purpose flour
- 1 teaspoon salt
- 1 teaspoon baking soda

FROSTING
- ¼ cup butter, softened
- 3 to 4 cups confectioners' sugar
- ½ teaspoon vanilla extract
- 3 to 4 tablespoons milk

Colored sprinkles

❋ In a mixing bowl, cream butter and suar. Add the eggs, one at a time, beatin well after each addition. Beat in ricot and vanilla. Combine flour, salt and baing soda; gradually add to the cream mixture.

❋ Drop by rounded teaspoonfuls 2 in. apa onto greased baking sheets. Bake at 35 for 10-12 minutes or until lightly browne Remove to wire racks to cool.

❋ In a mixing bowl, cream butter, sug and vanilla. Add enough milk until fros ing reaches spreading consistency. Fro cooled cookies and immediately decora with sprinkles. Store in the refrigerato YIELD: 8½ dozen.

ITALIAN CHRISTMAS COOKIES

ROSTED GINGERBREAD
UT COOKIES

RYN ROGERS, HEMET, CALIFORNIA
eceived the recipe for these soft
nger cookies from a dear lady, who
s since passed away. A comforting
ssic like this always satisfies.

- √2 **cup butter, softened**
- ⁄3 **cup sugar**
- 1 **egg**
- √2 **cup molasses**
- ⁄4 **cups all-purpose flour**
- 1 **teaspoon baking soda**
- 1 **teaspoon ground cinnamon**
- 1 **teaspoon ground ginger**
- √2 **teaspoon salt**
- ⁄4 **teaspoon ground cloves**
- √2 **cup buttermilk**
- √2 **cup chopped walnuts**

OSTING
- √2 **cups confectioners' sugar**
- √2 **teaspoons butter, softened**
- √2 **teaspoon vanilla extract**
- 2 **to 3 tablespoons half-and-half cream**

alnuts halves, optional

In a large mixing bowl, cream butter and sugar. Beat in the egg and molasses. Combine the flour, baking soda, cinnamon, ginger, salt and cloves; add to creamed mixture alternately with buttermilk. Stir in chopped walnuts.

Drop by tablespoonfuls 2 in. apart onto greased baking sheets. Bake at 350° for 10-12 minutes or until cookies spring back when lightly touched. Remove to wire racks to cool.

For frosting, in a small bowl, combine the confectioners' sugar, butter, vanilla and enough cream to achieve desired consistency. Frost cooled cookies. Top each with a walnut half if desired. YIELD: 5 dozen.

CRISP GRAHAM COOKIES

CRISP GRAHAM COOKIES

LORI DANIELS, BEVERLY, WEST VIRGINIA
I was delighted to find the recipe for these fun cookies. The peanut butter makes them extra special.

- ½ **cup butter-flavored shortening**
- ½ **cup packed brown sugar**
- 1 **egg**
- 1½ **teaspoons vanilla extract**
- 1 **can (14 ounces) sweetened condensed milk**
- 3 **tablespoons creamy peanut butter**
- 1½ **cups all-purpose flour**
- 1 **cup graham cracker crumbs**
- 1 **teaspoon baking soda**
- 1 **teaspoon salt**
- 2 **cups (1 pound) plain M&M's**
- ½ **cup chopped pecans**

❊ In a mixing bowl, cream shortening and brown sugar; beat in egg. Add vanilla and milk. Blend in peanut butter. Combine dry ingredients; add to the creamed mixture. Stir in the M&M's and nuts.

❊ Drop by teaspoonfuls 1 in. apart onto ungreased baking sheets. Bake at 350° for 10-12 minutes or until golden brown. Remove to wire racks to cool. YIELD: 7 dozen.

BEST☀LOVED
COOKIES
&BARS

ORANGE COOKIES

ORANGE COOKIES

DIANE MYERS, MERIDIAN, IDAHO
Dozens of these citrusy delights travel along with me to the school and church functions I attend during the holidays. The orange flavor is so refreshing.

- 1 **cup shortening**
- 1½ **cups sugar**
- 1 **cup buttermilk**
- 3 **eggs**
- ⅔ **cup orange juice**
- 4½ **teaspoons grated orange peel**
- 3 to 3½ **cups all-purpose flour**
- 1 **teaspoon baking soda**
- 1 **teaspoon baking powder**

ICING
- 4¼ **cups confectioners' sugar**
- ¼ **teaspoon orange extract**
- ⅓ to ½ **cup orange juice**

❈ In a mixing bowl, cream shortening and sugar. Add the buttermilk, eggs, orange juice and peel. Combine the dry ingredients; gradually add to creamed mixture.

❈ Drop by teaspoonfuls 2 in. apart onto ungreased baking sheets. Bake at 375° for 10 minutes or until lightly browned. Remove to wire racks to cool.

❈ For icing, combine the confectioners' sugar, orange extract and enough orange juice to achieve desired consistency. Spread over cooled cookies. YIELD: about 12 dozen.

TWO-MINUTE COOKIES

KERRY BOUCHARD, SHAWMUT, MONTANA
My mom used to pack these cookies into our school lunches. They're inexpensive and easy to prepare, so seven of us children learned to make them. Now they're also a favorite of my children.

- ½ **cup butter**
- ½ **cup milk**
- 2 **cups sugar**
- 3 **cups dry quick-cooking** or **rolled oats**
- 5 **tablespoons unsweetened cocoa**
- ½ **cup raisins, chopped nuts** or **coconut**

❈ In a large saucepan, heat butter, m and sugar. Bring to a boil, stirring occ sionally. Boil for 1 minute. Remove fro the heat.

❈ Stir in oats, cocoa and raisins, nuts or c conut. Drop by tablespoonsful on waxed paper. Cool. YIELD: about 3 doze

STRAWBERRY COOKIES

NANCY SHELTON, BOAZ, KENTUCKY
My family finds these fruity cookies to be a light treat in summer. But they enjoy them so much, I whip up a batc year-round. I sometimes use lemon cake mix in place of the strawberry.

- 1 **package (18¼ ounces) strawberry cake mix**
- 1 **egg, lightly beaten**
- 1 **carton (8 ounces) frozen whipped topping, thawed**
- 2 **cups confectioners' sugar**

❈ In a mixing bowl, combine the cake m egg and whipped topping until well co bined. Place confectioners' sugar in shallow dish.

❈ Drop dough by tablespoonfuls into sug turn to coat. Place 2 in. apart on greas baking sheets. Bake at 350° for 10- minutes or until lightly browned arou the edges. Remove to wire racks to co YIELD: about 5 dozen.

TUFFED DATE DROPS

RICE SCHWEITZER, SUN CITY, ARIZONA

my recipe collection, these chewy
op cookies with date-nut centers are
d under "E" for "extra-special."

- 2 pecans *or* walnut halves
- 4 pitted whole dates
- 2 tablespoons butter, softened
- 3 cup packed brown sugar
- 1 egg yolk
- 4 cup all-purpose flour
- 4 teaspoon baking powder
- 4 teaspoon baking soda
- 3 cup sour cream

OWN BUTTER FROSTING

- 2 tablespoons butter
- 4 cup confectioners' sugar
- 2 teaspoon vanilla extract
- 2 to 2 teaspoons milk

Cut pecan or walnut halves lengthwise;
stuff into dates and set aside. In a mixing
bowl, cream butter and brown sugar. Beat
in egg yolk. Combine flour, baking powder and baking soda; add to creamed
mixture alternately with sour cream. Stir in
stuffed dates.

Drop by tablespoonfuls, with one date
per cookie, onto greased baking sheets.
Bake at 375° for 7-9 minutes or until gold-
en brown. Remove to wire racks to cool.

In a saucepan, cook butter over medium
heat until golden brown, about 5 minutes.
Gradually stir in sugar, vanilla and milk.
Frost cookies. YIELD: 2 dozen.

HOCOLATE MINT REAMS

NE REVERS, OMAHA, NEBRASKA

ce chocolate-mint is my favorite
vor combination, I sometimes eat
ese dainty shortbread-like treats by
e dozen. But I manage to save some
company.

- 4 cup butter, softened
- 1 cup confectioners' sugar
- 2 squares (1 ounce *each*)
  unsweetened chocolate, melted
  and cooled
- ¼ teaspoon peppermint extract
- 1½ cups all-purpose flour
- 1 cup miniature semisweet chocolate
  chips

ICING

- 2 tablespoons butter, softened
- 1 cup confectioners' sugar
- 1 tablespoon milk
- ¼ teaspoon peppermint extract
- 1 to 2 drops green food coloring

DRIZZLE

- ½ cup semisweet chocolate chips
- ½ teaspoon shortening

✳ In a large mixing bowl, cream butter and
confectioners' sugar. Beat in chocolate
and mint extract. Gradually add flour.
Stir in chocolate chips (dough will be soft).

✳ Drop by tablespoonfuls 2 in. apart onto
ungreased baking sheets. Bake at 375° for
6-8 minutes or until firm. Cool for 2 minutes before removing to wire racks to cool
completely.

✳ Meanwhile, combine icing ingredients;
spread over cooled cookies. Let set. In a
microwave, melt chocolate chips and
shortening; stir until smooth. Drizzle over
cookies. YIELD: 4½ dozen.

CHOCOLATE MINT DREAMS

cooling cookies and sheets

Unless otherwise direct-
ed, let cookies cool for
1 minute on the baking
sheet before removing
to a wire rack. Cool
completely before stor-
ing. Let baking sheets
cool before placing the
next batch of cookie
dough on it. Other-
wise, the heat from the
baking sheet will soften
the dough and cause it
to spread.

shaping drop cookies

Fill a teaspoon or table-spoon with dough. Use another spoon or small rubber spatula to push the mound of dough off the spoon onto a cool baking sheet. Place dough 2 to 3 in. apart or as the recipe directs.

MOCHA FUDGE COOKIES

BERNIECE WALLACE, VAN METER, IOWA

These rich, soft cookies are convenient to make ahead. The dough and cookies freeze well. This is particularly helpful around the holidays. And the recipe yields such a large number!

- 2 **cups butter**
- 4 **cups (24 ounces) semisweet chocolate chips, _divided_**
- 3 **cups sugar**
- 1 **cup baking cocoa**
- 1 **tablespoon instant coffee granules**
- 3 **cups packed brown sugar**
- 8 **eggs, beaten**
- 3 **tablespoons vanilla extract**
- 8 **cups all-purpose flour**
- 2 **teaspoons baking powder**
- 1 **teaspoon salt**
- 1½ **cups chopped walnuts**

✣ In a Dutch oven over low heat, melt butter and 2 cups of chocolate chips. Remove from the heat and stir until smooth. Combine the sugar, cocoa and coffee; add to butter mixture. Stir in brown sugar. Stir in eggs and vanilla. Combine flour, baking powder and salt; gradually add to chocolate mixture. Stir in the walnuts and remaining chocolate chips.

MOCHA FUDGE COOKIES

✣ Drop by rounded teaspoonfuls 2 in. ap onto ungreased baking sheets. Bake 350° for 10-11 minutes or until edges set. Remove to wire racks to cool. YIE 18½ dozen.

SPONGE CAKE COOKIES

TERRY CARPENTER, VINELAND, NEW JERSEY

My heart's warmed by these cookies because the recipe comes from my grandmother. No wedding, shower c holiday gathering went by without o caring matriarch or her pretty little treats.

- 1 **cup butter, softened**
- 1½ **cups sugar**
- 8 **eggs**
- 2 **tablespoons lemon extract**
- 4 **cups all-purpose flour**
- ¼ **cup baking powder**

FROSTING

- ½ **cup butter, softened**
- 3¾ **cups confectioners' sugar**
- 1 **teaspoon lemon extract**
- ⅛ **teaspoon salt**
- 3 **to 4 tablespoons milk**

Food coloring, optional

- 4 **cups flaked coconut, optional**

✣ In a mixing bowl, cream butter and s ar. Add eggs, one at a time, beating v after each addition. Beat in the extra Combine flour and baking powder; gr ually add to the creamed mixture.

✣ Drop by teaspoonfuls 3 in. apart o ungreased baking sheets. Bake at 400° 6-8 minutes or until the edges are lig browned. Remove to wire racks to co

✣ In a mixing bowl, cream butter, sugar, tract and salt. Add enough milk to achi spreading consistency. Tint with food oring if desired. Frost cooled cooki Sprinkle with coconut if desired. YIE 11 dozen.

HOCOLATE CHIP UMPKIN COOKIES

IDI HARRINGTON, STEUBEN, MAINE

; a fun alternative to pumpkin pie, I ten make these easy drop cookies. e chocolate chips and harvest-fresh odness make them special enough r a holiday dessert.

- **4 cups all-purpose flour**
- **2 cups sugar**
- **2 teaspoons ground cinnamon**
- **2 teaspoons baking soda**
- **1 teaspoon salt**
- **1 can (16 ounces) solid-pack pumpkin**
- **1 cup vegetable oil**
- **2 eggs**
- **2 tablespoons milk**
- **2 teaspoons vanilla extract**
- **2 cups (12 ounces) semisweet chocolate chips**
- **1 cup chopped walnuts**

In a mixing bowl, combine flour, sugar, cinnamon, baking soda and salt. Add pumpkin, oil, eggs, milk and vanilla; beat on medium speed until well mixed. Stir in chocolate chips and nuts.

Drop by tablespoonfuls onto greased baking sheets. Bake at 375° for 13-14 minutes or until edges just begin to brown. Cool for 2 minutes; remove to a wire rack to cool completely. YIELD: about 7 dozen.

RIPLE-CHOCOLATE ROWNIE COOKIES

IDA ROBINSON, NEW BRAUNFELS, TEXAS

ur family of chocolate lovers gets ply excited when these cookies come it of the oven. They have the texture d taste of fudge brownies, and the ocolate chip-based drizzle make em look so tempting.

- **3/4 cup butter, cubed**
- **4 squares (1 ounce *each*) unsweetened chocolate**
- **2 cups sugar**
- **4 eggs**
- **1/2 cups all-purpose flour**

TRIPLE-CHOCOLATE BROWNIE COOKIES

- **1/2 cup baking cocoa**
- **2 teaspoons baking powder**
- **1/2 teaspoon salt**
- **2 cups (12 ounces) semisweet chocolate chips, *divided***
- **2 teaspoons shortening**

In a small saucepan over low heat, melt butter and unsweetened chocolate; cool. Transfer to a large mixing bowl; add sugar and eggs. Beat until smooth. Combine the flour, cocoa, baking powder and salt; gradually add to chocolate mixture. Stir in 1 1/2 cups chocolate chips. Cover and refrigerate for 2 hours or until dough is easy to handle.

Drop by tablespoonfuls 2 in. apart onto greased baking sheets. Bake at 350° for 7-9 minutes or until edges are set and tops are slightly cracked. Cool for 2 minutes before removing from pans to wire racks to cool completely.

In a microwave-safe bowl, heat shortening and remaining chocolate chips on high for 1 minute or until chips are melted; stir until smooth. Drizzle over cookies. Let stand for 30 minutes or until chocolate is set. Store in an airtight container. YIELD: 6 dozen.

FAMILY-FAVORITE OATMEAL COOKIES

FAMILY-FAVORITE OATMEAL COOKIES

VIRGINIA BODNER, SANDUSKY, OHIO

My mother got this recipe in about 1910 when she was a housekeeper and cook for the local physician. The doctor's wife was an excellent cook and taught my mother a lot of her cooking techniques. The cookies soon became a favorite in our home and now are a favorite with my children's families.

1 cup shortening
2 cups packed brown sugar
3 eggs
3 cups all-purpose flour
1 teaspoon salt
1 teaspoon baking powder
1 teaspoon baking soda
1 teaspoon ground cinnamon
1 cup buttermilk
2 cups rolled oats
1 cup raisins
1 cup chopped walnuts

❊ In a large mixing bowl, cream shortening and sugar. Add eggs, one at a time, mixing well after each addition. Combine flour, salt, baking powder, baking soda and c namon; add alternately with buttermilk the creamed mixture. Stir in oats, rais and nuts.

❊ Drop dough by heaping tablespoonf onto greased baking sheets. Bake at 3! for about 12 minutes or until ligh browned. Remove to wire racks to co YIELD: about 5 dozen.

CHOCOLATE MACADAMI NUT COOKIES

ARLIENE HILLINGER
RANCHO PALOS VERDES, CALIFORNIA

I've been hosting an annual Christma cookie exchange for over 35 years now. Each guest brings 6 dozen cookies to share. This recipe is always a favorite.

10 tablespoons butter, softened
3/4 cup packed brown sugar
1 teaspoon vanilla extract
1 egg, lightly beaten
1 cup all-purpose flour
3/4 teaspoon baking powder
1/8 teaspoon baking soda
1/8 teaspoon salt
1 1/2 cups semisweet chocolate chips
3/4 cup coarsely chopped macadamia nuts
3/4 cup coarsely chopped pecans

CARAMEL GLAZE
12 caramel candies
2 tablespoons heavy whipping crea

❊ In a mixing bowl, cream butter, sug and vanilla. Add egg. Combine flour, ba ing powder, baking soda and salt; add creamed mixture and mix well. Fold chocolate chips and nuts.

❊ Drop by teaspoonfuls 2 in. apart on greased baking sheets. Bake at 350° 10 to 12 minutes or until golden. Remo to wire racks to cool.

❊ For glaze, melt the caramels and cream a saucepan over low heat, stirring ur smooth. Drizzle over cooled cooki YIELD: 12 servings.

CHOCOLATE MARSHMALLOW COOKIES

JANE FORMANEK, BELLE PLAINE, IOWA

What fun! These double-chocolaty delights have a surprise inside! Atop the chocolate cookie base, marshmallow peeks out under chocolate icing. Kids love them!

1/2 cup butter, softened
1 cup sugar
1 egg
1/4 cup milk
1 teaspoon vanilla extract
1 3/4 cups all-purpose flour
1/3 cup baking cocoa
1/2 teaspoon baking soda
1/2 teaspoon salt
16 to 18 large marshmallows

ICING
6 tablespoons butter, softened
2 tablespoons baking cocoa
1/4 cup milk
1 3/4 cups confectioners' sugar
1/2 teaspoon vanilla extract
Pecan halves

✳ In a large mixing bowl, cream butter and sugar. Add egg, milk and vanilla; mix well. Combine the flour, cocoa, baking soda and salt; beat into creamed mixture.

✳ Drop by rounded teaspoonfuls onto ungreased baking sheets. Bake at 350° for 8 minutes. Meanwhile, cut marshmallows in half. Press a marshmallow half cut side down onto each cookie. Return to the oven for 2 minutes. Cool completely on a wire rack.

✳ For icing, in a small saucepan, combine butter, cocoa and milk . Bring to a boil; boil for 1 minute, stirring constantly. Cool slightly; transfer to a small mixing bowl. Beat in confectioners' sugar and vanilla until smooth. Spread over the cooled cookies. Top each with a pecan half. YIELD: about 3 dozen.

CHOCOLATE MARSHMALLOW COOKIES

keep cookies constant

For even baking, it's important that you make cookies the same size. Use a teaspoon or tablespoon from your flatware set or a small ice cream scoop.

COCONUT PECAN COOKIES

COCONUT PECAN COOKIES

DIANE SELICH, VASSAR, MICHIGAN

With chocolate chips and coconut in the batter and a yummy pecan-coconut frosting, these cookies will remind you of German chocolate cake. A drizzle of chocolate tops them off in a festive way.

- 1 **egg, lightly beaten**
- 1 **can (5 ounces) evaporated milk**
- ⅔ **cup sugar**
- ¼ **cup butter, cubed**
- 1¼ **cups flaked coconut**
- ½ **cup chopped pecans**

COOKIE DOUGH

- 1 **cup butter, softened**
- ¾ **cup sugar**
- ¾ **cup packed brown sugar**
- 2 **eggs**
- 1 **teaspoon vanilla extract**
- 2¼ **cups all-purpose flour**
- 1 **teaspoon baking soda**
- 1 **teaspoon salt**
- 4 **cups (24 ounces) semisweet chocolate chips,** *divided*
- ¼ **cup flaked coconut**

❋ For frosting, in a large saucepan, combine the egg, milk, sugar and butter. Cook and stir over medium-low heat for 10-12 minutes or until slightly thickened and mix-

ture reaches 160°. Stir in coconut a pecans. Set aside.

❋ In a large mixing bowl, cream butter a sugars. Add eggs, one at a time, beat well after each addition. Beat in van Combine the flour, baking soda and s gradually add to creamed mixture. Sti 2 cups chips and coconut.

❋ Drop by tablespoonfuls 2 in. apart o ungreased baking sheets. Bake at 350° 8-10 minutes or until lightly brown Cool for 10 minutes before removing wire racks to cool completely.

❋ In a microwave, melt the remain chocolate chips; stir until smooth. Fr cooled cookies; drizzle with mel chocolate. YIELD: 6½ dozen.

MICHIGAN CHERRY DROPS

CAROL BLUE, BARNESVILLE, PENNSYLVANIA

I usually double this recipe so that I have plenty to share during the holidays. Pretty pink cookies such as these are a wonderful treat.

- 1 **cup butter, softened**
- 1 **cup sugar**
- ½ **cup packed brown sugar**
- 4 **eggs**
- 1½ **teaspoons vanilla extract**
- 4 **cups all-purpose flour**
- 1 **teaspoon salt**
- 1 **teaspoon ground cinnamon**
- ½ **teaspoon ground nutmeg**
- 3½ **cups chopped walnuts**
- 3 **cups chopped maraschino cherrie**
- 2⅔ **cups raisins**

❋ In a large mixing bowl, cream the but and sugars. Add eggs, one at a tin beating well after each addition. Bea vanilla. Combine flour, salt, cinnamon a nutmeg; gradually add to the cream mixture. Transfer to a large bowl if n essary. Stir in walnuts, cherries and rais

❋ Drop by tablespoonfuls 2 in. apart or ungreased baking sheets. Bake at 350° 16-18 minutes or until lightly browne Remove to wire racks to cool. Store in airtight container. YIELD: about 14 doz

OFT GINGERSNAPS

ONNA LEE LEONARD
WER SACKVILLE, NOVA SCOTIA

ese soft, cake-like spice cookies are elightfully old-fashioned, which makes hard to believe they're low in fat. ey're still so full of flavor, though, no e guesses it's a lighter recipe.

- **½ cups all-purpose flour**
- **½ cup whole wheat flour**
- **2 teaspoons baking soda**
- **1 teaspoon ground cinnamon**
- **1 teaspoon ground cloves**
- **1 teaspoon ground ginger**
- **¼ teaspoon salt**
- **gg substitute equivalent to 2 eggs**
- **½ cup sugar**
- **¼ cup packed brown sugar**
- **¼ cup vegetable oil**
- **¼ cup molasses**

In a mixing bowl, combine flours, baking soda, cinnamon, cloves, ginger and salt. Combine the egg substitute, sugars, oil and molasses; mix well. Add to dry ingredients; mix well.

Drop by teaspoonfuls 2 in. apart onto baking sheets coating with nonstick cooking spray.

Bake at 350° for 8-10 minutes or until cookies spring back when lightly touched. Cool for 5 minutes; remove from pans to wire racks to cool completely. YIELD: 3 dozen.

CED CINNAMON CHIP COOKIES

ATIE JEAN BOYD, ROACHDALE, INDIANA

take these cookies to family atherings and socials and give them gifts to friends. The cinnamon flavor nd soft frosting make them special. ly mom helped me bake my first atch of cookies when I was 8. She's y role model.

- **1 cup butter, softened**
- **¾ cup packed brown sugar**
- **¾ cup sugar**
- **2 eggs**
- **1 teaspoon vanilla extract**
- **3 cups all-purpose flour**
- **1 teaspoon baking soda**
- **1 teaspoon salt**
- **1 package (10 ounces) cinnamon baking chips**

ICING

- **¼ cup butter, melted**
- **¼ cup shortening**
- **1¼ cups confectioners' sugar**
- **1 tablespoon milk**
- **¾ teaspoon vanilla extract**

In a large mixing bowl, cream butter and sugars. Beat in eggs and vanilla. Combine the flour, baking soda and salt; gradually add to creamed mixture and mix well. Fold in cinnamon chips.

Drop by rounded tablespoonfuls 2 in. apart onto ungreased baking sheets. Bake at 350° for 10-12 minutes or until golden brown. Remove to wire racks to cool.

In a small mixing bowl, combine icing ingredients; beat on high speed for 1-2 minutes or until fluffy. Spread over cookies. YIELD: 46 cookies.

ICED CINNAMON CHIP COOKIES

SUPER CHUNKY COOKIES

REBECCA JENDRY, SPRING BRANCH, TEXAS

Chocolate lovers will go crazy over these cookies—they have four kinds of chocolate! When friends ask me to make "those" cookies, I know they mean this recipe. One of these will keep you going until mealtime.

- ½ **cup butter-flavored shortening**
- ½ **cup butter, softened**
- 1 **cup packed brown sugar**
- ¾ **cup sugar**
- 2 **eggs**
- 2 **teaspoons vanilla extract**
- 2½ **cups all-purpose flour**
- 1 **teaspoon baking soda**
- ⅛ **teaspoon salt**
- 1 **cup miniature semisweet chocolate chips**
- 1 **cup milk chocolate chips**
- 1 **cup vanilla *or* white chips**
- 4 **squares (1 ounces *each*) bittersweet chocolate, coarsely chopped**
- ¾ **cup English toffee bits *or* almond brickle chips**
- ½ **cup chopped pecans**

❊ In a mixing bowl, cream shortening, butter and sugars. Add eggs, one at a time, beating well after each addition. Beat in vanilla. Combine flour, baking soda and salt; gradually add to the creamed mixture. Stir in the remaining ingredients.

❊ Drop by tablespoonfuls 3 in. apart onto ungreased baking sheets. Bake at 350° for 10-12 minutes or until lightly browned.

SUPER CHUNKY COOKIES

Cool for 2-3 minutes before removing wire racks to cool completely. YIELD: 8 dozen.

WHITE CHOCOLATE PUMPKIN DREAMS

JEAN KLECKNER, SEATTLE, WASHINGTON

If you like pumpkin pie, you'll love these delicious pumpkin cookies dotted with white chocolate chips and chopped pecans. Topped with a brown sugar frosting, they're irresistible.

- 1 **cup butter, softened**
- ½ **cup sugar**
- ½ **cup packed brown sugar**
- 1 **egg**
- 2 **teaspoons vanilla extract**
- 1 **cup canned pumpkin**
- 2 **cups all-purpose flour**
- 3½ **teaspoons pumpkin pie spice**
- 1 **teaspoon baking powder**
- 1 **teaspoon baking soda**
- ¼ **teaspoon salt**
- 1 **package (11 ounces) vanilla *or* white chips**
- 1 **cup chopped pecans**

BROWN SUGAR FROSTING

- ½ **cup packed brown sugar**
- 3 **tablespoons butter**
- ¼ **cup milk**
- 1½ **to 2 cups confectioners' sugar**

❊ In a mixing bowl, cream butter and sugars. Beat in egg, vanilla and pumpkin. Combine dry ingredients; gradually add to the creamed mixture. Stir in chips and pecans.

❊ Drop by rounded teaspoonfuls 2 in. apart onto ungreased baking sheets. Bake at 350° for 12-14 minutes or until firm. Remove to wire racks to cool.

❊ For frosting, combine brown sugar and butter in a saucepan. Bring to a boil; cook over medium heat for 1 minute or until slightly thickened. Cool for 10 minutes. Add milk; beat until smooth. Beat in enough confectioners' sugar to reach desired consistency. Frost cookies. YIELD: about 4½ dozen.

SOFT CHOCOLATE MINT COOKIES

JUSTIN VINCENT, OREM, UTAH

If you don't care for crisp cookies that crumble when you take a bite, give this soft variety a try. No one can resist the fudgy, minty flavor.

- 1/2 **cup butter**
- 3 **squares (1 ounce** *each***) unsweetened chocolate**
- 1/2 **cup sugar**
- 1/2 **cup packed brown sugar**
- 1 **egg**
- 1/4 **cup buttermilk**
- 1 **teaspoon peppermint extract**
- 1 3/4 **cups all-purpose flour**
- 1/2 **teaspoon baking powder**
- 1/4 **teaspoon baking soda**
- 1/4 **teaspoon salt**

In a microwave or heavy saucepan, melt butter and chocolate; stir until smooth. In a mixing bowl, beat sugars and egg; add buttermilk and peppermint extract. Beat in chocolate mixture.

Combine the flour, baking powder, baking soda and salt; gradually add to sugar mixture. Let stand for 15 minutes or until dough becomes firmer.

Drop by tablespoonfuls 3 in. apart onto ungreased baking sheets. Bake at 350° for 8-10 minutes or until edges are firm. Cool for 2 minutes before removing from pans to wire racks. YIELD: about 3 dozen.

FROSTED CRANBERRY DROP COOKIES

SHIRLEY KIDD, NEW LONDON, MINNESOTA

I started making these treats after tasting a batch my friend whipped up. I immediately requested the recipe and have been baking them by the dozens ever since. The frosting is an ideal complement to the tart berries in the cookies.

- 1/2 **cup butter, softened**
- 1 **cup sugar**
- 3/4 **cup packed brown sugar**

FROSTED CRANBERRY DROP COOKIES

- 1/4 **cup milk**
- 1 **egg**
- 2 **tablespoons orange juice**
- 3 **cups all-purpose flour**
- 1 **teaspoon baking powder**
- 1/2 **teaspoon salt**
- 1/4 **teaspoon baking soda**
- 2 1/2 **cups chopped fresh** *or* **frozen cranberries**
- 1 **cup chopped walnuts**

FROSTING

- 1/3 **cup butter**
- 2 **cups confectioners' sugar**
- 1 1/2 **teaspoons vanilla extract**
- 2 **to 4 tablespoons hot water**

❈ In a mixing bowl, cream butter and sugars. Add milk, egg and orange juice; mix well. Combine the flour, baking powder, salt and baking soda; add to the creamed mixture and mix well. Stir in cranberries and nuts.

❈ Drop by tablespoonfuls 2 in. apart onto greased baking sheets. Bake at 350° for 12-15 minutes or until golden brown. Remove to wire racks to cool.

❈ For frosting, heat the butter in a saucepan over low heat until golden brown, about 5 minutes. Cool for 2 minutes; transfer to a small mixing bowl. Add sugar and vanilla. Beat in water, 1 tablespoon at a time, until frosting reaches desired consistency. Frost the cookies. YIELD: 5 dozen.

flattening drop cookies

Drop cookies generally melt and spread during baking. But sometimes a recipe may instruct you to flatten the cookies with the bottom of a glass dipped in sugar or with a fork to make a crisscross pattern.

BEST❈LOVED
cookies
& BARS

using an ice cream scoop to make drop cookies

An ice cream scoop is the perfect utensil for making uniformly-sized drop cookies. (A tablespoon-size ice cream scoop will result in a standard-size 2-in. cookie.) Just scoop the dough, even off the top with a flat-edge metal spatula and release onto a baking sheet.

APPLE BUTTER COOKIES

DOROTHY HAWKINS, SPRINGHILL, FLORIDA

My mother used to bake these mouth-watering cookies for an after-school treat. Though it's been many, many years since I first found out about them, I still savor the aroma that fills the house as these cookies bake. They stay moist and fresh for a long time, or the dough can be stored in the refrigerator for several days so you can bake as you need them.

- ¼ cup butter, softened
- 1 cup packed brown sugar
- 1 egg
- ½ cup quick-cooking oats
- ½ cup apple butter
- 1 cup all-purpose flour
- ½ teaspoon baking soda
- ½ teaspoon baking powder
- ½ teaspoon salt
- 2 tablespoons milk
- ½ cup chopped nuts
- ½ cup raisins

✤ In a small mixing bowl, cream butter and sugar. Beat in egg, oats and apple butter. Combine dry ingredients; gradually add to creamed mixture along with the milk; beat until blended. Stir in nuts and raisins. Cover and refrigerate until easy to handle.

✤ Drop by teaspoonfuls onto lightly greased baking sheets. Bake at 350° for 15 minutes or until set. Remove to wire racks to cool. YIELD: about 2½ dozen.

APPLE BUTTER COOKIES

DROP FRUITCAKE COOKIES

BONNIE MILNER, DE RIDDER, LOUISIANA

For folks who like fruitcake in small doses, this is the mouth-watering answe

- 1 cup butter, softened
- 1½ cups sugar
- 2 eggs
- 2½ cups all-purpose flour
- 1 teaspoon baking soda
- 1 teaspoon ground cinnamon
- ½ teaspoon salt
- 2 cups chopped pecans
- 1 package (8 ounces) chopped date
- 8 ounces candied cherries, halved
- 8 ounces candied pineapple, diced

✤ In a mixing bowl, cream butter and su ar. Add eggs; mix well. Combine flo baking soda, cinnamon and salt; add creamed mixture and mix well. Fold pecans, dates and fruit.

✤ Drop by rounded teaspoonfuls on greased baking sheets. Bake at 325° f 13-15 minutes or until lightly browne Remove to wire racks to cool. YIELD: dozen.

DATE NUT MERINGUES

ANTOINETTE CAPELLI, WILLISTON, FLORIDA

It's always nice to make different recipes to enhance my Christmas cookie selection each year. These no-fuss chews are a good choice.

- 3 egg whites
- 1 cup sugar
- ½ teaspoon vanilla extract
- 1 package (8 ounces) chopped dates
- 1½ cups chopped pecans

✤ In a mixing bowl, beat egg whites un soft peaks form. Gradually add suga beat until stiff peaks form, 6 minutes. Be in vanilla. Fold in dates and pecans.

✤ Drop by rounded teaspoonfuls 2 in. apa onto lightly greased baking sheets. Ba at 325° for 12-15 minutes or until firm the touch. Remove to wire racks to coo Store in an airtight container. YIELD: dozen.

ℲERRY CHOCOLATE COOKIES

ℲERRY CHOCOLATE OOKIES

ℲI WILLIAMS, FORT WAYNE, INDIANA

ɔ one can resist the chewy texture of ɛse fudgy cookies. I always double ɛ recipe because they disappear ickly around our house.

- **⁄2 cups butter, softened**
- **4 cups sugar**
- **4 eggs**
- **4 teaspoons vanilla extract**
- **4 cups all-purpose flour**
- **⁄2 cups baking cocoa**
- **2 teaspoons baking soda**
- **1 teaspoon salt**
- **1 package (12 ounces) miniature semisweet chocolate chips**
- **1 jar (16 ounces) maraschino cherries, drained and halved**

In a large mixing bowl, cream butter and sugar. Add eggs, one at a time, beating well after each addition. Beat in vanilla. Combine the flour, cocoa, baking soda and salt; gradually add to creamed mixture. Stir in chocolate chips.

❄ Drop by heaping tablespoonfuls 3 in. apart onto ungreased baking sheets. Top each with a cherry half. Bake at 350° for 10-12 minutes or until edges are firm. Remove to wire racks to cool. YIELD: about 6½ dozen.

CHOCOLATE CLUSTERS

SARA ANN FOWLER, ILLINOIS CITY, ILLINOIS

No-bake cookies are so easy to do. These chocolaty treats are a cross between a cookie and candy.

- **2 pounds white chocolate *or* almond bark**
- **1 cup creamy *or* chunky peanut butter**
- **2 cups salted dry roasted peanuts**
- **3 cups pastel miniature marshmallows**
- **4 cups crisp rice cereal**

❄ Melt white chocolate and peanut butter in microwave or double boiler, stirring often to mix well. Add all remaining ingredients; stir with wooden spoon to coat evenly. Drop by teaspoonsful onto waxed paper. YIELD: 11 dozen.

**WHITE CHOCOLATE CHIP
HAZELNUT COOKIES**

WHITE CHOCOLATE CHIP HAZELNUT COOKIES

DENISE DEJONG, PITTSBURGH, PENNSYLVANIA
This is a cookie you will want to make again and again. I like to take it to church get-togethers and family reunions. It's very delicious...crispy on the outside and chewy on the inside.

1¼ **cups whole hazelnuts, toasted,** *divided*

9 **tablespoons butter, softened,** *divided*

½ **cup sugar**

½ **cup packed brown sugar**

1 **egg**

1 **teaspoon vanilla extract**

1½ **cups all-purpose flour**

½ **teaspoon baking soda**

½ **teaspoon salt**

1 **cup white** *or* **vanilla chips**

✳ Coarsely chop ½ cup hazelnuts; set aside. Melt 2 tablespoons butter. In a food processor, combine melted butter and remaining hazelnuts. Cover and process until the mixture forms a crumbly paste; set aside.

✳ In a mixing bowl, cream the remaining butter. Beat in the sugars. Add egg and vanilla; beat until light and fluffy. Beat in ground hazelnut mixture until blended.

Combine the flour, baking soda and s[alt;] add to batter and mix just until combin[ed.] Stir in chips and chopped hazelnuts.

✳ Drop by rounded tablespoonfuls 2 [in.] apart onto greased baking sheets. Ba[ke] at 350° for 10-12 minutes or until ligh[tly] browned. Remove to wire racks to co[ol.] YIELD: 3 dozen.

COCONUT MACAROONS

NANCY TAFOYA, FT. COLLINS, COLORADO
I keep the ingredients for these easy-to-make cookies in my pantry. That w[ay] I can have a freshly made batch in minutes.

2½ **cups flaked coconut**

⅓ **cup all-purpose flour**

⅛ **teaspoon salt**

⅔ **cup sweetened condensed milk**

1 **teaspoon vanilla extract**

✳ In a bowl, combine the coconut, flour a[nd] salt. Add milk and vanilla; mix well (b[at-]ter will be stiff).

✳ Drop by tablespoonfuls 1 in. apart o[n] a greased baking sheet. Bake at 350° [for] 15-20 minutes or until golden brow[n.] Remove to wire racks to cool. YIELD: 1[½] dozen.

COCONUT MACAROONS

EANUT OAT COOKIES

ACIA MCLIMORE, INDIANAPOLIS, INDIANA

n not surprised when people say
ese are the best cookies they've ever
d...I agree! Oats make them hearty
d more delicious than traditional
eanut butter cookies.

- /4 **cups butter-flavored shortening**
- /4 **cups chunky peanut butter**
- /2 **cups packed brown sugar**
- 1 **cup sugar**
- 3 **eggs**
- /2 **cups old-fashioned oats**
- 2 **teaspoons baking soda**
- 1 **package (11½ ounces) milk chocolate chips**
- 1 **cup chopped peanuts**

In a mixing bowl, cream shortening, peanut butter and sugars. Add eggs, one at a time, beating well after each addition. Combine oats and baking soda; gradually add to creamed mixture. Stir in chocolate chips and peanuts.

Drop by tablespoonfuls 2 in. apart onto greased baking sheets. Bake at 350° for 10-12 minutes or until golden brown. Remove to wire racks to cool. YIELD: about 8 dozen.

HERRY DATE COOKIES

OPE HUGGINS, SANTA CRUZ, CALIFORNIA

y mother made these festive drop
ookies as far back as I can
member—80 years at least. We
lled them "the Christmas cookies,"
aybe because they're so full of fruit
d nuts.

- 1 **cup shortening**
- /2 **cups packed brown sugar**
- 3 **eggs**
- /2 **cups all-purpose flour**
- 1 **teaspoon baking soda**
- 1 **teaspoon ground cinnamon**
- /2 **teaspoon salt**
- 3 **tablespoons hot water**
- 1 **cup chopped walnuts**
- /2 **cup chopped dates**
- /2 **cup quartered maraschino cherries**

CREAM CHEESE DELIGHTS

* In a mixing bowl, cream shortening and brown sugar. Add eggs, one at a time, beating well after each addition. Combine the flour, baking soda, cinnamon and salt; add to creamed mixture alternately with water. Stir in walnuts, dates and cherries.

* Drop by rounded teaspoonfuls 2 in. apart onto ungreased baking sheets. Bake at 375° for 8-9 minutes or until golden brown. Remove to wire racks to cool. YIELD: 10½ dozen.

CREAM CHEESE DELIGHTS

AGNES GOLIAN, GARFIELD HEIGHTS, OHIO

So festive-looking topped with cherry halves, these light, airy cookies are easy enough to make for any occasion or just for dessert.

- ½ **cup butter-flavored shortening**
- 1 **package (3 ounces) cream cheese, softened**
- ½ **cup sugar**
- 1 **egg yolk**
- 1 **teaspoon vanilla extract**
- 1 **cup all-purpose flour**
- 1 **teaspoon salt**

Halved maraschino cherries *or* **candied cherries**

* In a small mixing bowl, cream shortening, cream cheese and sugar. Beat in egg yolk and vanilla. Combine flour and salt; gradually add to the creamed mixture.

* Drop by teaspoonfuls 2 in. apart onto greased baking sheets. Top each with a cherry half. Bake at 350° for 12-15 minutes or until lightly browned. Cool for 1 minute before removing to wire racks. YIELD: 2 dozen.

removing cookies from a baking sheet

- If cookies seem to crumble when you remove them from the baking sheet, let them cool for 1 to 2 minutes first.

- But be aware that if cookies cool too long, they become hard and can break when removed. If this happens, return the baking sheet to the oven to warm the cookies slightly so they'll release easily.

WHITE CHOCOLATE COOKIES

WHITE CHOCOLATE COOKIES

SHANA BOUNDS, MAGEE, MISSISSIPPI

Fixing desserts is my favorite kind of cooking. I usually make these cookies for Christmas—their pale-white adds a special touch to all the reds and greens.

- **1/2 cup butter**
- **1/2 cup shortening**
- **3/4 cup sugar**
- **1/2 cup packed brown sugar**
- **1 egg**
- **1 3/4 cups all-purpose flour**
- **1 teaspoon baking soda**
- **1/2 teaspoon salt**
- **2 teaspoons vanilla extract**
- **10 ounces white chocolate, coarsely chopped**
- **1/2 cup coarsely chopped macadamia nuts, lightly toasted**

❊ In a large mixing bowl, cream butter and shortening. Gradually add sugars, beating until light and fluffy. Add egg; mix well. Combine flour, baking soda and salt; add to creamed mixture. Blend in vanilla. Stir in chocolate and nuts. Cover and chill dough for 1 hour.

❊ Drop by heaping about 3 in. apart onto ungreased baking sheets. Bake at 350° for 12-14 minutes or until lightly browned. Let stand a few minutes before removing cookies to wire racks to cool. YIELD: ab 2 1/2 dozen.

HOLIDAY MACAROONS

KRISTINE CONWAY, MOGADORE, OHIO

These tasty coconut cookies have wonderful, old-fashioned goodness that is especially irresistible at holiday time.

- **4 eggs**
- **1 1/2 cups sugar**
- **2/3 cup all-purpose flour**
- **1/2 teaspoon baking powder**
- **1/4 teaspoon salt**
- **2 tablespoons butter, melted and cooled**
- **1 teaspoon vanilla extract**
- **5 cups flaked coconut**
- **1 jar (10 ounces) maraschino cherrie drained and halved**

❊ In a mixing bowl, beat the eggs ur foamy. Gradually add sugar, beating cc stantly until thick and pale yellow. Stir gether dry ingredients; fold into e mixture. Stir in butter, vanilla and cocon

❊ Drop by teaspoonfuls onto greased a floured baking sheets. Top with cherri Bake at 325° for 10-13 minutes. Remo to wire racks to cool. YIELD: about dozen.

MOCHA TRUFFLE COOKIE

SHERRIE PICKLE, KENT, WASHINGTON

Cocoa and coffee come together deliciously in these treats preferred by my husband. I like to make extras to tu in gift baskets for friends and family.

- **1/2 cup butter**
- **1 1/2 cups (9 ounces) semisweet chocolate chips, *divided***
- **2 to 3 teaspoons instant coffee granules**
- **2 eggs**
- **3/4 cup sugar**
- **3/4 cup packed brown sugar**
- **2 teaspoons vanilla extract**
- **2 cups all-purpose flour**
- **1/3 cup baking cocoa**

teaspoon baking powder

teaspoon salt

In a saucepan over low heat, melt butter and ½ cup chocolate chips. Remove from the heat; stir until smooth. Stir in coffee granules; cool for 5 minutes. Stir in eggs, sugars and vanilla. Combine flour, cocoa, baking powder and salt; fold into the chocolate mixture. Add the remaining chocolate chips.

Drop by rounded teaspoonfuls 2 in. apart onto greased baking sheets. Bake at 350° for 9-11 minutes or until tops appear lightly dry and cracked. Cool for 1 minute before removing to wire racks. YIELD: about 5½ dozen.

MACADAMIA ALMOND DELIGHTS

MEL MARSHALL, SALEM, OREGON

"A few years ago, I decided to liven up a basic chocolate chip cookie recipe by adding macadamia nuts, white chocolate chips and almond paste. Since the scrumptious results got such rave reviews from my 26 grandchildren, I've designated this version a keeper."

⅓ cup butter, softened

⅓ cup shortening

1 cup sugar

1 cup packed brown sugar

2 eggs

2 teaspoons vanilla extract

1 cup almond paste

3 cups plus 3 tablespoons all-purpose flour

1 teaspoon baking soda

1 teaspoon salt

2 cups macadamia nuts, chopped

1 package (11 ounces) vanilla or white chips

In a mixing bowl, cream the butter, shortening and sugars. Add eggs, one at a time, beating well after each addition. Beat in the vanilla and almond paste. Combine flour, baking soda and salt; gradually add to the creamed mixture and mix well. Stir in nuts and chips.

✳ Drop by heaping tablespoonfuls 2 in. apart onto ungreased baking sheets. Bake at 350° for 12-15 minutes or until lightly browned. Remove to wire racks to cool. YIELD: 4 dozen.

AMISH SUGAR COOKIES

SYLVIA FORD, KENNETT, MISSOURI

These easy-to-make cookies simply melt in your mouth! After I gave the recipe to my sister, she entered the cookies in a local fair and won the "best of show" prize!

1 cup butter, softened

1 cup vegetable oil

1 cup sugar

1 cup confectioners' sugar

2 eggs

1 teaspoon vanilla

4½ cups all-purpose flour

1 teaspoon baking soda

1 teaspoon cream of tartar

✳ Combine butter, oil and sugars in large mixing bowl; mix well. Add eggs; beat 1 minute until well blended. Add vanilla; beat well. In separate bowl, combine flour, baking soda and cream of tartar; add to creamed mixture, mixing well.

✳ Drop by small teaspoonfuls onto ungreased baking sheets. Bake at 375° for 8-10 minutes. Remove to wire racks to cool. YIELD: 5 dozen.

AMISH SUGAR COOKIES

CRANBERRY OATMEAL COOKI

CRANBERRY OATMEAL COOKIES

PAT HABIGER, SPEARVILLE, KANSAS

Dotted with cranberries, orange peel and vanilla chips, these cookies are so colorful and fun to eat. They look lovely on a dessert tray and would be a great addition to your Christmas cookie lineup.

- 1 **cup butter, softened**
- 1½ **cups sugar**
- 2 **eggs**
- 1 **teaspoon vanilla extract**
- 2 **cups all-purpose flour**
- 1 **teaspoon baking powder**
- ½ **teaspoon salt**
- ¼ **teaspoon baking soda**
- 2 **cups quick-cooking oats**
- 1 **cup raisins**
- 1 **cup coarsely chopped fresh or frozen cranberries**
- 1 **tablespoon grated orange peel**
- 1 **package (12 ounces) vanilla or white chips**

✳ In a mixing bowl, cream butter and su ar. Add the eggs, one at a time, beati well after each addition. Beat in vani Combine flour, baking powder, salt a baking soda; add to the creamed mixtu Stir in oats, raisins, cranberries and oran peel. Stir in vanilla chips.

✳ Drop by rounded teaspoonfuls 2 in. ap onto greased baking sheets. Bake at 37 for 10-12 minutes or until the edges lightly browned. Remove to wire racks cool. YIELD: 6 dozen.

UTTY CHOCOLATE UGGETS

ANN WOLFE, TOLEDO, WASHINGTON

family can't get enough of these ewy, chocolaty drop cookies. They're quick and easy to fix that I can whip several batches, even during the sy holiday season.

- 4 **cup butter, softened**
- 2 **cup sugar**
- 1 **egg**
- 2 **teaspoons vanilla extract**
- 2 **squares (1½ ounces *each*) unsweetened chocolate, melted and cooled**
- 2 **cup all-purpose flour**
- 4 **teaspoon baking powder**
- 2 **teaspoon salt**
- 2 **cups chopped walnuts *or* pecans**

In a mixing bowl, cream butter and sugar. Beat in egg and vanilla. Stir in chocolate. Combine the flour, baking powder and salt; gradually add to chocolate mixture. Stir in the nuts.

Drop by rounded teaspoonfuls 2 in. apart onto ungreased baking sheets. Bake at 350° for 10-11 minutes or until edges are firm. Remove to wire racks to cool. YIELD: about 3½ dozen.

EMON SNOWFLAKES

DA BARRY, DIANNA, TEXAS

ur ingredients is all it takes to make ese delightful cookies.

- 1 **package (18¼ ounces) lemon cake mix with pudding**
- 4 **cups frozen whipped topping, thawed**
- 1 **egg**

nfectioners' sugar

In a mixing bowl, combine cake mix, whipped topping and egg. Beat with electric mixer on medium speed until blended. Batter will be very sticky.

Drop by teaspoonfuls into confectioners' sugar; roll lightly to coat. Place on ungreased baking sheets. Bake at 350° for 10-12 minutes or until lightly browned.

Remove to wire racks to cool. YIELD: 5-6 dozen.

PEANUT BUTTER CHOCOLATE CHIP COOKIES

CLARICE SCHWEITZER, SUN CITY, ARIZONA

Here's a different version of the traditional favorite cookie that I think is especially good.

- ½ **cup butter, softened**
- ½ **cup sugar**
- ⅓ **cup packed brown sugar**
- ½ **cup chunky peanut butter**
- 1 **egg**
- 1 **teaspoon vanilla extract**
- 1 **cup all-purpose flour**
- ½ **cup old-fashioned oats**
- 1 **teaspoon baking soda**
- ¼ **teaspoon salt**
- 1 **cup (6 ounces) semisweet chocolate chips**

✻ In a mixing bowl, cream butter and sugars; beat in peanut butter, egg and vanilla. Combine flour, oats, baking soda and salt; stir into the creamed mixture. Stir in chocolate chips.

✻ Drop by rounded tablespoonfuls onto ungreased baking sheets. Bake at 350° for 10-12 minutes or until golden brown. Cool 1 minute before removing to wire racks to cool. YIELD: 2 dozen.

PEANUT BUTTER CHOCOLATE CHIP COOKIES

CHOCOLATE CHIP MINT COOKIES

CHOCOLATE CHIP MINT COOKIES

PATRICIA KASETA
BROCKTON, MASSACHUSETTS

I jazz up a packaged cookie mix, then let Junior Mints melt on top of the warm treats to create an easy frosting. These delicious cookies are requested at every gathering.

- 1 **package (17½ ounces) chocolate chip cookie mix**
- 3 **tablespoons water**
- 1 **egg**
- ¼ **cup vegetable oil**
- ½ **cup semisweet chocolate chips**
- ½ **cup vanilla or white chips**
- ½ **cup chopped walnuts**
- 1 **package (5½ ounces) Junior Mints**

❋ In a mixing bowl, combine cookie mix, water, egg and oil; mix well. Stir in the chips and nuts. Drop by tablespoonfuls 2 in. apart onto ungreased baking sheets. Bake at 350° for 7-9 minutes or until edges are golden brown.

❋ Remove from the oven; place one candy on each cookie. Remove from pans to wire racks. When candy is melted, spread over cookie. Cool completely. YIELD: about 4 dozen.

CRANBERRY WALNUT COOKIES

JOYCE LARSON, KIESTER, MINNESOTA

When I brought these cookies in for the holiday open house at work, they simply disappeared—150 dozen of them!

- 1 **cup butter-flavored shortening**
- 1 **cup sugar**
- ⅔ **cup packed brown sugar**
- 2 **eggs**
- 1 **tablespoon orange juice concentrate**
- 1 **tablespoon grated orange peel**
- 2 **teaspoons vanilla extract**
- 2½ **cups all-purpose flour**
- 1 **teaspoon cream of tartar**
- 1 **teaspoon baking soda**
- 1 **teaspoon salt**
- 1 **cup coarsely chopped fresh cranberries**
- 1 **cup chopped walnuts**

❋ In a large mixing bowl, cream shortening and sugars. Beat in eggs, one at a time, beating well after each addition. Add orange juice concentrate, orange peel and vanilla. Combine the flour, cream of tartar, baking soda and salt; gradually add to creamed mixture and mix well. Stir in cranberries and walnuts. Cover and refrigerate 2 hours or until easy to handle.

❋ Drop by tablespoonfuls onto greased baking sheets. Bake at 350° for 14- minutes or until lightly browned. Remove to wire racks to cool. YIELD: 4 dozen.

RASPBERRY KISSES

RUTH VANDERBERG, LIBERTY, MISSOURI

These light and airy drops, bursting with bits of chocolate, have long been a holiday favorite at our house. I often make them for luncheons and teas the rest of the year as well.

- 3 **egg whites**
- ⅛ **teaspoon salt**
- ¾ **cup sugar**
- 3 **tablespoons plus 2 teaspoons raspberry gelatin powder**

1 tablespoon white vinegar

1 cup miniature chocolate chips

In a mixing bowl, beat egg whites and salt until foamy. Combine sugar and gelatin powder; gradually add to egg whites, beating until stiff peaks form and sugar is dissolved. Beat in vinegar. Fold in the chocolate chips.

Drop by teaspoonfuls 2 in. apart onto parchment paper-lined baking sheets. Bake at 250° for 25 minutes. Turn oven off, leaving kisses in the oven 20 minutes longer. Remove to wire racks to cool. YIELD: about 6 dozen.

HOCOLATE
EPPERMINT COOKIES

LIA TRUE, FOREST RANCH, CALIFORNIA
anything can get you in the
hristmas spirit, these minty chocolate
ip cookies can. A sprinkle of
ppermint candy adds an extra-
stive touch. They're excellent for
nking.

1 cup butter, softened

¾ cup sugar

¾ cup packed brown sugar

2 eggs

2 teaspoons vanilla extract

½ cups whole wheat flour

1 teaspoon baking soda

½ teaspoon salt

1 cup (6 ounces) semisweet chocolate chips

½ cup crushed peppermint candy

dditional crushed peppermint candy, optional

In a large mixing bowl, cream butter and sugars. Beat in eggs and vanilla. Combine flour, baking soda and salt; gradually add to creamed mixture. Stir in chocolate chips and crushed candy.

Drop by rounded teaspoonfuls 2 in. apart onto ungreased baking sheets. Sprinkle with additional candy if desired.

Bake at 350° for 9-10 minutes or until cookies spring back when lightly touched. Remove to wire racks to cool. YIELD: about 7½ dozen.

DEVIL'S FOOD COOKIES

MELANIE VAN DEN BRINK, ROCK RAPIDS, IOWA
Most people don't realize that these cookies are lower in fat. You actually get more than 2 dozen of the treats from a cake mix and just four other common ingredients.

1 package (18¼ ounces) devil's food cake mix

2 eggs

2 tablespoons butter, softened

3 tablespoons water

½ cup miniature semisweet chocolate chips

✳ In a large mixing bowl, combine the cake mix, eggs, butter and water (batter will be thick). Fold in chocolate chips.

✳ Drop by tablespoonfuls 2 in. apart onto baking sheets coated with nonstick cooking spray. Bake at 350° for 10-13 minutes or until set and edges are lightly browned. Cool for 2 minutes before removing to wire racks. YIELD: 28 cookies.

DEVIL'S FOOD COOKIES

JUMBO CHOCOLATE CHIP COOKIES

JACKIE RUCKWARDT, COTTAGE GROVE, OREGON
These gourmet cookies are my "most asked for" recipe. Chockfull of coconut and chocolate chips and dipped in white candy coating, they are truly a chocolate-lover's delight.

- 1 cup butter, softened
- 1 cup sugar
- 1 cup packed brown sugar
- 2 eggs
- 2 teaspoons vanilla extract
- 2½ cups all-purpose flour
- 1 teaspoon baking soda
- 1 teaspoon baking powder
- 1 teaspoon salt
- 2⅔ cups flaked coconut
- 1 cup (6 ounces) semisweet chocolate chips
- ½ cup milk chocolate chips
- 5 ounces white candy coating, chopped, optional

❋ In a large mixing bowl, cream butter a sugars. Add eggs, one at a time, beati well after each addition. Beat in vani Combine the flour, baking soda, baki powder and salt; gradually add to creamed mixture. Stir in the coconut a chips. Shape 3 tablespoonfuls of dou into a ball; repeat with remaining doug

❋ Place balls 3 in. apart on ungreased b ing sheets. Bake at 350° for 12-18 minu or until lightly browned. Remove to w racks to cool.

❋ In a microwave-safe bowl, melt can coating if desired. Dip one end of cool cookies in candy coating. Allow exce to drip off. Place on waxed paper; stand until set. YIELD: 2 dozen.

JUMBO CHOCOLATE CHIP COOKIES

OFT MACAROONS

RBARA SCHINDLER, NAPOLEON, OHIO

ake 22 types of cookies at ristmas, and these macaroons are e most requested. People can't lieve I use sherbet and cake mix to ake the simple sweets.

- **1 pint pineapple *or* orange sherbet, softened**
- **2 teaspoons almond extract**
- **1 package (18¼ ounces) white cake mix**
- **6 cups flaked coconut**

In a large mixing bowl, combine sherbet, almond extract and dry cake mix; mix well. Stir in the coconut.

Drop by tablespoonfuls 2 in. apart onto greased baking sheets. Bake at 350° for 12-15 minutes or until edges are lightly browned. Remove to wire racks to cool. YIELD: about 6 dozen.

ELLY-TOPPED UGAR COOKIES

NE QUINN, KALAMAZOO, MICHIGAN

n busy days, I appreciate this fast-to-drop sugar cookie. Top each cookie th your favorite flavor of jam or jelly.

- **2 eggs**
- **¼ cup vegetable oil**
- **2 teaspoons vanilla extract**
- **1 teaspoon lemon extract**
- **1 teaspoon grated lemon peel**
- **¼ cup sugar**
- **2 cups all-purpose flour**
- **2 teaspoons baking powder**
- **½ teaspoon salt**
- **½ cup jam *or* jelly**

In a mixing bowl, combine eggs, oil, extracts and lemon peel until well blended. Beat in sugar (mixture will become thick). Combine the flour, baking powder and salt; gradually add to egg mixture. Drop by rounded tablespoonfuls 2 in. apart onto ungreased baking sheets.

Spray the bottom of a glass with non-stick cooking spray, then dip in sugar. Flatten cookies with glass, redipping in sugar as needed. Place ¼ teaspoon jelly in the center of each cookie.

❄ Bake at 400° for 8-10 minutes or until set. Remove to wire racks to cool. YIELD: about 3½ dozen.

CRANBERRY CHIP COOKIES

JO ANN MCCARTHY, CANTON, MASSACHUSETTS

I received these delightful cookies for Christmas a few years ago. I was watching my diet, but I couldn't stay away from them! The tart cranberries blend beautifully with the sweet chocolate and vanilla chips.

- **½ cup butter, softened**
- **½ cup shortening**
- **¾ sugar**
- **¾ cup packed brown sugar**
- **2 eggs**
- **1 teaspoon vanilla extract**
- **2¼ cups all-purpose flour**
- **1 teaspoon baking soda**
- **½ teaspoon salt**
- **1 cup semisweet chocolate chips**
- **1 cup vanilla *or* white chips**
- **1 cup dried cranberries**
- **1 cup chopped pecans**

❄ In a mixing bowl, cream butter, shortening and sugars. Add eggs, one at a time, beating well after each addition. Beat in vanilla. Combine flour, baking soda and salt; gradually add to the creamed mixture. Stir in the chips, cranberries and pecans.

❄ Drop by tablespoonfuls 2 in. apart onto ungreased baking sheets. Bake at 375° for 9-11 minutes or until golden brown. Cool for 2 minutes before removing to wire racks to cool completely. YIELD: 9 dozen.

CRANBERRY CHIP COOKIES

BEST LOVED
cookies
& BARS

SHAPED
cookies

LEMON DREAMS
PAGE 50

WHITE CHOCOLATE-
CRANBERRY BISCOTTI
PAGE 60

FUDGE-FILLED TOFFEE COOKIES
PAGE 69

storing cookies

- Allow cookies to cool completely before storing.

- Store soft cookies and crisp cookies in separate airtight containers. If stored together, the moisture from the soft cookies will soften the crisp cookies, making them lose their crunch.

- Flavors can also blend during storage, so don't store strong-flavored cookies with delicate-flavored ones.

- Layer the cookies in a container, separating each layer with waxed paper.

- Allow icing on cookies to completely dry before storing.

APRICOT CHEESE CRESCENTS

RUTH GILHOUSEN, KNOXDALE, PENNSYLVANIA
Traditionally, I bake these for Christmas. A cross between sweet bread and cookies, they're also something that I have been asked to make for weddings.

- 2 cups all-purpose flour
- ½ teaspoon salt
- 1 cup cold butter
- 1 cup (8 ounces) small-curd cottage cheese

FILLING
- 1 package (6 ounces) dried apricots
- ½ cup water
- ½ cup sugar

TOPPING
- ¾ cup finely chopped almonds
- ½ cup sugar
- 1 egg white, lightly beaten

✳ In a large bowl, combine flour and salt; cut in butter until crumbly. Add cottage cheese; mix well. Shape into 1-in. balls. Cover and refrigerate several hours or overnight.

✳ For the filling, combine apricots and water in a saucepan. Cover and simmer for 20 minutes. Cool for 10 minutes.

✳ Pour into a blender; cover and process on high speed until smooth. Transfer to a bowl; stir in sugar. Cover and chill.

APRICOT CHEESE CRESCENTS

✳ For topping, combine almonds and sugar; set aside. On a floured surface, roll the balls into 2½-in. circles. Spoon about teaspoon of filling onto each. Fold dough over filling and pinch edges to seal.

✳ Place on greased baking sheets. Brush tops with egg white; sprinkle with almond mixture. Bake at 375° for 12-15 minutes or until lightly browned. Remove to wire racks to cool. YIELD: 4½ dozen.

CHOCOLATE MACADAMIA MELTAWAYS

BARBARA SEPCICH, GALT, CALIFORNIA
I came up with this recipe by accident one day when I wanted to make some cookies. I decided to use some ingredients already in my cupboard, and these were the delicious result.

- ½ cup butter, softened
- ¼ cup confectioners' sugar
- ½ teaspoon vanilla extract
- 1¼ cups all-purpose flour
- 1 jar (3½ ounces) macadamia nuts, finely chopped

FILLING
- 1 cup (6 ounces) semisweet chocolate chips
- ½ cup coarsely chopped macadamia nuts

Additional confectioners' sugar

✳ In a small mixing bowl, cream butter and sugar. Beat in vanilla. Gradually add flour. Stir in nuts (dough will be stiff); set aside.

✳ For filling, melt chocolate chips. Stir in nuts; cool slightly. Drop by ½ teaspoonfuls onto a waxed paper-lined baking sheet; cover and refrigerate for 30 minutes.

✳ Shape teaspoonfuls of dough around each piece of chocolate-nut mixture so it is completely covered. Place 2 in. apart on ungreased baking sheets. Bake at 375° for 12-14 minutes or until lightly browned. Roll warm cookies in confectioners' sugar. Remove to wire racks to cool. YIELD: 2½ dozen.

storing cookies
(continued)

- Unfrosted cookies can be stored in a cool dry place in airtight containers for about 3 days. Cookies topped with a cream cheese frosting should be stored in the refrigerator.

- For longer storage, wrap unfrosted cookies in plastic wrap, stack in an airtight container, seal and freeze for up to 3 months. Thaw wrapped cookies at room temperature before frosting and serving.

- If your crisp cookies became soft during storage, crisp them up by heating in a 300° oven for 5 minutes.

CHOCOLATE-FILLED POPPY SEED COOKIES
CHOCOLATE MACADAMIA MELTAWAYS

CHOCOLATE-FILLED POPPY SEED COOKIES

AREN MEAD, GRANVILLE, NEW YORK
Vhile it's been around for years, this ecipe remains enjoyable to this day. A o-worker prepared these at a cookie xchange a while back...they were the iggest hit of the party!

- 1 cup butter, softened
- ½ cup sugar
- 2 egg yolks
- 1 teaspoon vanilla extract
- 2 cups all-purpose flour
- 3 tablespoons poppy seeds
- ¼ teaspoon salt
- 1 cup (6 ounces) semisweet chocolate chips, melted

✳ In a small mixing bowl, cream butter and sugar. Beat in egg yolks and vanilla. Combine the flour, poppy seeds and salt; gradually add to the creamed mixture.

✳ Roll into 1-in. balls. Place 2 in. apart on ungreased baking sheets. Using the end of a wooden spoon handle, make an indentation in the center of each.

✳ Bake at 375° for 10-12 minutes or until lightly browned. Immediately make an indentation in the center again. Remove to wire racks to cool slightly; fill with melted chocolate. YIELD: 6½ dozen.

shaping cookie dough into balls

Roll the dough between your palms until it forms a ball. A 1-in. ball requires about 2 teaspoons of dough. If the dough is sticky, you can refrigerate it until it is easy to handle, lightly flour your hands or spray your hands with nonstick cooking spray.

BUTTER COOKIE SNOWMEN

BUTTER COOKIE SNOWMEN

KATHLEEN TAUGHER, EAST TROY, WISCONSIN
It was great fun making these tasty cookies with my grandchildren one Christmas. The dough is easy to shape.

- 1 cup butter, softened
- 1/2 cup sugar
- 1 tablespoon milk
- 1 teaspoon vanilla extract
- 2 1/4 cups all-purpose flour
Red and yellow paste food coloring
Miniature chocolate chips

❋ In a mixing bowl, cream butter and sugar. Add the milk and vanilla; mix well. Gradually add flour. Remove 1/3 cup of dough to a small bowl; tint with red food coloring. Repeat with 1/3 cup of dough and yellow food coloring; set aside.

❋ For snowmen, shape white dough into 24 balls, 1 1/4 in. each; 24 balls, about 1/2 in. each; and 24 balls, about 1/8 in. each. For bodies, place large balls on two un-greased baking sheets; flatten to 3/8-in. thickness. Place 1/2-in. balls above bodies for heads; flatten.

❋ Shape red dough into 24 balls, 1/8 in. each, and 24 triangles. Place triangles above heads for hats; attach 1/8-in. white balls for tassels. Place red balls on heads for noses.

Divide the yellow dough into 24 piec[es] shape into scarves and position on sno[w]men. Add chocolate chip eyes and bu[t]tons. Bake at 325° for 13-16 minutes [or] until set. Cool for 2 minutes before car[e]fully removing to wire racks. YIELD: [2] dozen.

FROSTED PEANUT BUTTER COOKIES

TASTE OF HOME TEST KITCHEN
Are you looking for a quick way to dress up an ordinary cookie mix? Try this trick! The frosting can be used on [a] variety of cookies, including sugar an[d] chocolate chip.

- 1 package (17 1/2 ounces) peanut butter cookie mix
- 2 cups confectioners' sugar
- 1/4 cup baking cocoa
- 1/4 cup hot water
- 1 teaspoon vanilla extract
Sliced almonds or pecan halves

❋ In a large mixing bowl, prepare cook[ie] dough according to package direction[s.] Shape into 1-in. balls. Place 2 in. apa[rt] on ungreased baking sheets.

❋ Bake at 375° for 8-10 minutes or unt[il] edges are golden brown. Cool for [1] minute before removing to wire racks.

❋ For frosting, in a bowl, combine the co[n]fectioners' sugar, cocoa, water and vani[l]la. Spread over cookies; top with nut[s.] YIELD: about 2 dozen.

FROSTED PEANUT BUTTER COOKIES

HIP-TOPPED
UTTER COOKIES

TH HODGDON, EAST QUOGUE, NEW YORK

e chocolate center in these crisp
tter cookies makes them a winner.
nbellish them with a quick dusting of
nfectioners' sugar if you like.

- /2 **cup butter, softened**
- /4 **cup sugar**
- 1 **cup all-purpose flour**
- /3 **cup semisweet chocolate chips**

onfectioners' sugar, optional

In a large mixing bowl, cream butter and
sugar. Add flour and beat until well mixed.
Shape into 1-in. balls. Place 1 in. apart
on ungreased baking sheets. Using the
end of a wooden spoon handle, make a
wide indentation in the center of each
ball; fill with five chocolate chips.

Bake at 350° for 12-15 minutes or until
edges are lightly browned. Cool for 2 minutes before removing from pans to wire
racks. Just before serving, dust with confectioners' sugar if desired. YIELD: 3
dozen.

EANUT BUTTER TREATS

DY STANTON, THONOTOSASSA, FLORIDA

u can't miss with these no-fuss
okies. People are surprised to see
e short list of ingredients. These
okies are fragile, so store them
arefully when completely cooled.

- 2 **cups peanut butter**
- 1/4 **cups sugar**
- 2 **eggs**
- 52 **milk chocolate stars or kisses**

In a mixing bowl, cream peanut butter
and sugar. Add eggs, one at a time, beating well after each addition (dough will be
sticky). With floured hands, roll tablespoonfuls into 1 1/4-in. balls. Place 2 in.
apart on ungreased baking sheets.

Bake at 350° for 14-16 minutes or until
tops are cracked. Remove to wire racks.
Immediately press a chocolate star in the
center of each. Cool. YIELD: 4 1/2 dozen.

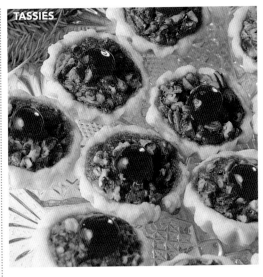

TASSIES

TASSIES

JOY CORIE, RUSTON, LOUISIANA

Any cookie tray will be perked up with
the addition of these pretty tarts. If you
don't have miniature tart pans, use
miniature muffin pans instead.

PASTRY
- 1 **package (3 ounces) cream cheese,
  softened**
- 1/2 **cup butter**
- 1 **cup all-purpose flour**

FILLING
- 3/4 **cup packed brown sugar**
- 1 **tablespoon butter, softened**
- 1 **egg**
- 1 **teaspoon vanilla extract**

Dash salt
- 2/3 **cup finely chopped pecans, divided**

Maraschino cherries, halved, optional

❊ For pastry, blend cream cheese and butter until smooth; stir in flour. Cover and refrigerate for about 1 hour.

❊ Roll into twenty-four 1 in. balls. Place in
ungreased miniature muffin tins or small
cookie tarts; press the dough against bottom and sides to form shell. Set aside.

❊ In a bowl, beat brown sugar, butter and
egg until combined. Add vanilla, salt and
half the pecans; spoon into pastry. Top
with remaining pecans. Bake at 375° for 20
minutes or until filling is set and pastry is
light golden brown. Remove to wire racks
to cool. Top each with a maraschino cherry half if desired. YIELD: 24 tarts.

BEST LOVED
COOkies
& BARS

MINIATURE PEANUT BUTTER TREATS

JODIE MCCOY, TULSA, OKLAHOMA

This recipe is one of my family's favorites, and I make these treats a lot, especially at Christmas. I have three children and eight grandchildren, and every one of them loves those "peanut butter thingies," as the grandchildren call them!

COOKIE
- ½ cup butter, softened
- ½ cup sugar
- ½ cup packed brown sugar
- 1 egg
- ½ cup creamy peanut butter
- ½ teaspoon vanilla
- 1¼ cups all-purpose flour
- ¾ teaspoon baking soda
- ½ teaspoon salt

FILLING
About 42 miniature peanut butter-chocolate cups

MINIATURE PEANUT BUTTER TREATS

❄ Combine butter, sugars, egg, peanut butter and vanilla in mixing bowl; beat until smooth. In separate bowl, combine flour, baking soda and salt; add to creamed mixture. Cover dough and chill.

❄ When cold enough to handle easily, roll into small (walnut-sized) balls; place each ball in greased miniature muffin tin. Bake at 375° for 8-9 minutes.

❄ Remove from oven; gently press one peanut butter cup into each cookie to make depression. Cool in pan 10 minutes; remove from pan and cool on rack. Store in cool place until serving time. YIELD: about 3½ dozen.

PFEFFERNUESSE

BETTY HAWKSHAW, ALEXANDRIA, VIRGINIA

These mild spice cookies, perfect for dunking, come from an old family recipe.

- 1 cup butter, softened
- 1 cup sugar
- 2 eggs
- ½ cup light corn syrup
- ½ cup molasses
- ⅓ cup water
- 6⅔ cups all-purpose flour
- ¼ cup crushed aniseed
- 1 teaspoon baking soda
- 1 teaspoon ground cinnamon
- ½ teaspoon ground nutmeg
- ¼ teaspoon ground cloves
- ¼ teaspoon ground allspice

Confectioners' sugar

❄ In a mixing bowl, cream butter and sugar. Add eggs, one at a time, beating well after each addition. In a bowl, combine corn syrup, molasses and water; set aside. Combine the flour, aniseed, baking soda and spices; add to creamed mixture alternately with molasses mixture. Cover and refrigerate overnight.

❄ Roll into 1-in. balls. Place 2 in. apart on greased baking sheets. Bake at 400° for 11 minutes or until golden brown. Roll warm cookies in confectioners' sugar. Cool on wire racks. YIELD: 8 dozen.

PRITZ WREATHS

JUDITH SCHOLOVICH, WAUKESHA, WISCONSIN

These make a nice addition to a cookie exchange, bake sale or gift tray.

- **1 cup butter, softened**
- **⅔ cup sugar**
- **1 egg, lightly beaten**
- **¼ cups all-purpose flour**
- **½ teaspoon baking powder**
- **1 teaspoon almond extract**
- **Red and green candied cherries**

In a mixing bowl, cream butter and sugar. Add egg and mix well. Combine flour and baking powder; add to creamed mixture. Add extract.

Using a cooking press fitted with a star-shaped disk, form dough into long ropes. Cut into 3¼-in. pieces; shape into wreaths. Decorate with cherries.

Place on ungreased baking sheets. Bake at 375° for 8-10 minutes. Remove to wire racks to cool. YIELD: 6-7 dozen.

HAZELNUT CRESCENTS

BEVERLY LAUNIUS, SANDWICH, ILLINOIS

My mom and I make these delicate cookies every Christmas. Hazelnuts have a little different flavor from the usual pecans.

- **1 cup butter, softened**
- **¼ cup sugar**
- **1 teaspoon vanilla extract**
- **2 cups all-purpose flour**
- **1 cup whole hazelnuts, ground**
- **Confectioners' sugar**

In a mixing bowl, cream butter, sugar and vanilla. Gradually add the flour and nuts. Cover and refrigerate for 2 hours or until easy to handle.

Shape dough by teaspoonfuls into 2-in. rolls. Form into crescents. Place 2 in. apart on ungreased baking sheets. Bake at 350° for 12 minutes or until lightly browned. Cool for 2 minutes before removing from pans to wire racks. Dust with confectioners' sugar. YIELD: about 10 dozen.

NUTMEG SUGAR CRISPS

NUTMEG SUGAR CRISPS

KRISTI THORPE, PORTLAND, OREGON

My grandma shared her recipe for these old-fashioned sugar cookies with the unexpected taste of nutmeg. They are light, crunchy and so delicious. That's why they're always a part of our Christmas tradition.

- **1 cup butter, softened**
- **¾ cup sugar**
- **½ cup confectioners' sugar**
- **1 egg**
- **1 teaspoon vanilla extract**
- **2½ cups all-purpose flour**
- **½ teaspoon baking soda**
- **½ teaspoon cream of tartar**
- **¼ to ½ teaspoon ground nutmeg**
- **⅛ teaspoon salt**

❋ In a mixing bowl, cream butter and sugars. Beat in egg and vanilla; mix well. Combine the flour, baking soda, cream of tartar, nutmeg and salt; add to the creamed mixture and mix well. Refrigerate for 1 hour.

❋ Shape into ¾-in. balls; place 2 in. apart on greased baking sheets. Flatten with a glass dipped in sugar. Bake at 350° for 10-12 minutes or until lightly browned. Remove to wire racks to cool. YIELD: about 6 dozen.

LEMON DREAM

LEMON DREAMS

KAREN SCAGLIONE, NANUET, NEW YORK

A buttery cookie with a luscious lemon filling is simply hard to resist. Every time I serve these elegant cookies, I'm asked for the recipe. I'm glad to share it because these are great!

 1 cup butter, softened
⅓ cup confectioners' sugar
 1 teaspoon vanilla extract
1⅔ cups all-purpose flour

FILLING
⅔ cup sugar
1½ teaspoons cornstarch
 1 teaspoon grated lemon peel
¼ teaspoon salt
 1 egg, beaten
 3 tablespoons lemon juice

 1 tablespoon butter, melted
Confectioners' sugar, optional

❊ In a small mixing bowl, cream butter ar confectioners' sugar. Beat in vanill Gradually add flour. Cover and refrigera for 30 minutes or until easy to handle.

❊ Roll into 1-in. balls. Place 2 in. apart on u greased baking sheets. Using the end a wooden spoon handle, make an inde tation in the center of each. Bake at 35 for 12-14 minutes or until lightly browne Remove to wire racks to cool.

❊ For filling, combine the sugar, cornstarc lemon peel and salt in a saucepan. Stir egg, lemon juice and butter until smoot Cook over medium-high heat until thic ened. Reduce heat; cook and stir 2 mi utes longer. Cool. Spoon ½ teaspoonf into each cookie. Dust with confectioner sugar if desired. YIELD: 3 dozen.

BEST★LOVED
COOKIES
&BARS

LMOND CRESCENTS

NDI MURRAY, BISMARCK, NORTH DAKOTA
me, it isn't Christmas until my
chen is filled with these almond
okies baking by the dozens. My
sband, children and grandchildren
oleheartedly agree!

1 cup butter, softened
/3 cup sugar
/3 cups all-purpose flour
/4 cup finely ground almonds
/4 teaspoon salt
/2 cup confectioners' sugar
1 teaspoon ground cinnamon

In a mixing bowl, cream butter and sugar. Combine flour, almonds and salt; gradually add to the creamed mixture. Cover and refrigerate for 1 hour or until easy to handle. Divide the dough into fourths. Roll out each portion into a long rope, about ¼ in. diameter. Cut into 2-in. lengths.

Place 2 in. apart on lightly greased baking sheets; form each into a crescent. Bake at 325° for 14-16 minutes or until set. Cool for 2 minutes. Combine confectioners' sugar and cinnamon; dip warm cookies in sugar mixture. Place on wire racks to cool. YIELD: about 10 dozen.

NGLISH TEA CAKES

VERLY CHRISTIAN, FORT WORTH, TEXAS
ese unique cookies are baked in
uffin cups, giving them a perfectly
und shape. I sometimes omit the
cans and decorate the cookies for
lidays.

2 cups butter, softened
1 cup sugar
2 teaspoons vanilla extract
4 cups all-purpose flour
0 walnut or pecan halves, toasted

In a large mixing bowl, cream butter and sugar. Beat in vanilla. Gradually add flour. Drop by heaping tablespoonfuls into greased miniature muffin cups; flatten slightly. Press a walnut half into the center of each.

⁂ Bake at 350° for 10-12 minutes or until edges are lightly browned. Cool for 2 minutes before removing from pans to wire racks. YIELD: 5 dozen.

PEPPERMINT KISSES

LYNN BERNSTETTER, LAKE ELMO, MINNESOTA
These cookies really melt in your mouth. They're great when you don't want something rich and heavy.

2 egg whites
⅛ teaspoon salt
⅛ teaspoon cream of tartar
½ cup sugar
2 peppermint candy canes (one green, one red), crushed

⁂ In a mixing bowl, beat egg whites until foamy. Add salt and cream of tartar; beat until soft peaks form. Beat in sugar, 1 tablespoon at a time, until stiff and glossy.

⁂ Spoon meringue into a pastry bag or a resealable plastic bag. If using a plastic bag, cut a 1-in. hole in a corner.

⁂ Squeeze 1½-in. kisses of meringue onto ungreased foil-lined baking sheets. Sprinkle half with red crushed candy canes and half with green candy canes.

⁂ Bake at 225° for 1½ to 2 hours or until dry but not brown. Cool; remove from foil. Store in an airtight container. YIELD: 3 dozen.

PEPPERMINT KISSES

PECAN HORNS

top with a scant teaspoon of filling. Fo[ld]
dough over filling; seal and shape like [a]
horn.

❈ Place on ungreased baking shee[t.]
Combine remaining pecans and sug[ar.]
Brush egg white over horns; sprinkle w[ith]
pecan mixture. Bake at 350° for 25 m[in]-
utes or until lightly browned. Remove [to]
wire racks to cool. YIELD: 4 dozen.

SNOWBALLS

MADELINE SCHOLFIELD, WINCHESTER, ILLINO[IS]
I first tried this recipe because it's low
in fat, but now I make these no-bake
cookies for their fruity taste of apricot[s]
and raisins. My friends love them.

    4 cups All-Bran® cereal
    1 cup dried pitted prunes
1²/₃ cups raisins
1¹/₂ cups dried apricots
    2 cups chopped pecans

Confectioners' sugar

❈ Place cereal and prunes in a food proce[s]-
sor or blender; cover and process until c[e]-
real is crumbled. Add raisins, apricots a[nd]
pecans; process until finely chopped.

❈ Shape in 1-in. balls; roll in confectione[rs']
sugar. Store in an airtight container [in]
the refrigerator. Roll again in sugar befo[re]
serving if desired. YIELD: about 5¹/₂ doze[n.]

PECAN HORNS

DOLORES GRUENEWALD, GROVE, OKLAHOMA
These cookies have a nutty, slightly
sweet taste. They go well served with
coffee or tea at festive get-togethers.

    2 cups all-purpose flour
1¹/₂ tablespoons sugar
 ¹/₂ teaspoon salt
    1 cup cold butter
    1 egg plus 1 egg yolk
    1 teaspoon vanilla extract

FILLING/TOPPING

1¹/₂ cups ground pecans, *divided*
 ¹/₂ cup sugar, *divided*
 ¹/₄ teaspoon grated lemon peel
 ¹/₄ cup milk
    1 egg white, beaten

❈ In a mixing bowl, combine flour, sugar and
salt. Cut in butter until mixture resembles coarse crumbs. Combine egg, yolk
and vanilla; add to flour mixture. Mix
well and form into a ball. Chill about 1
hour or until firm enough to handle.

❈ Meanwhile, for filling, combine 1¹/₄ cups
pecans, ¹/₄ cup sugar, lemon peel and
milk; set aside. Cut dough into four sec-
tions; shape 12 balls out of each section.
Flatten each ball into a 2¹/₂-in. round;

SNOWBALLS

CHOCOLATE CHERRY COOKIES

ROL HEMKER, PHENIX CITY, ALABAMA

juicy maraschino cherry peeks out
om under a creamy frosting in this
ocolate cookie. I've been making
em for years and they've never failed
satisfy.

- /2 cup butter, softened
- 1 cup sugar
- 1 egg
- 2 teaspoons maraschino cherry juice
- /2 teaspoons vanilla extract
- /2 cups all-purpose flour
- /2 cup baking cocoa
- /4 teaspoon salt
- /4 teaspoon baking powder
- /4 teaspoon baking soda
- :4 maraschino cherries, drained and halved

OSTING

- 1 cup (6 ounces) semisweet chocolate chips
- /2 cup sweetened condensed milk
- 1 teaspoon maraschino cherry juice

In a large mixing bowl, cream butter and
sugar. Beat in the egg, cherry juice and
vanilla. Combine the flour, cocoa, salt,
baking powder and baking soda; gradually add to the creamed mixture.

Roll into 1-in. balls. Place 2 in. apart on ungreased baking sheets. Using the end of
a wooden spoon handle, make an indentation in the center of each. Place a cherry half in each indentation.

In a small saucepan over low heat, melt
chocolate chips with milk, stirring constantly. Remove from the heat; stir in cherry juice until blended. Spoon about 1
teaspoon over each cherry (frosting will
spread over cookies during baking). Bake
at 350° for 9-11 minutes or until set.
Remove to wire racks to cool. YIELD: 4
dozen.

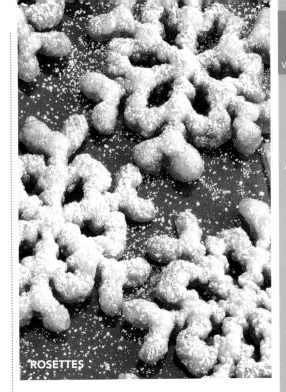

ROSETTES

ROSETTES

RITA CHRISTIANSON
GLENBURN, NORTH DAKOTA

Shaped like delicate snowflakes, these
crisp rosettes make a lovely winter
snack. We make these Norwegian treats
for Christmas and special occasions.

- 2 eggs
- 1 cup milk
- 1 teaspoon sugar
- 1/4 teaspoon salt
- 1 cup all-purpose flour

Oil for deep-fat frying

Confectioners' sugar

※ In a small mixing bowl, beat the eggs,
milk, sugar and salt. Add flour; beat until
smooth. In a deep-fat fryer or electric skillet, heat 2½ in. of oil to 375°. Place
rosette iron in hot oil for 30 seconds.

※ Blot iron on paper towels, then dip iron in
batter to three-fourths the way up the
sides (do not let batter run over top of
iron). Immediately place in hot oil; loosen
rosette with fork and remove iron.

※ Fry for 1-2 minutes on each side or until
golden brown. Remove to a wire rack covered with paper towels. Repeat with remaining batter. Sprinkle with confectioners' sugar before serving. YIELD: about 2½
dozen.

tips for making shaped cookies

- Refrigerate cookie dough until it is chilled for easier handling. If there is a high butter content in the dough, the heat
from your hands can soften the butter in the dough, making it
harder to shape.

- Dust hands lightly with flour to prevent dough from sticking
while shaping it.

PEPPERY SNAPS

JOANIE ELBOURN, GARDNER, MASSACHUSETTS

I love to bake and spend most of my time at it. I have a job as a baker and keep my family supplied with baked goods. My father-in-law said he'd love a cookie that was "real snappy," so I combined recipes to get this one.

1¼ **cups all-purpose flour**
1 **cup whole wheat flour**
1½ **teaspoons baking soda**
1 **teaspoon ground aniseseed**
½ **teaspoon salt**
½ **teaspoon ground ginger**
¼ **teaspoon pepper**
1 **cup packed light brown sugar**
3 **tablespoons light molasses**
¾ **cup butter, softened**
1 **egg**
Sugar

❋ Combine first seven ingredients; set aside. In a mixing bowl, beat brown sugar, molasses, butter and egg. Stir in dry ingredients; mix well. Chill for 1 hour.

❋ Shape into 1-in. balls. Roll in sugar and place on ungreased baking sheets. Bake at 350° for 10-13 minutes. Cool cookies about 1 minute before removing to wire racks. YIELD: 6-7 dozen.

PEPPERY SNAPS

CARDAMOM SWEDISH RUSKS

JULIANNE JOHNSON, GROVE CITY, MINNESO

Cardamom, which has a lemony ging flavor, is a popular spice in many Scandinavian foods. It gives a pleasantly pungent flavor to these cri cookies. Similar to biscotti, they're great "dunkers" for a cup of steaming coffee.

1 **cup butter, softened**
1 **cup sugar**
2 **eggs**
1 **tablespoon heavy whipping cream**
¾ **teaspoon almond extract**
3 **cups all-purpose flour**
1 **teaspoon baking powder**
½ **to ¾ teaspoon ground cardamom**
½ **teaspoon salt**
⅛ **teaspoon baking soda**

❋ In a mixing bowl, cream butter and su ar. Add the eggs, cream and extrac Combine the remaining ingredients; gra ually add to creamed mixture (batter v be thick).

❋ Spoon into three greased 5¾-in. x 3- x 2-in. loaf pans. Bake at 350° for 35- minutes or until a toothpick inserted ne the center comes out clean. Cool in pa for 10 minutes.

❋ Remove to a cutting board; cut each lc into nine slices with a serrated knife. Pla cut side down on an ungreased bakir sheet. Bake for 10 minutes. Turn slice bake 10 minutes longer or until crisp a golden brown. Remove to wire racks cool. Store in an airtight container. YIEL 27 cookies.

BUTTER BALL CHIFFONS

MYLA HARVEY, STANTON, MICHIGAN

The combination of lemon pudding and toffee candy bars sets these crisp cookies apart from all others. Keep th ingredients on hand for when you nee a treat in a hurry.

1 **cup butter, softened**
¼ **cup confectioners' sugar**

1 package (3.4 ounces) instant lemon pudding mix

2 teaspoons water

1 teaspoon vanilla extract

2 cups all-purpose flour

1 cup chopped pecans *or* walnuts

2 Heath candy bars (1.4 ounces *each*), chopped

Additional confectioners' sugar

In a mixing bowl, cream butter and confectioners' sugar. Beat in the pudding mix, water and vanilla. Gradually add flour. Stir in nuts and chopped candy bars.

Roll into 1-in. balls. Place 2 in. apart on ungreased baking sheets. Bake at 325° for 12-15 minutes or until lightly browned. Cool for 3 minutes before removing to wire racks. Sprinkle with additional confectioners' sugar. YIELD: 5 dozen.

EDITOR'S NOTE: This recipe does not use eggs.

CHEWY OATMEAL COOKIES
INGA AUSTIN, LODI, NEW JERSEY

With just a few simple ingredients from the pantry, you can whip up a batch of these sweet morsels in no time! It's such a yummy recipe. Not only is it easy, it makes dozens without much fuss.

3 cups butter, softened

3 cups packed brown sugar

3 cups all-purpose flour

1 tablespoon baking soda

6 cups quick-cooking oats

1/2 cup sugar

In a large mixing bowl, cream butter and brown sugar. Combine flour and baking soda; gradually add to creamed mixture. Transfer to a large bowl; knead in oats.

Shape into 1 1/2-in. balls, then roll in sugar. Place 2 in. apart on ungreased baking sheets. Flatten with a glass. Bake at 350° for 10-12 minutes or until golden brown. Remove to wire racks to cool. YIELD: about 8 dozen.

CRISPY NORWEGIAN BOWS

CRISPY NORWEGIAN BOWS
JANIE NORWOOD, ALBANY, GEORGIA

I've been fixing these cookies for so long, I don't recall where the recipe came from. They're a "must" at our house come Christmas.

3 egg yolks

3 tablespoons sugar

3 tablespoons heavy whipping cream

1/2 teaspoon ground cardamom

1 to 1 1/4 cups all-purpose flour

Oil for deep-frying

Confectioners' sugar

❋ In a large mixing bowl, beat egg yolks and sugar until light and lemon-colored. Add cream and cardamom; mix well. Gradually add flour until dough is firm enough to roll.

❋ On a lightly floured surface, roll into a 15-in. square. Using a pastry wheel or knife, cut into 15-in. x 1 1/2-in. strips; cut diagonally at 2 1/2-in. intervals. In the center of each diamond, make a 1-in. slit; pull one end through slit.

❋ In an electric skillet or deep-fat fryer, heat oil to 375°. Fry bows, a few at a time, for 20-40 seconds or until golden brown on both sides. Drain on paper towels. Dust with confectioners' sugar. YIELD: 4 dozen.

BEST LOVED cookies & BARS

PEPPERMINT TWIST KISSES

TRACI WYNNE, BEAR, DELAWARE

As rosy as Santa's cheeks, these merry morsels with the chocolate kisses on top are a delightful Yuletide favorite and one of my most-requested recipes.

- ½ cup butter, softened
- ⅓ cup sugar
- 1 egg yolk
- ½ teaspoon peppermint extract
- ½ teaspoon vanilla extract
- 1¼ cups all-purpose flour
- ¼ teaspoon salt
- 4 to 8 drops red food coloring
- 36 chocolate kisses

✳ In a large mixing bowl, cream butter and sugar. Add the egg yolk and extracts; mix well. Combine flour and salt; gradually add to creamed mixture. Divide dough in half; tint one portion red. Divide each into four portions. Cover and refrigerate for 1 hour.

✳ Shape each portion into a 9-in. log. Place one red log next to one white log; twist gently to create one swirled roll. Roll gently until roll becomes one log. Repeat with remaining dough.

✳ Cut each log into nine slices; roll each into to a ball. Place 1 in. apart on ungreased baking sheets. Flatten slightly with a glass.

✳ Bake at 350° for 10-12 minutes or until edges are lightly browned. Press chocolate kisses into the center of warm cookies. Remove to wire racks to cool. YIELD: 3 dozen.

PEPPERMINT TWIST KISSES

ALYPSO CUPS

. FRANK KACZMAREK
UBENVILLE, OHIO

ese are great cookies to prepare for
rties throughout the year. I simply
t the frosting for the occasion—red
 Valentine's Day, pastel colors for
by showers and green for Christmas
d St. Patrick's Day.

- 1 cup butter, softened
- 2 packages (3 ounces *each*) cream cheese, softened
- 2 cups all-purpose flour

ING

- 2 cup flaked coconut
- 2 cup sugar
- 2 teaspoons cornstarch
- 1 can (8 ounces) crushed pineapple, undrained
- 1 egg

OSTING

- 2 cups confectioners' sugar
- 2 cup shortening
- 1 teaspoon vanilla extract
- 3 to 4 tablespoons milk

ely chopped walnuts *and/or*
dditional flaked coconut, optional

In a mixing bowl, cream butter and cream cheese. Gradually add flour. Cover and refrigerate for 1 hour or until the dough is easy to handle.

Roll into 1-in. balls. Press onto the bottom and up the sides of greased miniature muffin cups. Combine filling ingredients; spoon into cups. Bake at 350° for 15-20 minutes or until the edges are lightly browned. Cool in pans on wire racks.

For frosting, combine the sugar, shortening and vanilla; add enough milk to achieve spreading consistency. Remove cooled cups from pans. Frost; sprinkle with walnuts and additional flaked coconut if desired. YIELD: 4 dozen.

CHERRY SNOWBALLS

CHERRY SNOWBALLS

EVY ADAMS, WEST SENECA, NEW YORK

A juicy maraschino cherry is the pleasant surprise tucked inside these unique cookies. My mother clipped this recipe out of the newspaper more than 30 years ago.

- 1 cup butter, softened
- 1/2 cup confectioners' sugar
- 1 tablespoon water
- 1 teaspoon vanilla extract
- 2 cups all-purpose flour
- 1 cup quick-cooking oats
- 1/2 teaspoon salt
- 36 maraschino cherries, well drained

COATING

- 2 cups confectioners' sugar
- 1/4 to 1/3 cup milk
- 2 cups flaked coconut, finely chopped

* In a mixing bowl, cream butter, sugar, water and vanilla. Combine flour, oats and salt; gradually add to creamed mixture.

* Shape a tablespoonful of dough around each cherry, forming a ball. Place 2 in. apart on ungreased baking sheets. Bake at 350° for 18-20 minutes or until bottoms are browned. Remove to wire racks to cool.

* Combine sugar and enough milk to achieve smooth dipping consistency. Dip cookies, then roll in coconut. YIELD: 3 dozen.

FENNEL TEA COOKIES

NUTTY FINGERS

ELSIE HENDRICKSON, HAYS, KANSAS

These classic Christmas cookies have stood the test of time. The recipe makes a smaller-sized batch, which gets you in and out of the kitchen.

- ½ **cup butter, softened**
- ⅓ **cup confectioners' sugar**
- 1 **teaspoon vanilla extract**
- 1 **cup all-purpose flour**
- ¼ **teaspoon salt**
- 1 **cup finely chopped pecans**

Additional confectioners' sugar

❋ In a small mixing bowl, cream butter a sugar. Beat in vanilla. Combine flour a salt; gradually add to creamed mixtu Stir in pecans. Shape tablespoonfuls dough into 2-in. logs. Place 2 in. ap on ungreased baking sheets.

❋ Bake at 375° for 9-11 minutes or ur edges are lightly browned. Roll wa cookies in confectioners' sugar. Remo to wire racks to cool. YIELD: abou dozen.

OATMEAL PECAN COOKIE

DEBBI SMITH, CROSSETT, ARKANSAS

It's hard to stop munching on these delightful cookies once you start.

- 1 **cup shortening**
- 1 **cup packed brown sugar**
- 1 **cup sugar**
- 2 **eggs**
- 1 **teaspoon vanilla extract**
- 1½ **cups all-purpose flour**
- 1 **teaspoon baking soda**
- 1 **teaspoon salt**
- 3 **cups old-fashioned oats**
- 1 **cup chopped pecans**

❋ In a mixing bowl, cream shortening a sugars. Add eggs and vanilla. Combi flour, baking soda and salt; gradually a to creamed mixture. Stir in oats and nu Chill for 30 minutes.

❋ Shape into 1½-in. balls; place 2 in. ap on greased baking sheets. Bake at 35 for 10-12 minutes or until golden brov Remove to wire racks to cool. YIELD dozen.

FENNEL TEA COOKIES

SUSAN BECK, NAPA, CALIFORNIA

These tender, buttery tea cookies have a lovely fennel flavor and add a touch of elegance to any holiday cookie tray. Rolled in confectioners' sugar, they look like snowballs!

- 1 **tablespoon fennel seed, crushed**
- 2 **tablespoons boiling water**
- ¾ **cup butter, softened**
- ⅔ **cup packed brown sugar**
- 1 **egg**
- 2 **cups all-purpose flour**
- ½ **teaspoon baking soda**

Confectioners' sugar

❋ In a small bowl, soak fennel seed in boiling water; set aside. In a mixing bowl, cream butter and brown sugar. Beat in egg. Drain fennel seed. Combine the flour, baking soda and fennel seed; gradually add to creamed mixture.

❋ Roll into 1-in. balls; place 2 in. apart on ungreased baking sheets. Bake at 350° for 10-12 minutes or until lightly browned. Roll warm cookies in confectioners' sugar. Remove to wire racks to cool. YIELD: 3 dozen.

REAM CHEESE DAINTIES

INE STEWART, JULIAN, PENNSYLVANIA

eam cheese and butter make these
nder treats just melt in your mouth.
th just four ingredients, these lovely
okies could not be easier to make.
ey've very impressive-looking on a
ssert tray and always generate
mpliments. I really enjoy the fruit
ng tucked into the rich cookies.

1 cup butter, softened

**1 package (8 ounces) cream cheese,
softened**

2 cups all-purpose flour

**2 cup 100% apricot spreadable fruit
or seedless raspberry preserves**

In a large mixing bowl, cream the butter
and cream cheese. Gradually add flour
to the creamed mixture. Divide dough
into four portions; cover and refrigerate
until easy to handle.

On a lightly floured surface, roll one portion of dough at a time into a 10-in. x
7½-in. rectangle. Trim edges if necessary.
Cut into 2½-in. squares.

Place ¼ teaspoon spreadable fruit or preserves near each end of two diagonal corners. Moisten the remaining two corners
with water; fold over and press lightly.

Place on ungreased baking sheets. Bake
at 350° for 12-15 minutes or until corners
are lightly browned. Cool 2-3 minutes before removing to wire racks. YIELD: about
4 dozen.

ARAMEL-FILLED
HOCOLATE COOKIES

B WALSH, CABERY, ILLINOIS

ese yummy chocolate cookies have
asty caramel surprise inside. With
cans on top and a contrasting white
ocolate drizzle, they're almost too
etty to eat!

1 cup butter, softened

1 cup plus 1 tablespoon sugar, *divided*

1 cup packed brown sugar

2 eggs

1 teaspoon vanilla extract

2 cups all-purpose flour

¾ cup baking cocoa

1 teaspoon baking soda

1¼ cups chopped pecans, *divided*

1 package (13 ounces) Rolo candies

**4 squares (1 ounce *each*) white
baking chocolate, melted**

✳ In a large mixing bowl, cream butter, 1
cup sugar and brown sugar. Add the
eggs, one at a time, beating well after
each addition. Beat in vanilla. Combine
the flour, cocoa and baking soda; gradually add to the creamed mixture, beating
just until combined. Stir in ½ cup pecans.

✳ Shape a tablespoonful of dough around
each candy, forming a ball. In a small
bowl, combine the remaining sugar and
pecans; dip each cookie halfway. Place
nut side up 2 in. apart on greased baking
sheets.

✳ Bake at 375° for 7-10 minutes or until tops
are slightly cracked. Cool for 3 minutes
before removing to wire racks to cool
completely. Drizzle with melted white
chocolate. YIELD: 5 dozen.

CARAMEL-FILLED CHOCOLATE COOKIES

WHITE CHOCOLATE-CRANBERRY BISCOTTI

BRENDA KEITH, TALENT, OREGON

The original version of this recipe was handed down from my great-aunt. Through the years, my mother and I have tried different flavor combinations...this is a favorite for all.

- ½ **cup butter, softened**
- 1 **cup sugar**
- 4 **eggs**
- 1 **teaspoon vanilla extract**
- 3 **cups all-purpose flour**
- 1 **tablespoon baking powder**
- ¾ **cup dried cranberries**
- ¾ **cup vanilla** *or* **white chips**

❉ In a large mixing bowl, cream butter and sugar. Add eggs, one at a time, beating well after each addition. Beat in vanilla. Combine flour and baking powder; gradually add to creamed mixture. Stir in cranberries and vanilla chips. Divide dough into three portions.

❉ On ungreased baking sheets, shape each portion into a 10-in. x 2-in. rectangle. Bake at 350° for 20-25 minutes or until lightly browned. Cool for 5 minutes.

❉ Transfer to a cutting board; cut diagonally with a serrated knife into 1-in. slices. Place cut side down on ungreased baking sheets. Bake for 15-20 minutes or until golden brown. Remove to wire racks to cool. Store in an airtight container. YIELD: 2½ dozen.

WHITE CHOCOLATE-CRANBERRY BISCOTTI

SOFT AND CHEWY MOLASSES COOKIES

SOFT AND CHEWY MOLASSES COOKIES

DEBBIE RACETTE, ANTICOCH, ILLINOIS

These cookies are delicious served warm right from the oven! I usually make them around Christmastime or on cold snowy days here in the Midwest.

- 1 **cup plus 3 tablespoons butter**
- 1¼ **cups sugar,** *divided*
- ¼ **cup molasses**
- 1 **egg**
- 2½ **cups all-purpose flour**
- 2 **teaspoons baking soda**
- 1 **teaspoon ground cinnamon**
- 1 **teaspoon ground ginger**
- ¾ **teaspoon ground cloves**

❉ In a large mixing bowl, cream butter a 1 cup sugar. Blend in molasses and e Combine flour, baking soda, cinnam ginger and cloves; add to creamed m ture. Mix until well blended.

❉ Shape dough into 1¼-in. balls. Roll b in remaining sugar. Place on greased b ing sheets. Press flat with a fork. Bake 350° about 10-12 minutes or until s Remove to wire racks to cool. YIELD: ab 4 dozen.

NICKERDOODLES

TE OF HOME TEST KITCHEN

e history of this whimsically named
at is widely disputed, but the
pularity of this classic cinnamon-
gar-coated cookie is undeniable!

- 2 cup butter, softened
- 1 cup plus 2 tablespoons sugar, *divided*
- 1 egg
- 2 teaspoon vanilla extract
- 2 cups all-purpose flour
- 4 teaspoon baking soda
- 4 teaspoon cream of tartar
- 1 teaspoon ground cinnamon

In a large mixing bowl, cream butter and
1 cup sugar until light and fluffy. Beat in
egg and vanilla. Combine the flour, baking soda and cream of tartar; gradually
add to the creamed mixture. In a small
bowl, combine cinnamon and remaining
sugar.

Shape dough into 1-in. balls; roll in cinnamon-sugar. Place 2 in. apart on ungreased
baking sheets. Bake at 375° for 10-12 minutes or until lightly browned. Remove to
wire racks to cool. YIELD: 2½ dozen.

WEDISH SPRITZ

MGARD SINN, SHERWOOD PARK, ALBERTA

touch of almond extract gives these
ritz wonderful flavor. For Christmas,
u could tint half of the dough with
d food coloring and the other half
th green.

- 1 cup butter, softened
- ⅓ cup sugar
- 1 egg
- ½ teaspoon almond extract
- ½ teaspoon vanilla extract
- ¼ cups all-purpose flour
- 1 teaspoon baking powder

epared frosting

In a large mixing bowl, cream butter and
sugar until light and fluffy. Beat in egg and
extracts. Combine the flour and baking
powder; gradually add to the creamed
mixture.

※ Using a cookie press fitted with the disk
of your choice, press dough 1 in. apart onto ungreased baking sheets. Bake at 400°
for 7-9 minutes or until edges are firm and
lightly browned. Remove to wire racks to
cool. Frost as desired. YIELD: 4-5 dozen.

COOKIE JAR GINGERSNAPS

DEB HANDY, POMONA, KANSAS

My grandma kept two cookie jars in
her pantry. One of the jars, which I now
have, always had these crisp and chewy
gingersnaps in it.

- ¾ cup shortening
- 1 cup sugar
- 1 egg
- ¼ cup molasses
- 2 cups all-purpose flour
- 2 teaspoons baking soda
- 1½ teaspoons ground ginger
- 1 teaspoon ground cinnamon
- ½ teaspoon salt

Additional sugar

※ In a large mixing bowl, cream the shortening and sugar. Beat in the egg and molasses. Combine flour, baking soda, ginger, cinnamon and salt; gradually add to
creamed mixture.

※ Roll teaspoonfuls of dough into balls.
Dip one side of each ball into sugar; place
with sugar side up on a greased baking
sheet. Bake at 350° for 12-15 minutes or
until lightly browned and crinkly. Remove
to wire racks to cool. YIELD: 3-4 dozen.

COOKIE JAR GINGERSNAPS

PUMPKIN PECAN TASSIES

PUMPKIN PECAN TASSIES

PAT HABIGER, SPEARVILLE, KANSAS

These delicious mini tarts are lovely for Christmas or to serve at a tea. They're worth the extra time it takes to make them.

- ½ **cup butter, softened**
- 1 **package (3 ounces) cream cheese, softened**
- 1 **cup all-purpose flour**

FILLING

- ¾ **cup packed brown sugar,** *divided*
- ¼ **cup canned pumpkin**
- 4 **teaspoons plus 1 tablespoon butter, melted,** *divided*
- 1 **egg yolk**
- 1 **tablespoon half-and-half cream**
- 1 **teaspoon vanilla extract**
- ¼ **teaspoon rum extract**
- ⅛ **teaspoon ground cinnamon**
- ⅛ **teaspoon ground nutmeg**
- ½ **cup chopped pecans**

✳ In a small mixing bowl, cream butter and cream cheese. Beat in flour. Shape into 24 balls. With floured fingers, press onto the bottom and up the sides of greased miniature muffin cups.

✳ Bake at 325° for 8-10 minutes or ur edges are lightly browned.

✳ Meanwhile, in a bowl, combine ½ c brown sugar, pumpkin, 4 teaspoons b ter, egg yolk, cream, extracts, cinnam and nutmeg. Spoon into warm cuj Combine the pecans and remaini brown sugar and butter; sprinkle over t filling.

✳ Bake 23-27 minutes longer or until set a edges are golden brown. Cool for 10 m utes before removing from pans to w racks. YIELD: 2 dozen.

SECRET KISS COOKIES

KAREN OWEN, RISING SUN, INDIANA

Here's a recipe that's literally sealed with a "kiss." This cookie's bound to tickle any sweet tooth.

- 1 **cup butter, softened**
- ½ **cup sugar**
- 1 **teaspoon vanilla extract**
- 2 **cups all-purpose flour**
- 1 **cup finely chopped walnuts**
- 1 **package (8 ounces) milk chocolate kisses**
- 1⅓ **cups confectioners' sugar,** *divided*
- 2 **tablespoons baking cocoa**

✳ In a mixing bowl, cream butter, sug and vanilla. Gradually add flour. Fold walnuts. Refrigerate dough for 2-3 hou or until firm.

✳ Shape into 1-in. balls. Flatten balls ar place a chocolate kiss in the center each; pinch dough together around kis Place 2 in. apart on ungreased bakir sheets.

✳ Bake at 375° for 12 minutes or until s but not browned. Cool for 1 minute; r move from pans to wire racks.

✳ Sift ⅔ cup confectioners' sugar and c coa. While cookies are still warm, roll ha in cocoa mixture and half in remainin confectioners' sugar. Cool completel Store in an airtight container. YIELD: abo 2½ dozen.

NGERBREAD TEDDIES

ITH SCHOLOVICH, WAUKESHA, WISCONSIN

s of all ages will be delighted to see
se roly-poly teddy bears adorning
ur holiday table! I've been using this
gerbread recipe for as long as I can
member.

2 cups all-purpose flour, *divided*
2 cups packed brown sugar
2 cups shortening
2 cup molasses
2 eggs
2 teaspoons baking soda
2 teaspoons ground cinnamon
2 teaspoons ground ginger
1 teaspoon ground cloves
misweet chocolate chips

n a large mixing bowl, combine 2¼ cups
flour, brown sugar, shortening, molasses,
eggs, baking soda, cinnamon, ginger

and cloves. Beat on high speed until combined. Beat in remaining flour. Cover and refrigerate for at least 2 hours.

❋ Shape dough into 12 balls, 1¾ in. each; 12 balls, 1¼ in. each; 72 balls, ½ in. each; and 60 balls, ⅜ in. each. Place the 1¾-in. balls on three foil-lined baking sheets for the body of 12 bears; flatten to ½-in. thickness.

❋ Attach six ½-in. balls to each bear for arms, legs and ears. Attach four ⅜-in. balls for paws. Attach one ⅜-in. ball for nose. Add chocolate chips for eyes and belly buttons. Make three cuts halfway through the dough on the end of each paw; make an indentation in each ear with a wooden spoon handle.

❋ Bake at 350° for 12-16 minutes or until set. Cool for 10 minutes before carefully removing from pans to wire racks to cool completely (cookies will be fragile while warm). YIELD: 1 dozen.

GINGERBREAD TEDDIES

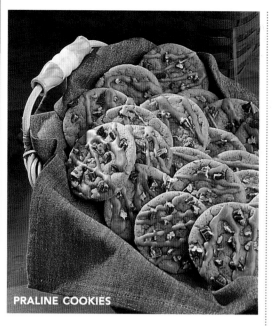

PRALINE COOKIES

PRALINE COOKIES

MELODY SROUFE, WICHITA, KANSAS
These cookies are both crisp and chewy. They can be frozen after they're iced for real convenience. With two small children, that's a great way to have my baking done ahead of time for holidays or special occasions. The only problem is hiding them so my husband can't find them!

- ½ **cup butter, softened**
- 1½ **cups packed brown sugar**
- 1 **egg**
- 1 **teaspoon vanilla extract**
- 1½ **cups all-purpose flour**
- 1½ **teaspoons baking powder**
- ¼ **teaspoon salt**
- 1 **cup pecans, coarsely chopped**

ICING
- 1 **cup packed brown sugar**
- ½ **cup heavy whipping cream**
- 1 **cup confectioners' sugar**

❄ In a mixing bowl, cream the butter and brown sugar. Add egg and vanilla; mix well. Combine flour, baking powder and salt; add to creamed mixture. Mix well. Cover and chill until dough is easy to handle, about 1 hour.

❄ Form into 1-in. balls; place 2 in. apart on greased baking sheets. Flatten cookies

slightly with fingers; sprinkle each wit[h] teaspoon pecans. Bake at 350° for [ ] minutes. Remove to wire racks to cool[.]

❄ Meanwhile, for icing, combine the bro[wn] sugar and cream in a saucepan. Cook o[ver] medium-high heat until sugar dissolv[es] and mixture comes to a boil, stirring co[n]stantly. Remove from the heat; blen[d in] confectioners' sugar until smooth. Driz[zle] over the top of the cooled cookies. YIE[LD:] 4 dozen.

JEWELED THUMBPRINTS

MARIA DEBONO, NEW YORK, NEW YORK
When I moved here from Malta more than 20 years ago, a kind neighbor la[dy] took me under her wing and baked many cookies for me. This is one of h[er] recipes that I treasure.

- ¾ **cup butter, softened**
- ¾ **cup confectioners' sugar**
- 1 **egg yolk**
- ½ **teaspoon almond extract**
- 1¾ **cups all-purpose flour**
- ½ **cup raspberry** *or* **apricot preserve[s]**

❄ In a mixing bowl, cream butter and su[g]ar. Beat in egg yolk and extract. Gradua[lly] add flour. Cover and refrigerate fo[r 2] hours or until easy to handle.

❄ Roll into ¾-in. balls. Place 1 in. apart [on] greased baking sheets. Using the end [of]

JEWELED THUMBPRINTS

a wooden spoon handle, make an indentation in the center of each ball.

Bake at 350° for 12-14 minutes or until edges are lightly browned. Remove to wire racks to cool. Fill with preserves. YIELD: 6 dozen.

INGERBREAD BISCOTTI

STE OF HOME TEST KITCHEN

anberries and almonds pair well with e mild gingerbread flavor in these okies. The crisp cookies taste terrific th a steaming cup of coffee.

- 3 eggs
- 1 cup sugar
- /3 cup vegetable oil
- /4 cup molasses
- /4 cups all-purpose flour
- 3 teaspoons baking powder
- 3 teaspoons ground ginger
- /4 teaspoons ground cinnamon
- /4 teaspoon ground nutmeg
- /4 cup slivered almonds
- /2 cup dried cranberries

In a large mixing bowl, beat the eggs, sugar, oil and molasses. Combine the flour, baking powder, ginger, cinnamon and nutmeg; gradually add to the egg mixture. Turn onto a floured surface. Knead in almonds and cranberries.

Divide dough in half; shape each portion into a 14-in. x 3-in. rectangle. Transfer to a greased baking sheet. Bake at 375° for 24-26 minutes or until lightly browned. Cool for 5 minutes.

Transfer to a cutting board; with a serrated knife, cut each rectangle into 18 slices. Place slices cut side down on greased baking sheets. Bake for 10-15 minutes or until firm and crisp, turning once. Remove to wire racks to cool. Store in an airtight container. YIELD: 3 dozen.

SANDBAKKELSE (SAND TARTS)

KAREN HOYLO, DULUTH, MINNESOTA
Translated from Norwegian, the name of these cookies is "sand tarts." They're most attractive if baked in authentic sandbakkelse molds, which can be purchased in a Scandinavian import shop. Most any decorative cookie mold will do, though, and the interesting shapes will make these tarts the focus of your cookie tray!

- 1 cup plus 2 tablespoons butter, softened
- 1 cup sugar
- 1 egg
- 1 teaspoon almond extract
- ½ teaspoon vanilla extract
- 3 cups all-purpose flour

✳ In a mixing bowl, cream butter and sugar. Add egg and extracts. Blend in flour. Cover and chill for 1-2 hours or overnight. Using ungreased sandbakkelse molds, press about 1 tablespoon dough into each mold.

✳ Bake at 375° for 10-12 minutes or until cookies appear set and just begin to brown around the edges. Cool for 2-3 minutes in molds. When cool to the touch, remove cookies from molds. To remove more easily, gently tap with a knife and carefully squeeze it. YIELD: about 8 dozen.

SANDBAKKELSE (SAND TARTS)

BEST LOVED
cookies
& BARS

perfectly shaped spritz

If you are making spritz cookies for the first time, it may take a little practice with the cookie press to make perfectly shaped cookies.

Just Right. When just the right amount of dough is pressed out, the baked cookie will have a uniform design and crisp indentations.

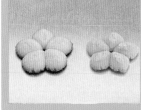

Too Small. When too little dough is pressed out, the design will not meet at all the indentations. The cookie will be too small and break easily.

Too Big. When too much dough is pressed out, the design will lose its form.

ORANGE SPRITZ COOKIES

SEAN FLEMING, ST. CHARLES, ILLINOIS

Brown sugar gives these spritz cookies a lovely light caramel tint. With a hint of orange flavor, this variation has a rich, buttery shortbread taste with less fat than other Christmas treats. They are a delightful addition to my holiday cookie tray.

- 1/2 cup butter, softened
- 1 package (3 ounces) cream cheese, softened
- 1/2 cup packed brown sugar
- 2 teaspoons grated orange peel
- 1/2 teaspoon orange *or* vanilla extract
- 1 1/2 cups all-purpose flour
- 1/4 teaspoon salt

Colored sugar

❋ In a large mixing bowl, cream the butter, cream cheese and brown sugar until light and fluffy. Beat in orange peel and extract. Combine flour and salt; gradually add to creamed mixture.

❋ Using a cookie press fitted with the disk of your choice, press cookies 1 in. apart onto ungreased baking sheets. Sprinkle with colored sugar. Bake at 375° for 6-9 minutes or until lightly browned. Cool for 2 minutes before removing to wire racks. YIELD: about 5 1/2 dozen.

ORANGE SPRITZ COOKIES

SUGARCOATED MELTAWAYS

CHARLOTTE WRIGHT, LEBANON, CONNECTIC

I have fond memories of my parents spending days in the kitchen baking Christmas cookies. It's a tradition that my husband and I now happily carry o

- 1/2 cup orange juice
- 1 tablespoon grated orange peel
- 3/4 cup butter, softened
- 1/4 cup sugar
- 1 tablespoon cold water
- 1 teaspoon vanilla extract
- 1 3/4 cups all-purpose flour
- 1/8 teaspoon salt
- 1 cup miniature semisweet chocolat chips
- 1 cup finely chopped walnuts

Additional sugar

❋ In a small bowl, combine orange juice a peel; set aside. In a mixing bowl, crea butter and sugar. Beat in water and var la. Combine flour and salt; gradually a to creamed mixture. Stir in chocola chips and walnuts.

❋ Roll into 1-in. balls. Place 1 in. apart on u greased baking sheets. Bake at 325° 12-15 minutes or until lightly browne Remove to wire racks to cool.

❋ Strain reserved orange juice. Dip cooki in juice, then roll in additional sugar. L dry. Store in an airtight container. YIEI 3 1/2 dozen.

RASPBERRY 'N' VANILLA CHIP COOKIES

DEANN ALLEVA, HUDSON, WISCONSIN

Many holiday cookies are fancy and time-consuming. So I appreciate this basic recipe featuring raspberry chocolate chips. I know your family will like them, too.

- 1/2 cup butter, softened
- 1 cup sugar
- 2 eggs
- 3 teaspoons vanilla extract
- 2 cups all-purpose flour

1 teaspoon baking soda

½ teaspoon salt

2 cups raspberry chocolate chips

½ cup vanilla or white chips

In a large mixing bowl, cream butter and sugar. Add eggs, one at a time, beating well after each addition. Beat in vanilla. Combine the flour, baking soda and salt; gradually add to the creamed mixture. Stir in chips.

Roll into 1½-in. balls. Place 2 in. apart on lightly greased baking sheets. Bake at 350° for 12-15 minutes or until lightly browned. Remove to wire racks to cool. YIELD: about 3½ dozen.

MOCHA-PECAN BUTTER BALLS

KATHLEEN PRUITT, HOOPESTON, ILLINOIS

When I was a little girl, one of my mother's co-workers would bring tins of assorted Christmas cookies for my sister and me. These were the ones I reached for first.

⅓ cup butter, softened

1 package (3 ounces) cream cheese, softened

⅓ cup instant chocolate drink mix

⅓ cup confectioners' sugar

1 teaspoon instant coffee granules

2 teaspoons vanilla extract

¼ cups all-purpose flour

¼ teaspoon salt

1 cup finely chopped pecans

Additional confectioners' sugar

In a mixing bowl, cream butter, cream cheese, drink mix, sugar and coffee granules. Beat in vanilla. Combine flour and salt; gradually add to creamed mixture. Stir in pecans. Cover and refrigerate for 1 hour or until easy to handle.

Roll into 1-in. balls. Place 1 in. apart on ungreased baking sheets. Bake at 350° for 15-18 minutes or until firm. Cool on pan for 1-2 minutes. Roll warm cookies in confectioners' sugar; Remove to wire racks to cool. YIELD: 4 dozen.

PECAN MELTAWAYS

PECAN MELTAWAYS

ALBERTA MCKAY, BARTLESVILLE, OKLAHOMA

These sugared nut-filled balls are a tradition of ours at Christmastime, but they are great any time of year. And, they melt in your mouth!

1 cup butter, softened

½ cup confectioners' sugar

1 teaspoon vanilla extract

2¼ cups all-purpose flour

¼ teaspoon salt

¾ cup chopped pecans

Additional confectioners' sugar

❋ In a mixing bowl, cream the butter, sugar and vanilla; mix well. Combine the flour and salt; add to creamed mixture. Stir in pecans. Chill.

❋ Roll into 1-in. balls and place on ungreased baking sheets. Bake at 350° for 10-12 minutes. Roll in confectioners' sugar while still warm. Cool; roll in sugar again. YIELD: about 4 dozen.

FRUITY PASTEL COOKIES

CONNA DUFF, LEXINGTON, VIRGINIA

Lime gelatin tints the dough and gives these wreaths a hint of fruity flavor. Try other flavors and shapes, too.

- ¾ **cup butter, softened**
- ½ **cup sugar**
- 1 **package (3 ounces) lime gelatin *or* flavor of your choice**
- 1 **egg**
- ½ **teaspoon vanilla extract**
- 1¾ **cups all-purpose flour**
- ½ **teaspoon baking powder**

Red and green colored sugar *and/or* sprinkles

❋ In a large mixing bowl, cream butter, sugar and gelatin powder. Beat in egg and vanilla. Combine flour and baking powder; gradually add to creamed mixture and mix well.

❋ Using a cookie press fitted with the disk of your choice, press dough 2 in. apart onto ungreased baking sheets. Decorate as desired with colored sugar and/or sprinkles. Bake at 400° for 6-8 minutes or until set (do not brown). Remove to wire racks to cool. YIELD: 6 dozen.

FRUITY PASTEL COOKIES

JEWELED COCONUT DROPS

ELLEN MARIE BYLER
MUNFORDVILLE, KENTUCKY

Red raspberry preserves add a festive flair to these tender coconut cookies. Perfect for potlucks and cookie exchanges, these shaped cookies never last long when I make them for my husband and sons.

- ⅓ **cup butter, softened**
- 1 **package (3 ounces) cream cheese, softened**
- ¾ **cup sugar**
- 1 **egg yolk**
- 2 **teaspoons orange juice**
- 1 **teaspoon almond extract**
- 1¼ **cups all-purpose flour**
- 1½ **teaspoons baking powder**
- ¼ **teaspoon salt**
- 3¾ **cups flaked coconut, *divided***
- 1 **cup seedless raspberry preserves, warmed**

❋ In a large mixing bowl, cream the butter, cream cheese and sugar. Beat in the egg yolk, orange juice and almond extract. Combine the flour, baking powder and salt; gradually add to creamed mixture. Stir in 3 cups of coconut. Refrigerate for 30 minutes or until easy to handle.

❋ Shape dough into 2-in. balls; roll in remaining coconut. Place 2 in. apart on ungreased baking sheets. Using the end of a wooden spoon handle, make an indentation in the center of each ball.

❋ Bake at 350° for 8-10 minutes or until lightly browned. Remove to wire racks to cool. Fill each cookie with preserves. YIELD: 3½ dozen cookies.

JDGE-FILLED TOFFEE COOKIES

JDGE-FILLED
OFFEE COOKIES

REN BARTO, CHURCHVILLE, VIRGINIA

ombined three recipes to come up
th these crisp cookies topped with a
eet chocolate center. They're a nice
dition to a holiday cookie tray.

'2 cup butter, softened

'2 cup sugar

'2 cup confectioners' sugar

'2 cup vegetable oil

1 egg

'2 teaspoon almond extract

'4 teaspoon coconut extract

'4 cups all-purpose flour

'2 cup whole wheat flour

'2 teaspoon salt

'2 teaspoon baking soda

'2 teaspoon cream of tartar

'4 cup English toffee bits *or* almond
   brickle chips

'3 cup chopped pecans

'3 cup flaked coconut

Additional sugar

FILLING

1½ **cups semisweet chocolate chips,
   melted**

 ¾ **cup sweetened condensed milk**

1½ **teaspoons vanilla extract**

1¼ **cups pecan halves**

❄ In a large mixing bowl, cream butter and
   sugars. Beat in the oil, egg and extracts.
   Combine the flours, salt, baking soda and
   cream of tartar; gradually add to the
   creamed mixture. Stir in the toffee bits,
   pecans and coconut. Cover and refrigerate for 1 hour or until easy to handle.

❄ Shape dough into 1-in. balls; roll in sugar. Place 2 in. apart on ungreased baking
   sheets. Using the end of a wooden spoon
   handle, make an indentation in the center
   of each.

❄ In a bowl, combine the melted chocolate,
   milk and vanilla until smooth. Spoon 1 teaspoon into the center of each cookie. Top
   with a pecan half. Bake at 350° for 12-14
   minutes or until lightly browned. Remove
   to wire racks to cool. YIELD: 5½ dozen.

DOUBLE CHOCOLATE CHIP COOKIES

DOUBLE CHOCOLATE CHIP COOKIES

DIANE HIXON, NICEVILLE, FLORIDA

The cocoa in the batter gives these treats a double dose of chocolate. They disappear fast from my cookie jar.

- 1 **cup butter, softened**
- 1 **cup sugar**
- ½ **cup packed dark brown sugar**
- 1 **teaspoon vanilla extract**
- 1 **egg**
- ⅓ **cup baking cocoa**
- 2 **tablespoons milk**
- 1¾ **cups all-purpose flour**
- ¼ **teaspoon baking powder**
- 1 **cup chopped walnuts**
- 1 **cup (6 ounces) semisweet chocolate chips**

❊ In a large mixing bowl, cream the butter, sugars and vanilla. Beat in egg. Add cocoa and milk. Combine flour and baking powder; fold into creamed mixture with walnuts and chocolate chips.

❊ Roll teaspoonfuls of dough into balls; place 2 in. apart on ungreased baking sheets. Bake at 350° for 10-12 minutes. Cool for 5 minutes before removing to wire racks. YIELD: 3-4 dozen.

CHOCOLATE-DIPPED SPRITZ

NANCY ROSS, ALVORDTON, OHIO

Some of my sisters and I get together for a weekend during the holidays to do nothing but bake cookies. These cookies always make an appearance i the goody baskets that we give as gif

- 1 **cup butter, softened**
- ¾ **cup sugar**
- 1 **egg**
- 1 **teaspoon vanilla extract**
- 2¼ **cups all-purpose flour**
- ½ **teaspoon salt**
- ¼ **teaspoon baking powder**
- 11 **ounces dark, white *or* milk chocolate candy coating**

Chopped walnuts *or* colored sprinkles, optional

❊ In a large mixing bowl, cream butter a sugar. Beat in egg and vanilla. Combi the flour, salt and baking powder; grac ally add to creamed mixture.

❊ Using a cookie press fitted with the d of your choice, press dough 2 in. apart to ungreased baking sheets. Bake at 37 for 7-9 minutes or until set (do not brow Remove to wire racks to cool.

❊ In a microwave-safe bowl, melt can coating; dip each cookie halfway. Sprin with nuts or sprinkles. Place on waxed p per until set. YIELD: about 6 dozen.

CHOCOLATE-DIPPED SPRIT

ATMEAL SHORTBREAD

LIAN MACHACEK, TABER, ALBERTA

unchy oats give this traditional ortbread recipe a new twist. These ttery confections are simply good to e very last crumb—especially with a of hot coffee or eggnog. I've also rned that they keep for months...if u hide them well enough!

- 2 **cups butter, softened**
- 1 **cup sugar**
- 1 **cup quick-cooking oats**
- 4 **cups all-purpose flour**
- 2 **teaspoon ground cinnamon**
- 4 **teaspoon salt**

ditional sugar

n a large mixing bowl, cream butter and sugar. Place the oats in a blender or food processor; process until ground. Add to creamed mixture.

Combine the flour, cinnamon and salt; gradually add to oat mixture. Cover and refrigerate for 1 hour.

Roll dough into 1-in. balls; roll in sugar. Place 2 in. apart on ungreased baking sheets; flatten slightly. Bake at 325° for 15-20 minutes or until golden brown. Remove to wire racks to cool. YIELD: about 4½ dozen.

ECAN-TOPPED UGAR COOKIES

TTY LECH, ST. CHARLES, ILLINOIS

is recipe dresses up refrigerated okie dough with cream cheese and conut. Folks love the almond flavor.

- 1 **can (8 ounces) almond paste**
- 1 **package (3 ounces) cream cheese, softened**
- 4 **cup flaked coconut**
- 1 **tube (18 ounces) refrigerated sugar cookie dough**
- 1 **cup pecan halves**

In a mixing bowl, beat almond paste and cream cheese. Add coconut; mix well. Cut cookie dough into ½-in. slices; divide each slice into four portions.

Roll into balls. Place 2 in. apart on greased

KIPPLENS

baking sheets. Shape ½ teaspoonfuls of almond mixture into balls; place one on each ball of dough. Lightly press pecans into tops.

✳ Bake at 350° for 10-12 minutes or until lightly browned. Remove to wire racks to cool. YIELD: about 3½ dozen.

KIPPLENS

SUSAN BOHANNON, KOKOMO, INDIANA

My Great-Aunt Hilda makes this recipe every Christmas, and everybody just raves about it! Kipplens taste a lot like Mexican wedding cakes, but I like them better.

- 2 **cups butter**
- 1 **cup sugar**
- 5 **cups all-purpose flour**
- 2 **teaspoons vanilla extract**
- 2 **cups chopped pecans**
- ¼ **teaspoon salt**

Confectioners' sugar

✳ In a mixing bowl, cream butter and sugar; add flour, vanilla, pecans and salt. Mix well. Roll dough into 1-in. balls and place on ungreased baking sheets.

✳ Bake at 325° for 17-20 minutes or until lightly browned. Cool cookies slightly before rolling them in confectioners' sugar. YIELD: 12 dozen.

making crescent-shaped cookies

Shape rounded tea-spoonfuls of dough into 2½-in. logs, then bend slightly to form the crescent shape.

DIPPED VANILLAS

DIPPED VANILLAS

KAREN BOURNE, MAGRTH, ALBERTA

A touch of chocolate makes these classics stand out on the holiday cookie tray. They're a tradition at our home for Christmas.

- ½ **cup butter, softened**
- ½ **cup ground almonds**
- ¼ **cup sugar**
- 1 **teaspoon vanilla extract**
- 1 **cup all-purpose flour**
- 2 **tablespoons cornstarch**
- 2 **squares (1 ounce *each*) semisweet chocolate**
- ½ **teaspoon shortening**

✻ In a mixing bowl, cream butter, almonds, sugar and vanilla; add flour and corn-starch. Roll into 1-in. balls; shape into cres-cents. Place on greased baking sheets.

✻ Bake at 375° for 8-10 minutes or until lightly browned. Cool completely on wire racks.

✻ Melt chocolate and shortening in a mi-crowave or double boiler; stir until smooth. Dip one end of each crescent into chocolate; decorate as desired. Cool on waxed paper. Refrigerate for about 30 minutes to firm the chocolate. YIELD: about 2½ dozen.

HONEY SPICE KRINKLES

DONALD SHOPSHIRE
SALTON SEA BEACH, CALIFORNIA

Sugar and spice make these Christma cookies among the nicest I've ever tried. Deliciously old-fashioned, they' been our family favorites for years. Busy holiday bakers will be pleased t know that the dough is very easy to work with.

- ¾ **cup butter, softened**
- 1 **cup packed brown sugar**
- 1 **egg**
- ¼ **cup honey**
- 2¼ **cups all-purpose flour**
- 1½ **teaspoons baking soda**
- 1 **teaspoon ground ginger**
- 1 **teaspoon salt**
- ½ **teaspoon ground cinnamon**
- ¼ **teaspoon ground cloves**

Sugar

✻ In a mixing bowl, cream butter and bro⌐ sugar until fluffy. Beat in egg and hon⌐ Combine flour, baking soda, ginger, s⌐ cinnamon and cloves; gradually add creamed mixture and mix well. Cover a⌐ refrigerate for at least 2 hours.

✻ Shape into 1-in. balls. Dip half of each b⌐ into water and then into sugar. Pla⌐ with sugar side up 2 in. apart on u⌐ greased baking sheets.

✻ Bake at 350° for 15-17 minutes or ur⌐ lightly browned. Remove to wire racks cool. YIELD: about 5 dozen.

OATMEAL GINGERSNAPS

SHERRY HARKE, SOUTH BEND, INDIANA

I always get compliments on these delicious chewy cookies. The spicy aroma fills my kitchen when they're baking and never fails to set a warm holiday mood.

- ½ **cup shortening**
- ¼ **cup molasses**
- 1 **egg**
- 1½ **cups all-purpose flour**
- 1 **cup sugar**

4 cup quick-cooking oats
1 teaspoon baking soda
1 teaspoon ground ginger
4 teaspoon ground cloves
4 teaspoon salt
ditional sugar

n a mixing bowl, cream shortening, mo-
asses and egg. Combine dry ingredients;
stir into creamed mixture. Roll into 1-in.
balls; roll in sugar.

Place on greased baking sheets. Flatten
slightly with a flat-bottomed glass. Bake
at 350° for 10 minutes. Remove to wire
racks to cool. YIELD: about 3½ dozen.

JGARED CHERRY
EWELS

JNIFER BRANUM, O'FALLON, ILLINOIS

e texture and crunch of the sugar
ating make these chewy cookies
tra special. I love the bright cherry
nter and the fact that they look
ely in a holiday gift box or tin.

1 cup butter, softened
2 cup sugar
3 cup light corn syrup
2 eggs, *separated*
2 teaspoon vanilla extract
2 cups all-purpose flour
ditional sugar
1 jar (10 ounces) maraschino cherries,
  drained and halved

In a mixing bowl, cream butter and sugar. Beat in corn syrup, egg yolks and vanilla. Gradually add the flour. Cover and refrigerate for 1 hour or until easy to handle.

Roll into 1-in. balls. Beat egg whites until
foamy; roll balls in egg whites, then in
sugar. Place 2 in. apart on ungreased baking sheets. Using the end of a wooden
spoon handle, make an indentation in the
center of each. Press a cherry half in the
center.

Bake at 325° for 14-16 minutes or until
lightly browned. Remove to wire racks to
cool. YIELD: about 5 dozen.

CANDY CANE COOKIES

TASTE OF HOME TEST KITCHEN

Guests will have a merry time
munching these mild mint cookies. The
cute crunchy candy canes are easy to
form once you color the dough—just
roll into ropes and twist together.

1/2 cup butter, softened
1/2 cup shortening
  1 cup sugar
1/4 cup confectioners' sugar
1/2 cup milk
  1 egg
  1 teaspoon peppermint extract
  1 teaspoon vanilla extract
3½ cups all-purpose flour
1/4 teaspoon salt
Green and red food coloring

❄ In a bowl, cream butter, shortening and
sugars. Beat in milk, egg and extracts.
Gradually add flour and salt. Set aside half of
the dough. Divide remaining dough in half;
add the green food coloring to one portion
and red food coloring to the other. Wrap
each dough separately in plastic wrap.
Refrigerate for 1 hour or until easy to handle.

❄ Roll 1/2 teaspoonfuls of each color of
dough into 3-in. ropes. Place each green
rope next to a white rope; press together
gently and twist. Repeat with red ropes and
remaining white ropes.

❄ Place 2 in. apart on ungreased baking
sheets. Curve one end, forming a cane. Bake
at 350° for 11-13 minutes or until set. Cool
for 2 minutes; carefully remove to wire racks.
YIELD: about 6 dozen.

CANDY CANE COOKIES

MOCHA COOKIE PRETZELS

MOCHA COOKIE PRETZELS

TASTE OF HOME TEST KITCHEN

Looking for a little something special to bake up for the holidays? Try these elegant mocha-frosted cookies. They're wonderful with coffee and make an eye-catching addition to any cookie platter.

- ½ cup butter, softened
- ½ cup sugar
- 1 egg
- 2 squares (1 ounce *each*) unsweetened chocolate, melted and cooled
- 1 teaspoon vanilla extract
- 2 cups cake flour
- ¼ teaspoon salt

GLAZE

- 1 cup (6 ounces) semisweet chocolate chips
- 1 teaspoon shortening
- 1 teaspoon light corn syrup
- 1 cup confectioners' sugar
- 3 to 5 tablespoons hot brewed coffee
- 2 squares (1 ounce *each*) white baking chocolate, chopped

Green colored sugar, optional

❊ In a small mixing bowl, cream butter a sugar. Beat in egg. Beat in melted choc late and vanilla. Combine flour and sa gradually add to the creamed mixtu Cover and refrigerate for 1 hour or un dough is easy to handle.

❊ Divide dough into fourths; divide ea portion into 12 pieces. Shape each pie into a 6-in. rope; twist into a pretz shape. Place 1 in. apart onto ligh greased baking sheets. Bake at 400° 7-9 minutes or until set. Remove to w racks to cool.

❊ For glaze, in a microwave, melt the se sweet chips, shortening and corn syr stir until smooth. Stir in confectione sugar and enough coffee to achieve glaze consistency. Dip cookies in glaze; low excess to drip off. Place on waxed per until set.

❊ In a microwave, melt white chocola stir until smooth. Drizzle over cooki Decorate with green sugar if desired; stand until set. YIELD: 4 dozen.

FAVORITE MOLASSES COOKIES

MARJORIE JENKINS, LEES SUMMIT, MISSOURI

These cookies are chewy inside, yet crisp outside. The recipe ranks high with my family.

- 3/4 cup butter, softened
- 1 cup sugar
- 1/4 cup molasses
- 1 egg
- 2 cups all-purpose flour
- 2 teaspoons baking powder
- 1/2 teaspoon baking soda
- 1 teaspoon ground cinnamon
- 1/2 teaspoon ground cloves
- 1/2 teaspoon ground ginger

In a mixing bowl, cream butter and sugar. Beat in molasses and egg. Combine dry ingredients; gradually add to creamed mixture. Chill for 1 hour or until firm.

Shape into 1-in. balls; place on greased baking sheets. Press flat with a glass dipped in sugar. Bake at 375° for 8-10 minutes or until lightly browned. Remove to wire racks to cool. YIELD: 6 dozen.

HOLIDAY SPRITZ COOKIES

TASTE OF HOME TEST KITCHEN

These crisp, buttery cookies make a welcome gift or sweet party treat. Color the dough in Christmasy hues and use a cookie press to make all kinds of fun shapes.

- 1/2 cup butter, softened
- 1 cup sugar
- 1 egg
- 2 tablespoons milk
- 1/2 teaspoon vanilla extract
- 2 1/4 cups cake flour
- 1/2 teaspoon salt
- 1 tablespoon nonpareils

Food coloring, optional

In a mixing bowl, cream butter and sugar until fluffy. Add egg; mix well. Beat in milk and vanilla. Combine flour and salt; gradually add to creamed mixture just until combined. Stir in nonpareils and food coloring if desired. Cover and chill at least 2 hours.

* Fill cookie press and form into desired shapes on ungreased baking sheets. Bake at 400° for 8 minutes or until edges just begin to brown. Remove to wire racks to cool. YIELD: about 5 dozen.

CHOCOLATE SNOWBALLS

DEE DEREZINSKI, WAUKESHA, WISCONSIN

This is my favorite Christmas cookie recipe. The cookies remind me of the snowballs I'd pack as a child during winters here in Wisconsin.

- 3/4 cup butter, softened
- 1/2 cup sugar
- 1 egg
- 2 teaspoons vanilla extract
- 2 cups all-purpose flour
- 1/2 teaspoon salt
- 1 cup chopped nuts
- 1 cup (6 ounces) chocolate chips

Confectioners' sugar

* In a mixing bowl, cream butter and sugar. Add the egg and vanilla; mix well. Combine flour and salt; stir into creamed mixture. Fold in nuts and chips. Roll into 1-in. balls.

* Place on ungreased baking sheets. Bake at 350° for 15-20 minutes. Cool cookies slightly before rolling in confectioners' sugar. YIELD: about 4 dozen.

CHOCOLATE SNOWBALLS

CINNAMON SUGAR COOKIES

CINNAMON SUGAR COOKIES

LEAH COSTIGAN, OTTO, NORTH CAROLINA
My mom always had these cookies on hand. They're good with coffee or milk.

- 1 cup butter, softened
- 1 cup sugar
- 1 cup confectioners' sugar
- 1 cup vegetable oil
- 2 eggs
- 1 teaspoon vanilla extract
- 4⅓ cups all-purpose flour
- 1 teaspoon salt
- 1 teaspoon baking soda
- 1 teaspoon cream of tartar
- 1 teaspoon ground cinnamon
- 1 cup finely chopped pecans, optional

Colored sugar, optional

❋ In a large mixing bowl, cream the butter, sugars and oil. Add eggs and vanilla; mix well. Add flour, salt, baking soda, cream of tartar and cinnamon. Stir in the pecans if desired. Cover and refrigerate for 3 hours or until easy to handle.

❋ Roll into 1-in. balls. Place on greased baking sheets; flatten with the bottom of a glass dipped in sugar. Sprinkle with colored sugar if desired.

❋ Bake at 375° for 10-12 minutes. Remo to wire racks to cool. YIELD: about 8 doz

LEMON CREAM CHEESE SPRITZ

TASTE OF HOME TEST KITCHEN
We livened up ordinary spritz cookies with lemon extract and peel. The addition of cream cheese makes ever bite tasty and tender.

- 1 cup shortening
- 1 package (3 ounces) cream cheese, softened
- 1 cup sugar
- 1 egg yolk
- 1 teaspoon lemon extract
- 1 teaspoon grated lemon peel
- 2½ cups all-purpose flour
- ¼ teaspoon salt

❋ In a large mixing bowl, beat shorteni and cream cheese until blended. A sugar; beat until creamy. Beat in egg yo lemon extract and peel. Combine t flour and salt; gradually add to t creamed mixture.

❋ Using a cookie press fitted with the disk your choice, press dough 1 in. apart or ungreased baking sheets. Bake at 350° 9-12 minutes or until set (do not brow Remove to wire racks to cool. Decorate desired. YIELD: about 9 dozen.

SCANDINAVIAN DROPS

NAOMI FALCONE, LANCASTER, PENNSYLVAN
This traditional recipe has been in the family for years. Every Christmas, friends and family expect to see these attractive and delicious cookies on the table. I'm always happily oblige!

- 1 cup butter, softened
- ½ cup packed brown sugar
- 2 eggs, *separated*
- 1 teaspoon vanilla extract
- 2⅓ cups all-purpose flour
- 1 cup finely chopped walnuts
- ½ to ⅔ cup jam *or* jelly of your choi

❋ In a mixing bowl, cream butter and brow sugar. Add egg yolks, one at a time, bea

ng well after each addition. Beat in vanil-
a. Gradually add flour. Roll into 1-in. balls.
Beat egg whites until foamy.

Dip each ball halfway into egg whites,
then into walnuts. Place nut side up 2 in.
apart on ungreased baking sheets. Using
the end of a wooden spoon handle, make
an indentation in the center of each.

Bake at 375° for 10-12 minutes or until
lightly browned. Remove to wire racks. Fill
with jam; cool. YIELD: 5½ dozen.

UGARED DATE BALLS

NDRA VAUTRAIN, SUGAR LAND, TEXAS
hen I was a youngster, Mom always
ked these tender old-fashioned
okies dotted with chewy dates and
unchy walnuts. Much to the delight
my family, I've continued her
licious tradition.

2 **cup butter, softened**
3 **cup confectioners' sugar**
1 **tablespoon milk**
1 **teaspoon vanilla extract**
4 **cups all-purpose flour**
4 **teaspoon salt**
3 **cup chopped dates**
2 **cup chopped nuts**
dditional confectioners' sugar

In a mixing bowl, cream butter and sugar. Beat in milk and vanilla. Combine flour
and salt; gradually add to creamed mixture. Stir in dates and nuts.

Roll into 1-in. balls. Place 2 in. apart on ungreased baking sheets. Bake at 325° for
22-25 minutes or until bottoms are lightly browned. Roll warm cookies in confectioners' sugar; cool on wire racks. YIELD:
about 2½ dozen.

HOCOLATE PECAN
HUMBPRINTS

M RIES, MILWAUKEE, WISCONSIN
ery Christmas for over 30 years, I
ve rolled, cut, shaped and baked
tches of cookies for family and
ends. These melt-in-your-mouth
orsels with a dollop of chocolate in
e center are among my favorites.

½ **cup plus 1 tablespoon butter,
softened,** *divided*
¼ **cup packed brown sugar**
1 **egg yolk**
1 **teaspoon vanilla extract**
1 **cup all-purpose flour**
1 **egg white, lightly beaten**
¾ **cup finely chopped pecans**
¾ **cup semisweet chocolate chips**

❋ In a mixing bowl, cream ½ cup butter and
brown sugar. Beat in egg yolk and vanilla. Gradually add flour; mix well. Cover
and refrigerate for 2 hours or until easy to
handle.

❋ Roll dough into 1-in. balls. Dip in egg
white, then coat with pecans. Place 2 in.
apart on greased baking sheets. Using the
end of a wooden spoon handle, make a
½-in. indentation in the center of each
ball.

❋ Bake at 325° for 10 minutes. Press again
into indentations with the spoon handle.
Bake 10-15 minutes longer or until pecans
are golden brown. Remove to wire racks
to cool.

❋ In a microwave-safe bowl, heat the chocolate chips and remaining butter until melted; stir until blended and smooth. Spoon
into cooked cookies. YIELD: about 1½
dozen.

CHOCOLATE PECAN THUMBPRINTS

CHOCOLATE-DIPPED MAPLE LOGS

LORRAINE CALAND, THUNDER BAY, ONTARIO

For as long as I can remember, these fancy little maple logs have been a Christmas tradition at our house. My girls loved working the assembly line and dipping the ends in chocolate.

- ½ **cup butter, softened**
- ½ **cup shortening**
- ½ **cup confectioners' sugar**
- 1 **teaspoon vanilla extract**
- 1 **teaspoon maple flavoring**
- 1½ **cups all-purpose flour**
- 1 **cup quick-cooking oats**
- ½ **teaspoon salt**
- 1 **cup (6 ounces) semisweet chocolate chips**
- 3 **tablespoons milk**
- ¾ **cup ground walnuts**

❋ In a large mixing bowl, cream the butter, shortening and confectioners' sugar. Beat in vanilla and maple flavoring. Combine the flour, oats and salt; gradually add to creamed mixture.

CHOCOLATE-DIPPED MAPLE LOGS

❋ On a lightly floured surface, shape dou into ½-in.-wide logs. Cut into 2-in. piec Place 1 in. apart on ungreased baki sheets. Bake at 325° for 15-18 minu or until set and very lightly browne Remove to wire racks to cool.

❋ In a microwave, melt chocolate chips a milk; stir until smooth. Dip one end each cookie into chocolate, then rol walnuts. Place on waxed paper until s YIELD: about 6 dozen.

FRUITCAKE COOKIES

DORCAS WRIGHT, GUELPH, ONTARIO

My old-fashioned goodies are fun, colorful and chewy without being sticky. Even people who say they aren a fan of traditional fruitcake fall for these cookies!

- ½ **cup butter, softened**
- ½ **cup shortening**
- ½ **cup sugar**
- ½ **cup packed brown sugar**
- 1 **egg**
- 1 **teaspoon vanilla extract**
- 1 **cup all-purpose flour**
- ½ **teaspoon baking soda**
- ½ **teaspoon salt**
- 2 **cups old-fashioned oats**
- 1 **cup flaked coconut**
- ½ **cup chopped dates**
- ½ **cup *each* chopped red and green candied cherries**
- ½ **cup chopped candied pineapple**

❋ In a mixing bowl, cream butter, shorte ing and sugars. Add egg and vanilla; n well. Combine flour, baking soda, salt a oats; add to creamed mixture and m well. Stir in the coconut, dates, cherri and pineapple.

❋ Shape into 1-in. balls; place on greas baking sheets. Bake at 325° for 15 mi utes or until lightly browned. Remove wire racks to cool. YIELD: 5-6 dozen.

BUTTERY SPRITZ COOKIES

CHINESE ALMOND COOKIES

JANE GARING, TALLADEGA, ALABAMA

Each Christmas, my mother made lots of these tender butter cookies and stored them in clean coffee cans. When she passed away, I started giving our kids a can of these sentimental sweets.

- 1 cup butter, softened
- 1 cup sugar
- 1 egg
- 1 teaspoon almond extract
- 3 cups all-purpose flour
- 1 teaspoon baking soda
- ½ teaspoon salt
- ¼ cup sliced almonds
- 1 egg white
- ½ teaspoon water

❊ In a large mixing bowl, cream butter and sugar. Beat in egg and extract. Combine the flour, baking soda and salt; gradually add to creamed mixture.

❊ Roll into 1-in. balls. Place 2 in. apart on ungreased baking sheets. Flatten with a fork. Sprinkle with almonds.

❊ In a small bowl, beat egg white and water. Brush over cookies. Bake at 325° for 14-16 minutes or until edges and bottoms are lightly browned. Cool for 2 minutes before removing to wire racks. YIELD: about 5 dozen.

UTTERY SPRITZ COOKIES

VERLY LAUNIUS, SANDWICH, ILLINOIS

hese tender little cookies are very ve-catching on my Christmas cookie ay. The dough is easy to work with, so s fun to make these into a variety of stive shapes.

- 1 cup butter, softened
- ¼ cups confectioners' sugar
- 1 egg
- 1 teaspoon vanilla extract
- ½ teaspoon almond extract
- ½ cups all-purpose flour
- ½ teaspoon salt
- od coloring, optional
- olored sugar or decorating candies, optional

In a mixing bowl, cream butter and sugar until smooth. Beat in egg and extracts. Combine the flour and salt; gradually add to creamed mixture. Tint with food coloring if desired.

Using a cookie press fitted with the disk of your choice, press dough 2 in. apart onto ungreased baking sheets. Top with colored sugar and decorating candies if desired.

Bake at 375° for 6-8 minutes or until set (do not brown). Remove to wire racks to cool. YIELD: 7½ dozen.

CHINESE ALMOND COOKIES

RASPBERRY RIBBONS
PATSY WOLFENDEN
GOLDEN, BRITISH COLUMBIA

I make these attractive, buttery cookies to serve at our remote guest lodge, and all the girls in the kitchen are addicted to them!

   1 **cup butter, softened**
   ½ **cup sugar**
   1 **egg**
   1 **teaspoon vanilla extract**
2¼ **cups all-purpose flour**
   ½ **teaspoon baking powder**
   ¼ **teaspoon salt**
   ½ **cup raspberry jam**
GLAZE
   1 **cup confectioners' sugar**
   2 **tablespoons evaporated milk**
   ½ **teaspoon vanilla extract**

❉ In a mixing bowl, cream butter and su ar. Beat in egg and vanilla. Combine t flour, baking powder and salt; gradua add to creamed mixture and mix well.

❉ Divide dough into four portions; shap each into a 10-in. x 2½-in. log. Place in. apart on greased or foil-lined bakir sheets. Make a ½-in. depression dov the center of each log. Bake at 350° for minutes.

❉ Fill depressions with jam. Bake 10-15 mi utes longer or until lightly browned. Co for 2 minutes. Remove to a cutting boar cut into ¾-in. slices. Place on wire rack

❉ In a small bowl, combine glaze ingred ents until smooth. Drizzle over war cookies. Cool completely. YIELD: about dozen.

RASPBERRY RIBBONS

CHRISTMAS CASSEROLE COOKIES

IRA LINK, REEDS SPRING, MISSOURI

The batter for these specialty cookies is baked and then formed into balls. When my son-in-law and grandson are coming for a visit, I'm always sure to have these cookies on hand.

3 eggs
1 cup sugar
1 teaspoon vanilla extract
1/4 teaspoon almond extract
1 cup chopped dates
1 cup flaked coconut
1 cup chopped walnuts
Additional sugar

In a mixing bowl, beat eggs until lemon-colored. Gradually beat in sugar. Beat in extracts. Stir in the dates, coconut and walnuts. Pour into an ungreased deep 2-qt. baking dish.

Bake at 350° for 30-35 minutes. Remove from oven; stir with a wooden spoon (batter will appear moist and sticky). Place baking dish on a wire rack. When cool enough to handle, roll batter into 1-in. balls. Roll in sugar; place on waxed paper-lined baking sheets. YIELD: 4 dozen.

CINNAMON ALMOND CRESCENTS

JENNIFER BRANUM, O'FALLON, ILLINOIS

Set out these cookies as we open our gifts on Christmas Eve. Before long, the plate is empty and I'm being asked to refill it!

1 cup butter, softened
1/3 cup sugar
1/2 teaspoon vanilla extract
2/3 cups all-purpose flour
1/2 cup finely ground blanched almonds
TOPPING
1/2 cup sugar
1/2 teaspoon ground cinnamon

In a mixing bowl, cream butter and sugar. Beat in vanilla. Combine flour and almonds; gradually add to creamed mixture.

FLOURLESS PEANUT BUTTER COOKIES

❋ Roll into 1-in. balls; shape into crescents. Place 2 in. apart on lightly greased baking sheets. Bake at 350° for 10-12 minutes or until set (do not brown).

❋ Combine sugar and cinnamon in a small bowl. Roll warm cookies in cinnamon-sugar; remove to wire racks to cool. YIELD: about 3 1/2 dozen.

FLOURLESS PEANUT BUTTER COOKIES

MAGGIE SCHIMMEL, WAUWATOSA, WISCONSIN

When my mother (who's now a great-grandmother) gave me this recipe over 15 years ago, I was skeptical, because it calls for only three ingredients and no flour. But since then I've never had a failure, and I make them all the time!

1 egg, beaten
1 cup sugar
1 cup creamy peanut butter

❋ In a large bowl, mix all ingredients. Roll level tablespoons into balls. Place on ungreased baking sheets and flatten with a fork.

❋ Bake at 350° for about 18 minutes. Remove to wire racks to cool. YIELD: 2 dozen.

shaping peanut butter cookies

Peanut butter cookie dough is generally a stiff dough and needs to be flattened before baking. Using a floured fork, press the balls of dough until 3/8 in. thick. Press again in the opposite direction to make a crisscross pattern.

BERRY SHORTBREAD DREAMS

MILDRED SHERRER, FORT WORTH, TEXAS

Raspberry jam adds fruity sweetness to these rich-tasting cookies. They will absolutely melt in your mouth!

 1 **cup butter, softened**
 ⅔ **cup sugar**
 ½ **teaspoon almond extract**
 2 **cups all-purpose flour**
 ⅓ **to ½ cup seedless raspberry jam**

GLAZE

 1 **cup confectioners' sugar**
 2 **to 3 teaspoons water**
 ½ **teaspoon almond extract**

✳ In a mixing bowl, cream butter and sugar. Beat in extract; gradually add flour until dough forms a ball. Cover and refrigerate for 1 hour or until the dough is easy to handle.

✳ Roll into 1-in. balls. Place 1 in. apart on ungreased baking sheets. Using the end of a wooden spoon handle, make an indentation in the center. Fill with jam.

✳ Bake at 350° for 14-18 minutes or until edges are lightly browned. Remove to wire racks to cool. Spoon additional jam into cookies if desired. Combine glaze ingredients; drizzle over cookies. YIELD: about 3½ dozen.

BERRY SHORTBREAD DREAMS

CREAM FILBERTS

DEANNA RICHTER, ELMORE, MINNESOTA

These cookies remind me of a delicio[us] candy I used to buy with dimes Grandma gave me.

 1 **cup shortening**
 ¾ **cup sugar**
 1 **egg**
 1 **teaspoon vanilla extract**
 2½ **cups all-purpose flour**
 ½ **teaspoon baking powder**
 ⅛ **teaspoon salt**
 ¾ **cup whole filberts or hazelnuts**

GLAZE

 2 **cups confectioners' sugar**
 3 **tablespoons water**
 2 **teaspoons vanilla extract**

Granulated sugar or about 60 crushed sugar cubes

✳ In a mixing bowl, cream shortening a[nd] sugar. Add egg and vanilla; mix we[ll]. Combine the dry ingredients and add [to] creamed mixture.

✳ Roll heaping teaspoonfuls into balls; pre[ss] a filbert into each and reshape so dou[gh] covers nut. Place on ungreased baki[ng] sheets.

✳ Bake at 375° for 12-15 minutes or un[til] lightly browned. Remove to wire racks [to] cool. Combine first three glaze ingre[di]ents; dip entire top of cookies. Roll in su[g]ar. YIELD: about 5 dozen.

CHOCOLATE-TOPPED PEANUT BUTTER SPRITZ

DOLORES DEEGAN
POTTSTOWN, PENNSYLVANIA

Peanut butter make these delicious cookies different from other spritz. Th[e] chocolate drizzle makes them extra special.

 1 **cup butter, softened**
 1 **cup peanut butter**
 1 **cup sugar**
 1 **cup packed brown sugar**
 2 **eggs**
 2 **cups all-purpose flour**

1 teaspoon baking soda
2 teaspoon salt

OCOLATE TOPPING

2 cups semisweet chocolate chips
1 tablespoons shortening
opped peanuts

In a large mixing bowl, cream the butter, peanut butter and sugars. Beat in eggs, one at a time, beating well after each addition. Combine the flour, baking soda and salt; gradually add to creamed mixture. Chill for 15 minutes.

Using a cookie press fitted with bar disk, form dough into long strips on ungreased baking sheets. Cut each strip into 2-in. pieces (there is no need to separate the pieces). Bake at 350° for 6-8 minutes. (Watch carefully–cookies brown quickly.)

For topping, melt chocolate with shortening; stir until blended. Place in a heavy plastic bag; cut a small hole in the corner. Pipe a strip of chocolate down center of each cookie and sprinkle with chopped peanuts. YIELD: 16 dozen.

RISPY COFFEE COOKIES

MANE MOELLER
LORADO SPRINGS, COLORADO

reated this recipe because I wanted easy-to-make cookie that folks can't sist. These tempting treats have a nt of coffee flavor and aren't overly eet.

1 cup sugar
/4 cup vegetable oil
/3 cup instant coffee granules
2 tablespoons hot water
2 eggs
/2 cups all-purpose flour
/2 teaspoons baking powder
/4 teaspoon salt
dditional sugar

In a mixing bowl, combine sugar and oil. Dissolve coffee in water; add to sugar mixture and mix well. Add eggs, one at a time, beating well after each addition. Combine the flour, baking powder and salt; gradually add to the sugar mixture.

Roll into 3/4-in. balls, then roll in additional sugar. Place 2 in. apart on lightly greased baking sheets; flatten with a fork.

Bake at 400° for 8-10 minutes or until edges are firm. Remove to wire racks to cool. YIELD: about 5 dozen.

GROSSMUTTER'S PEPPERNUTS

GROSSMUTTER'S PEPPERNUTS

MARILYN KUTZLI, CLINTON, IOWA

Before Christmas, my grandmother would bake peppernuts and store them until the "big day." When we'd come home from school, the whole house would smell like anise and we knew the holiday season was about to begin.

3 eggs
2 cups sugar
2 3/4 cups all-purpose flour
1 teaspoon anise extract *or* crushed aniseseed

In a large mixing bowl, beat eggs and sugar on medium speed for 15 minutes. Reduce speed and slowly add flour and anise. Mix until well combined.

On a lightly floured surface, shape dough into ropes about 1/2 in. in diameter. Chill 1 hour.

Slice ropes into 1/2-in. lengths. Place on greased baking sheets. Bake at 350° for 6-8 minutes or until set. Cookies will harden upon standing. When cool, store in airtight containers; they are best if allowed to age before serving. YIELD: 30 dozen.

GREEK HOLIDAY COOKIES

NICOLE MOSKOV, NEW YORK, NEW YORK

I really enjoy these delicate butter cookies. They have a fun shape and subtle orange flavor.

- 1½ cups butter, softened
- 1¼ cups sugar
- 4 eggs
- 2 tablespoons orange juice
- 3 teaspoons vanilla extract
- 5¼ cups all-purpose flour
- 1½ teaspoons baking powder
- ¾ teaspoon baking soda

❄ In a large mixing bowl, cream butter and sugar. Add 2 eggs; beat well. Beat in orange juice and vanilla. Combine the flour, baking powder and baking soda; gradually add to creamed mixture. Cover and refrigerate for 1 hour or until easy to handle.

❄ Roll dough into 1¼-in. balls. Shape each into a 6-in. rope; fold in half and twist twice. Place 2 in. apart on ungreased baking sheets.

❄ In a small bowl, beat the remaining eggs; brush over dough. Bake at 350° for 7-12 minutes or until edges are golden brown. Remove to wire racks to cool. YIELD: about 6½ dozen.

HOLIDAY NUGGETS

ANNA MINEGAR, WAUCHULA, FLORIDA

My mother always made these cookies for Christmas when I was a little girl and now I make them for my family. The chopped nuts make them special.

- ½ cup butter, softened
- ½ cup margarine, softened
- ½ cup sifted confectioners' sugar
- 1 tablespoon vanilla extract
- 1 teaspoon almond extract
- 2 cups all-purpose flour
- ½ teaspoon salt
- ½ cup chopped nuts

Confectioners' sugar

Colored crystallized sugar

❄ In a mixing bowl, cream butter, margari[ne] and sugar. Blend in vanilla and almond [ex]tract. Gradually add flour and salt. Sti[r in] nuts. Shape into 1¼-in. balls; place on [un]greased baking sheets. Flatten sligh[tly] with fingers.

❄ Bake at 325° for 25 minutes or until t[he] bottoms are lightly browned. Remove [to] wire racks to cool. When cool, sprin[kle] with a mixture of confectioners' and c[ol]ored sugar. YIELD: 3½ dozen.

WHIPPED SHORTBREAD

JANE RICIUR, BOW ISLAND, ALBERTA

This version of shortbread is not too sweet and melts in your mouth. I mak[e] it for the holidays...but also for wedding showers and ladies' teas.

- 3 cups butter, softened
- 1½ cups confectioners' sugar, sifted
- 4½ cups all-purpose flour
- 1½ cups cornstarch

Nonpareils and/or halved candied cherries

❄ Using a heavy-duty mixer, beat butter [on] medium speed until light and fluf[fy]. Gradually add dry ingredients, beati[ng] constantly until well blended. Dust han[ds] lightly with additional cornstarch.

❄ Roll dough into 1-in. balls; dip in no[n]pareils and place on ungreased baki[ng] sheets. Press lightly with a floured fork. [To] decorate with cherries, place balls on ba[k]ing sheets and press lightly with fo[rk]. Top each with a cherry half.

❄ Bake at 300° for 20-22 minutes or un[til] cookie is set but not browned. Remove [to] wire racks to cool. YIELD: 16-18 dozen.

HOLIDAY NUGGETS

FRUIT-FILLED DAINTIES

FRUIT-FILLED DAINTIES

TASTE OF HOME TEST KITCHEN

Refrigerated cookie dough can be shaped into cookies or tarts in this scrumptious recipe. Use one filling or make them both.

CRAN-ORANGE FILLING

2 cups orange-flavored dried cranberries

9 tablespoons orange marmalade

APRICOT-ORANGE FILLING

9 tablespoons orange marmalade

2 teaspoons water

4 cups chopped dried apricots

DOUGH

1 tube (18 ounces) refrigerated sugar cookie dough, softened

4 cup all-purpose flour

Confectioners' sugar

Prepare either the cran-orange or apricot-orange filling. For cran-orange filling, combine cranberries and marmalade in a food processor; cover and process until finely chopped. For apricot-orange filling, combine the marmalade, water and apricots in a food processor; cover and process until finely chopped.

In a large mixing bowl, beat cookie dough and flour until smooth. Divide into thirds. Work with one portion at a time and keep remaining dough covered.

❈ To prepare cookies: On a floured surface, roll out one portion of dough to ⅛-in. thickness. Cut into 2½-in. squares or cut with a 2½-in. round cookie cutter. Place 1 in. apart on ungreased baking sheets. Repeat with remaining dough.

❈ Place a slightly rounded teaspoon of filling in the center of each square or circle. Shape by folding two opposite points of squares over one another or by folding edges of circles together; press to seal. Bake at 350° for 9-12 minutes or until lightly browned. Cool for 2 minutes before removing to wire racks. Dust with confectioners' sugar.

❈ TO PREPARE TARTS: Shape one portion of dough into twelve 1-in. balls. Press onto the bottom and up the sides of ungreased miniature muffin cups. Repeat with remaining dough. Bake at 350° for 10-12 minutes or until lightly browned.

❈ Using the end of a wooden spoon handle, gently make a ⅜- to ½-in.-deep indentation in the center of each tart. Cool for 10 minutes before removing from pans to wire racks. Dust with confectioners' sugar. Spoon about a tablespoon of filling into each tart. YIELD: 3 dozen.

EDITOR'S NOTE: Each type of filling makes enough to fill the entire batch of cookies. If you would like to use both fillings, make two batches of the dough.

piping meringue cookies

- Insert a decorating tip that has a large opening into a pastry bag or heavy-duty resealable plastic bag. (If using a plastic bag, first cut a small hole in the corner of the bag.)

- Fill the bag about halfway full with meringue. Smooth the meringue down toward the decorating tip to remove any air bubbles that could cause breaks in the design when piping. Twist the top of the bag shut.

- Line a baking sheet with parchment paper. Hold the pastry bag straight up and position the tip about 1/8 to 1/4 in. above the baking sheet. Hold the tip with one hand and squeeze the pastry bag with other. Stop squeezing before you lift up the decorating tip.

CHOCOLATE MERINGUE STARS

CHOCOLATE MERINGUE STARS

EDNA LEE, GREELEY, COLORADO

These light, delicate chewy cookies sure make for merry munching. Their big chocolate flavor makes it difficult to keep the kids away from them long enough to get any on the cookie tray.

- 3 egg whites
- 3/4 teaspoon vanilla extract
- 3/4 cup sugar
- 1/4 cup baking cocoa

GLAZE

- 3 squares (1 ounce *each*) semisweet chocolate
- 1 tablespoon shortening

✻ In a mixing bowl, beat egg whites and vanilla until soft peaks form. Gradually add sugar, about 2 tablespoons at a time, beating until stiff peaks form. Gently fold in cocoa. Place in a pastry bag with a large open star tip (#8b). Line baking sheets with foil and coat the foil with nonstick cooking spray. Pipe stars, about 1¼-in. diameter, onto foil, or drop by rounded teaspoonfuls. Bake at 300° for 30-35 minutes or until lightly browned. Remove from foil; cool on wire racks.

✻ In a microwave or double boiler, melt chocolate and shortening; stir until smooth. Dip the cookies halfway into glaze; place on waxed paper to harden. YIELD: about 4 dozen.

CINNAMON ALMOND STRIPS

FRED GROVER, LAKE HAVASU CITY, ARIZONA

When I was young, I could hardly wai for the holidays because I knew thes cookies would make an appearance the cookie tray. Now I make them for holidays throughout the year.

- 1½ cups butter, *softened*
- 1 cup sugar
- 3 eggs, *separated*
- 3 cups all-purpose flour

TOPPING

- 1½ cups sugar
- 1 cup finely chopped almonds
- 1½ teaspoons ground cinnamon

✻ In a mixing bowl, cream butter and su ar. Beat in egg yolks; mix well. Gradua add flour.

✻ Using a cookie press fitted with a bar di press dough into long strips onto greased baking sheets. Beat egg whi until stiff; brush over dough. Combi topping ingredients; sprinkle over stri Cut each strip into 2-in. pieces (there is need to separate the pieces).

✻ Bake at 350° for 8-10 minutes or ur edges are firm (do not brown). Cut ir pieces again if necessary. Remove to w racks to cool. YIELD: about 10 dozen.

PEANUT BUTTER KISS COOKIES

DEE DAVIS, SUN CITY, ARIZONA

These are great for little ones, and th keep adults guessing as to how they can be made with only five ingredient

- 1 cup peanut butter
- 1 cup sugar
- 1 egg
- 1 teaspoon vanilla extract
- 24 milk chocolate kisses

✻ In a large mixing bowl, cream peanut b ter and sugar. Add the egg and vani beat until blended.

✻ Roll into 1¼-in. balls. Place 2 in. apart ungreased baking sheets. Bake at 350° 10-12 minutes or until tops are sligh

PEANUT BUTTER KISS COOKIES

cracked. Immediately press one chocolate kiss into the center of each cookie. Cool for 5 minutes before removing from pans to wire racks. YIELD: 2 dozen.

EDITOR'S NOTE: Reduced-fat or generic brands of peanut butter are not recommended for this recipe.

CHOCOLATE PECAN TASSIES

MONA PORTER, OLIVE HILL, KENTUCKY

These cookies capture the wonderful flavor of pecan pie. The addition of chocolate chips makes them extra special.

- 1/2 cup butter, softened
- 1 package (3 ounces) cream cheese, softened
- 6 tablespoons sugar
- 1/2 cups all-purpose flour
- 3 tablespoons baking cocoa

PECAN FILLING

- 1 cup packed brown sugar
- 2 tablespoons butter, softened
- 2 eggs
- 2 teaspoons vanilla extract
- 1/3 cup chopped pecans
- 1/3 cup miniature semisweet chocolate chips

In a large mixing bowl, cream the butter, cream cheese and sugar. Combine the flour and cocoa; gradually add to the creamed mixture. Cover and refrigerate for 15 minutes. Meanwhile, for filling, combine the brown sugar and butter in a small mixing bowl. Beat in eggs and vanilla. Stir in the pecans and chocolate chips.

* Roll cream cheese mixture into 1-in. balls. Press onto the bottom and up the sides of ungreased miniature muffin cups. Spoon filling into cups.

* Bake at 325° for 20-25 minutes or until lightly browned. Cool for 10 minutes before carefully removing from pans to wire racks. YIELD: 3 dozen.

CRANBERRY CRISPIES

LAVERN KRAFT, LYTTON, IOWA

At holiday rush time, you can't go wrong with these simple cookies. They're a snap to stir up with a boxed quick bread mix, and they bake up crisp and delicious.

- 1 package (15.6 ounces) cranberry quick bread mix
- 1/2 cup butter, melted
- 1/2 cup finely chopped walnuts
- 1 egg
- 1/2 cup dried cranberries

* In a bowl, combine the bread mix, butter, walnuts and egg; mix well. Stir in cranberries. Roll into 1 1/4-in. balls. Place 3 in. apart on ungreased baking sheets. Flatten to 1/8 -in. thickness with a glass dipped in sugar.

* Bake at 350° for 10-12 minutes or until light golden brown. Remove to wire racks to cool. YIELD: 2 1/2 dozen.

CRANBERRY CRISPIES

CHERRY MOCHA BALL

CHERRY MOCHA BALLS

JEANA CROWELL, WHITEWATER, KANSAS

My mother-in-law gave me this recipe before my wedding. I've made mocha balls nearly every Christmas since then. Because they freeze so well, I will frequently bake some early and put them away to call on as last-minute holiday treats.

- **1 cup butter, softened**
- **1/2 cup sugar**
- **4 teaspoons vanilla extract**
- **2 cups all-purpose flour**
- **1/4 cup unsweetened cocoa**
- **1 tablespoon instant coffee granules**
- **1/2 teaspoon salt**
- **1 cup finely chopped pecans**
- **2/3 cup chopped red candied cherries**

Confectioners' sugar

- In a mixing bowl, cream butter. Gradua add sugar and vanilla; beat until lig and fluffy. Combine flour, cocoa, coff and salt; gradually add to creamed mi ture. Mix well. Stir in pecans and che ries. Chill dough until easy to handle.
- Shape into 1-in. balls and place on u greased baking sheets. Bake at 350° f 15 minutes or until cookies are se Remove to wire racks to cool. Dust wi confectioners' sugar. YIELD: about dozen.

PECIAL OATMEAL HIP COOKIES

ROL POSKIE, PITTSBURGH, PENNSYLVANIA

son dubbed these "the cookie" er just one taste, and they've come my signature cookie since en. I haven't shared my "secret" cipe until now.

1 cup butter, softened
1 cup peanut butter
1 cup sugar
1 cup packed brown sugar
2 eggs
1 teaspoon vanilla extract
3 cups old-fashioned oats
1 cup all-purpose flour
2 teaspoons ground cinnamon
1 teaspoon baking soda
4 teaspoon ground nutmeg
2 cups semisweet chocolate chips

ZZLE

1 cup white chocolate candy coating, melted
1 cup dark chocolate candy coating, melted

In a mixing bowl, cream butter, peanut butter and sugars. Add eggs, one at a time, beating well after each addition. Beat in vanilla. Combine oats, flour, cinnamon, baking soda and nutmeg; gradually add to the creamed mixture. Stir in chocolate chips.

Roll into 1-in. balls. Place 2 in. apart on greased baking sheets; flatten to 1/2-in. thickness. Bake at 350° for 10-12 minutes or until golden brown. Remove to wire racks to cool.

Drizzle with white coating in one direction, then with dark coating in the opposite direction to form a crisscross pattern. YIELD: about 5½ dozen.

IPPED GINGERSNAPS

JRA KIMBALL, WEST JORDAN, UTAH

et a great deal of satisfaction king and giving time-tested Yuletide ats like these soft, chewy cookies. pping them in white chocolate makes great gingersnaps even more special.

2 cups sugar
1½ cups vegetable oil
2 eggs
½ cup molasses
4 cups all-purpose flour
4 teaspoons baking soda
1 tablespoon ground ginger
2 teaspoons ground cinnamon
1 teaspoon salt
Additional sugar
2 packages (10 to 12 ounces each) vanilla or white chips
1/4 cup shortening

* In a large mixing bowl, combine sugar and oil. Beat in the eggs. Stir in molasses. Combine the flour, baking soda, ginger, cinnamon and salt; gradually add to creamed mixture and mix well.

* Shape into ¾-in. balls and roll in sugar. Place 2 in. apart on ungreased baking sheets. Bake at 350° for 10-12 minutes or until cookie springs back when touched lightly. Remove to wire racks to cool.

* In a small saucepan, melt chips with shortening over low heat, stirring until smooth. Dip the cookies halfway into the melted chips; shake off excess. Place on waxed paper-lined baking sheets until set. YIELD: 14½ dozen.

DIPPED GINGERSNAPS

GOLDEN RAISIN COOKIES

GOLDEN RAISIN COOKIES

ISABEL PODESZWA, LAKEWOOD, NEW JERSEY
Since my children are grown, I make these light butter cookies for the neighborhood kids.

1 cup butter, softened
1½ cups sugar
1 tablespoon lemon juice
2 eggs
3½ cups all-purpose flour
1½ teaspoons cream of tartar
1½ teaspoons baking soda
1 package (15 ounces) golden raisins (2½ cups)

❄ In a mixing bowl, cream butter and sugar. Add lemon juice and eggs. Combine dry ingredients; gradually add to creamed mixture. Stir in raisins. Roll into 1-in. balls.

❄ Place on greased baking sheets; flatten with a floured fork. Bake at 400° for 8-10 minutes or until lightly browned. Remove to wire racks to cool. YIELD: about 6 dozen.

DECORATED BUTTER COOKIES

DORIS SCHUMACHER
BROOKINGS, SOUTH DAKOTA
Tender, crisp and flavorful, these versatile cookies can be decorated to suit any season or occasion. Or you can just frost them lightly and top with toasted coconut.

1 cup butter, softened
½ cup sugar
½ cup packed brown sugar
1 egg
1 teaspoon vanilla extract
2 cups all-purpose flour
2 teaspoons cream of tartar
1 teaspoon baking soda
⅛ teaspoon salt
Colored sugar, ground nuts *and/or* chocolate *or* colored sprinkles

❄ In a mixing bowl, cream butter and su[gars]. Beat in egg and vanilla. Combine [the] flour, cream of tartar, baking soda a[nd] salt; gradually add to creamed mixtu[re.] Cover and refrigerate for 1 hour.

❄ Roll into 1-in. balls. Place 2 in. apart on [the] greased baking sheets. Flatten wit[h a] glass dipped in sugar; sprinkle with c[ol]ored sugar, nuts or sprinkles.

❄ Bake at 350° for 10-12 minutes or u[ntil] lightly browned. Remove to wire racks [to] cool. YIELD: 4 dozen.

LEMON-LIME CRACKLE COOKIES

ADA MERWIN, WATERFORD, MICHIGAN
You can taste the spirit of Christmas' past in these chewy old-time cookies with their crackle tops and lemony flavor. They're a luscious addition to cookie exchanges.

½ cup flaked coconut
2 teaspoons grated lemon peel
2 teaspoons grated lime peel
2 cups whipped topping
2 eggs
2 tablespoons whipped topping mi[x]
1 teaspoon lemon juice
1 package (18¼ ounces) lemon cak[e] mix
Confectioners' sugar

❄ In a blender or food processor, comb[ine] the coconut, lemon peel and lime pe[el.] Cover and process until finely chopp[ed,] about 30 seconds; set aside.

In a mixing bowl, combine whipped topping, eggs, dry whipped topping mix and lemon juice. Add dry cake mix and coconut mixture; mix well.

Drop by tablespoonfuls into a bowl of confectioners' sugar. Shape into balls. Place 2 in. apart on greased baking sheets. Bake at 350° for 10-12 minutes or until edges are golden brown. Remove to wire racks to cool. YIELD: about 3 dozen.

OOKIES ON A STICK

LORES WALLACE, JACOBSBURG, OHIO

folks munch on these peanut butter okies, they're delighted to uncover e candy bar surprise tucked inside.

/2 **cup butter, softened**
/2 **cup peanut butter**
/2 **cup sugar**
/2 **cup packed brown sugar**
1 **egg**
1 **teaspoon vanilla extract**
/2 **cups all-purpose flour**
/2 **teaspoon baking powder**
/2 **teaspoon baking soda**
0 **lollipop sticks**
0 **miniature Snickers candy bars**

In a large mixing bowl, cream the butter, peanut butter and sugars. Add egg; beat well. Beat in vanilla. Combine the flour, baking powder and baking soda; gradually add to creamed mixture.

Insert a lollipop stick into a side of each candy bar until stick is nearly at the opposite side. Press 1 heaping tablespoon of dough around each candy bar until completely covered. Press dough tightly around the end of the candy bar and the stick.

Place 3 in. apart on lightly greased baking sheets. Bake at 350° for 14-16 minutes or until cookies are set. Cool for 1-2 minutes before removing from pans to wire racks to cool completely. YIELD: about 20 cookies.

LEMON-BUTTER SPRITZ COOKIES

PAULA PELIS, LENHARTSVILLE, PENNSYLVANIA

This recipe makes a lot of terrific cookies! Using a cookie press may be too difficult for children to master. Instead, have them help sprinkle the cookies with colored sugar before baking.

2 **cups butter, softened**
1¼ **cups sugar**
2 **eggs**
Grated peel of 1 lemon
2 **teaspoons lemon juice**
1 **teaspoon vanilla extract**
5¼ **cups all-purpose flour**
¼ **teaspoon salt**
Colored sugar

✻ In a large mixing bowl, cream butter and sugar. Add the eggs, lemon peel, lemon juice and vanilla; mix well. Stir together flour and salt; gradually add to creamed mixture.

✻ Using a cookie press, shape into designs on ungreased baking sheets. Sprinkle with colored sugar. Bake at 400° for 8-10 minutes or until lightly browned around the edges. Remove to wire racks to cool. YIELD: about 12 dozen.

LEMON-BUTTER SPRITZ COOKIES

CUTOUT
cookies

**BUTTERSCOTCH
GINGERBREAD MEN
PAGE 95**

**APRICOT-FILLED TRIANGLES
PAGE 110**

**VANILLA BUTTER ROLLOUTS
PAGE 117**

GLAZED ANISE COOKIES

ARMETTA KEENEY, CARLISLE, IOWA

Years ago, my German neighbor made similar cookies and hung them on her Christmas tree for the neighbor kids to eat. I finally came up with my own recipe and have been very pleased with the results.

- ⅔ **cup butter, softened**
- 1 **cup sugar**
- 2 **eggs**
- 1 **tablespoon aniseed**
- 2 **teaspoons anise extract**
- 2½ **cups all-purpose flour**
- 1 **teaspoon baking powder**
- ½ **teaspoon salt**

GLAZE

- 2 **cups sugar**
- 1 **cup hot water**
- ⅛ **teaspoon cream of tartar**
- 1 **teaspoon anise extract**

Purple gel food coloring, optional

2½ **to 3 cups confectioners' sugar**

✷ In a large mixing bowl, cream butter and sugar. Add eggs, one at a time, beating well after each addition. Beat in aniseed and extract. Combine flour, baking powder and salt; gradually add to the creamed mixture. Cover and refrigerate for 1 hour or until easy to handle.

GLAZED ANISE COOKIES

✷ On a lightly floured surface, roll o dough to ¼-in. thickness. Cut with 2½- cookie cutters dipped in flour. Place 1 apart on ungreased baking sheets.

✷ Bake at 375° for 10-12 minutes or ur lightly browned. Remove to wire racks cool.

✷ In a large saucepan, combine sugar, wa and cream of tartar; bring to a boil ov low heat. Cook and stir until a candy the mometer reads 226° (thread stage). Co to 110° (do not stir). Stir in extract, fo coloring if desired, and enough confe tioners' sugar to achieve spreading co sistency. Spread over cookies. YIEL about 6 dozen.

MERRY NOTE COOKIES

NELLA PARKER, HERSHEY, MICHIGAN

These sweet treats were perfect to serve when I invited my four sisters ar their families over for a caroling them dinner. After we ate, we caroled and delivered cookies to shut-ins and our local police and fire departments.

- 1 **cup butter, softened**
- 1 **package (3 ounces) cream cheese, softened**
- 1 **cup sugar**
- 1 **egg**
- 1 **teaspoon vanilla extract**
- 2½ **cups all-purpose flour**
- ¼ **teaspoon salt**

Red and green colored sugar

✷ In a large mixing bowl, cream the butt cream cheese and sugar. Beat in egg ar vanilla. Combine the flour and salt; gra ually beat into creamed mixture. Cov and refrigerate the dough for 2 hours.

✷ On a lightly floured surface, roll o dough to ¼-in. thickness. Cut with a 3¾ in. x 2½-in. musical note cookie cutt dipped in flour. Place 2 in. apart on u greased baking sheets. Sprinkle with cc ored sugar.

✷ Bake at 375° for 8-10 minutes or until t edges are golden brown. Remove to wi racks to cool. YIELD: about 4 dozen.

BUTTERSCOTCH GINGERBREAD MEN

UTTERSCOTCH GINGERBREAD MEN

NE MCLEAN, BIRMINGHAM, ALABAMA

he addition of butterscotch pudding akes these a little different than most ngerbread cutout recipes.

- ½ cup butter, softened
- ½ cup packed brown sugar
- 1 package (3.4 ounces) instant butterscotch pudding mix
- 1 egg
- ½ cups all-purpose flour
- ½ teaspoons ground ginger
- ½ teaspoon baking soda
- ½ teaspoon ground cinnamon

OSTING

- 2 cups confectioners' sugar
- 3 tablespoons milk

✳ In a small mixing bowl, cream the butter, brown sugar and pudding mix. Beat in egg. Combine the flour, ginger, baking soda and cinnamon; gradually add to the creamed mixture. Cover and refrigerate overnight.

✳ On a lightly floured surface, roll out dough to ⅛-in. thickness. Cut with a 5-in. gingerbread man cookie cutter dipped in flour. Place 1 in. apart on ungreased baking sheets. Bake at 350° for 8-10 minutes or until edges are golden. Remove to wire racks to cool.

✳ In another small mixing bowl, combine the confectioners' sugar and milk until smooth. Decorate cookies as desired. YIELD: 1½ dozen.

CHERRY CHEESE WINDMILLS

CHERRY CHEESE WINDMILLS

HELEN MCGIBBON, DOWNERS GROVE, ILLINOIS
These pretty cookies look fancy, but they are really not much work. They're perfect for any occasion.

- ⅓ **cup butter, softened**
- ⅓ **cup shortening**
- ¾ **cup sugar**
- 1 **egg**
- 1 **tablespoon milk**
- 1 **teaspoon vanilla extract**
- 2 **cups all-purpose flour**
- 1½ **teaspoons baking powder**
- ¼ **teaspoon salt**

FILLING

- 1 **package (3 ounces) cream cheese, softened**
- ¼ **cup sugar**
- ¼ **teaspoon almond extract**
- ½ **cup finely chopped maraschino cherries**
- ¼ **cup sliced almonds, toasted and chopped**

✳ In a large mixing bowl, cream the butter, shortening and sugar until light and fluffy. Beat in the egg, milk and vanilla. Combine the flour, baking powder and salt; gradually add to creamed mixture. Divide dough in half. Cover and refrigerate for 3 hours or until easy to handle.

✳ In a small mixing bowl, beat the crea[m] cheese, sugar and extract. Fold in che[r]ries. On a floured surface, roll each po[r]tion of dough into a 10-in. square. With[a] sharp knife or pastry wheel, cut in[to] 2½-in. squares. Place 2 in. apart on u[n]greased baking sheets. Make 1-in. cu[ts] from each corner toward the center of t[he] dough.

✳ Drop teaspoonfuls of filling in the cent[er] of each square; sprinkle with almon[ds]. Fold alternating points to the center [to] form a windmill; moisten points with w[a]ter and pinch gently at center to se[al]. Bake at 350° for 8-10 minutes or un[til] set. Remove to wire racks to cool. YIEL[D:] about 2½ dozen.

EGGNOG COOKIES

MYRA INNES, AUBURN, KANSAS
This cookie's flavor fits right into the holiday spirit.

- 1 **cup butter, softened**
- 2 **cups sugar**
- 1 **cup store-bought eggnog**
- 1 **teaspoon baking soda**
- ½ **teaspoon ground nutmeg**
- 5½ **cups all-purpose flour**

EGGNOG COOKIES

1 egg white, lightly beaten

olored sugar

In a mixing bowl, cream butter and sugar. Beat in eggnog, baking soda and nutmeg. Gradually add flour and mix well. Cover and chill for 1 hour.

On a lightly floured surface, roll out half of the dough to 1/8-in. thickness. Cut into desired shapes; place on ungreased baking sheets. Repeat with remaining dough. Brush with egg white; sprinkle with colored sugar.

Bake at 350° for 6-8 minutes or until edges are lightly browned. Remove to wire racks to cool. YIELD: about 16 dozen.

HOLIDAY GINGER CUTOUTS

JOANNE MACVEY, BLUE GRASS, IOWA

ooking to get a little creative with our cookie decorating? Paint your wn masterpiece on a ginger cookie!

1 cup shortening

1 cup sugar

1 egg

1 cup molasses

2 tablespoons white vinegar

1/2 cups all-purpose flour

2 teaspoons ground ginger

1/2 teaspoons baking soda

1 teaspoon ground cinnamon

3/4 teaspoon ground cloves

1/2 teaspoon salt

ING

4 cups confectioners' sugar

2 tablespoons meringue powder

1/2 cup warm water

ssorted colors of liquid food coloring

ound pastry tip #2, #3 or #4

In a mixing bowl, cream shortening and sugar. Add the egg, molasses and vinegar; mix well. Combine dry ingredients; add to creamed mixture and mix well. Cover and refrigerate for 3 hours or overnight.

On a lightly floured surface, roll out dough to 1/8-in. thickness and cut into

HOLIDAY GINGER CUTOUTS

desired shapes. Place 1 in. apart on lightly greased baking sheets. Bake at 350° for 7-9 minutes or until set. Remove to wire racks to cool.

❊ For icing, sift confectioners' sugar and meringue powder into a large mixing bowl. Add water; beat on low speed until blended. Beat on high for 5-6 minutes or until soft peaks form. Place a damp paper towel over bowl and cover tightly until ready to use.

❊ Cut a small hole in the corner of a pastry or plastic bag; insert round tip. Fill bag with 1 cup icing. Outline each cookie with icing.

❊ Tint remaining icing with food coloring if desired. Add water, a few drops at a time, until the mixture is thin enough to flow smoothly. Prepare additional pastry or plastic bags with thinned icing. Fill in cookies, letting icing flow up to the outline.

❊ Let cookies dry at room temperature overnight. With food coloring and small new paintbrush, paint designs on dry icing. Store cookies in airtight containers. YIELD: about 6 dozen.

EDITOR'S NOTE: Meringue powder can be ordered by mail from Wilton Industries, Inc. Call 1-800-794-5866 or visit www.wilton.com.

decorating cookies with royal Icing

1. Cut a small hole in the corner of a pastry or plastic bag. Insert a round tip; fill bag with icing. Hold bag at a 45° angle to the cookie, and pipe a bead of icing around the edge. Stop squeezing the bag before you lift the tip from the cookie.

2. Thin remaining icing so that it will flow smoothly. Fill another bag with thinned icing. Starting in the middle, fill in the cookie with the thinned icing, letting icing flow up to the outline. Let cookies dry overnight.

3. With a new small paintbrush, paint your own designs on the cookies with liquid food coloring.

chill the dough

For easier handling, refrigerate dough before rolling. This is especially true if the dough was made with butter rather than shortening.

FROSTED BUTTER CUTOUTS

SANDY NACE, GREENSBURG, KANSAS

I have fond memories of baking and frosting these cutout cookies with my mom. Now I carry on the tradition with my kids. It's a messy but fun day!

- 1 **cup butter, softened**
- 2 **cups sugar**
- 2 **eggs**
- 1 **cup buttermilk**
- 1 **teaspoon vanilla extract**
- 1/2 **teaspoon almond extract**
- 5 **cups all-purpose flour**
- 2 **teaspoons baking powder**
- 1 **teaspoon baking soda**
- 1/4 **teaspoon salt**

FROSTING
- 1/4 **cup butter, softened**
- 2 **cups confectioners' sugar**
- 1/2 **teaspoon almond extract**
- 2 **to 3 tablespoons heavy whipping cream**

Green and red food coloring, optional

Red-hot candies, colored sugar, Cake Mate snowflake decors and colored sprinkles

✻ In a large mixing bowl, cream butter and sugar. Add eggs, one at a time, beating well after each addition. Beat in the buttermilk and extracts. Combine the flour, baking powder, baking soda and salt;

FROSTED BUTTER CUTOUTS

gradually add to creamed mixture. Cov[er] and refrigerate overnight or until easy [to] handle.

✻ On a lightly floured surface, roll o[ut] dough to 1/4-in. thickness. Cut with 2 1/2-i[n.] cookie cutters dipped in flour. Place 1 i[n.] apart on greased baking sheets. Bake [at] 350° for 6-7 minutes or until light[ly] browned. Remove to wire racks to cool.

✻ For frosting, in a small mixing bowl, com[bine] the butter, confectioners' suga[r,] extract and enough cream to achiev[e] spreading consistency. Add food colorin[g] if desired. Frost cookies and decorat[e] with candies. YIELD: about 8 1/2 dozen.

LEMON SUGAR COOKIES

VIVIAN HINES, NEW PHILADELPHIA, OHIO

These light cookies are crisp on the outside and soft inside, making it har[d] to eat just one! I most often bake the[m] for Christmas and Valentine's Day.

- 2 **cups butter, softened**
- 4 **cups confectioners' sugar**
- 4 **eggs**
- 3 **tablespoons lemon juice**
- 3 **tablespoons half-and-half cream**
- 2 **teaspoons grated lemon peel**
- 6 1/2 **cups all-purpose flour**
- 1 **teaspoon baking soda**
- 1/4 **teaspoon salt**

Sugar

✻ In a mixing bowl, cream butter and con[-] fectioners' sugar. Add the eggs, one at [a] time, beating well after each additio[n.] Beat in lemon juice, cream and lemo[n] peel.

✻ Combine flour, baking soda and sal[t;] gradually add to the creamed mixtur[e.] Cover and refrigerate for 2 hours or unt[il] easy to handle.

✻ On a lightly floured surface, roll ou[t] dough to 1/8-in. thickness. Cut with 2 1/2-i[n.] cookie cutters dipped in flour. Place 1 i[n.] apart on ungreased baking sheet[s.] Sprinkle with sugar.

✻ Bake at 350° for 8-10 minutes or unt[il] lightly browned. Remove to wire racks t[o] cool. YIELD: about 13 dozen.

PEPPERMINT BISCOTTI

PEPPERMINT BISCOTTI

ULA MARCHESI
NHARTSVILLE, PENNSYLVANIA

ipped in melted chocolate and rolled
crushed peppermint candy, this
avorful biscotti is a favorite. It's one of
e many sweets I make for Christmas.

- ¾ **cup butter, softened**
- ¾ **cup sugar**
- 3 **eggs**
- 2 **teaspoons peppermint extract**
- ¼ **cups all-purpose flour**
- 1 **teaspoon baking powder**
- ¼ **teaspoon salt**
- 1 **cup crushed peppermint candy**

ROSTING

- 2 **cups (12 ounces) semisweet**
  chocolate chips
- 2 **tablespoons shortening**
- ½ **cup crushed peppermint candy**

In a large mixing bowl, cream butter and
sugar. Add eggs, one at a time, beating
well after each addition. Beat in extract.
Combine the flour, baking soda and salt;
stir in peppermint candy. Gradually add to
creamed mixture, beating until blended
(dough will be stiff).

Divide dough in half. On an ungreased
baking sheet, roll each portion into a 12-
in. x 2½-in. rectangle. Bake at 350° for 25-
30 minutes or until golden brown.
Carefully remove to wire racks; cool for 15
minutes. Transfer to a cutting board; cut

diagonally with a sharp knife into ½-in.
slices. Place cut side down on ungreased
baking sheets. Bake for 12-15 minutes or
until firm. Remove to wire racks to cool.

✳ In a microwave safe bowl, melt chocolate
chips and shortening; stir until smooth.
Dip one end of each cookie in chocolate;
roll in candy. Place on waxed paper until
set. Store in an airtight container. YIELD:
about 3½ dozen.

SCOTTISH SHORTBREAD

ROSE MABEE, SELKIRK, MANITOBA
My mother, who is of Scottish heritage,
passed this recipe, as with most of my
favorite recipes, on to me. When I
entered the cookie at our local fair, it
won a red ribbon.

- 1 **pound butter, softened**
- 1 **cup packed brown sugar**
- 4 **to 4½ cups all-purpose flour**

✳ In a mixing bowl, cream the butter and
brown sugar. Add 3¾ cups flour; mix well.
Sprinkle a board with some of the
remaining flour. Knead for 5 minutes,
adding enough remaining flour to make a
soft, non-sticky dough.

✳ Roll to ½-in. thickness. Cut into 3-in. x 1-
in. strips. Place 1 in. apart on ungreased
baking sheets. Prick with fork. Bake at
325° for 20-25 minutes or until lightly
browned. Remove to wire racks to cool.
YIELD: about 4 dozen.

SCOTTISH SHORTBREAD

BEST✳LOVED
cookies
& BARS

frosting tips

- To fill a pastry or re-sealable plastic bag with frosting, insert a decorating tip if desired and place the bag in a measuring cup. Roll down top edge to make a cuff. Fill about half full with frosting. Roll up cuff.

- Smooth filling down toward tip to remove air bubbles, which will cause breaks in the design when piping. Twist top of bag shut.

STAINED GLASS COOKIE ORNAMENTS

STAINED GLASS COOKIE ORNAMENTS

TASTE OF HOME TEST KITCHEN

These fancy, jewel-colored cookie ornaments look great on the tree, hanging in a window or on a stand as a holiday centerpiece. They're not that tricky to make. They could become a fun family tradition.

1½ cups butter, softened
1½ cups sugar
2 eggs
3 teaspoons vanilla extract
4½ cups all-purpose flour
1 teaspoon baking soda
1 teaspoon cream of tartar
1 teaspoon salt
Assorted colors of Jolly Rancher hard candies
1 tablespoon meringue powder
3 tablespoons plus ½ teaspoon water
2⅔ cups confectioners' sugar

❋ In a large mixing bowl, cream butter and sugar. Add eggs, one at a time, beating well after each addition. Beat in vanill Combine the flour, baking soda, crea of tartar and salt; gradually add to th creamed mixture. Divide into three po tions; cover and refrigerate for 30 minut or until easy to handle.

❋ On a lightly floured surface, roll out o portion to ¼-in. thickness. Cut wi 2½-in. ornament-shaped cookie cutte dipped in flour. Cut out centers with ½-in. cookie cutter. Place larger cutouts in. apart on greased baking sheets. Pol a small hole in the top of each cooki Repeat with remaining dough; reroll sm cutouts if desired.

❋ Place the same color of hard candies small resealable plastic bags; crush ca dies. Sprinkle in center of each. Bake 350° for 8-10 minutes or until light browned. Cool for 2-3 minutes or un candies are set before carefully removir to wire racks.

❋ In a small mixing bowl, beat meringu powder and water until soft peaks for Gradually add the confectioners' suga Decorate cookies with icing. YIELD: abo 7 dozen.

FRIEDA'S MOLASSES COOKIES

INA SANDERS, DALY CITY, CALIFORNIA

This recipe has been in our family for a long time. During the 1930s and 1940s, my mother baked a batch of these delicious cookies at least once a week. Neighborhood children who passed our house on the way to school looked forward to stopping on their way home for those cookies, still warm from the oven. Dunked in a glass of cold milk, they were a scrumptious snack.

- 1 cup sugar
- 1 cup shortening
- 1 cup light molasses
- 1 tablespoon white vinegar
- 5 cups all-purpose flour
- 1 teaspoon ground ginger
- 1 teaspoon ground cinnamon
- 1/4 teaspoon salt
- 2 teaspoons baking soda
- 1/3 cup boiling water

In a large bowl, cream the sugar and shortening. Add molasses and vinegar. Combine flour, ginger, cinnamon and salt; add alternately with baking soda and water to the creamed mixture.

On a lightly floured surface, roll dough to 1/4-in. thickness. Cut with a 2 1/2-in. cookie cutter dipped in flour. Place on greased baking sheets.

Bake at 375° for 8 minutes. Remove to wire racks to cool. YIELD: 6-7 dozen.

POINSETTIA COOKIES

TRICIA ECKARD, SINGERS GLEN, VIRGINIA

I must make 30 different kinds of cookies during the Christmas season—many to give away as gifts. Judging from the comments I get, these pretty pink poinsettias with a hint of cinnamon flavor are not just my own favorite!

- 1 cup butter, softened
- 1 cup confectioners' sugar
- 1 egg
- 2 to 3 drops red food coloring

- 2 1/3 cups all-purpose flour
- 3/4 teaspoon salt
- 1/4 cup finely crushed red-hot candies

FROSTING
- 1 cup confectioners' sugar
- 4 teaspoons milk

Additional red-hot candies

❈ In a large mixing bowl, cream butter and confectioners' sugar. Beat in egg and food coloring. Combine flour and salt; gradually add to the creamed mixture. Stir in red-hots. Divide dough in half; wrap in plastic wrap. Refrigerate for at least 1 hour or until firm.

❈ On a lightly floured surface, roll out one portion of dough into a 12-in. x 10-in. rectangle. With a sharp knife or pastry wheel, cut dough into 2-in. squares. Place 1 in. apart on lightly greased baking sheets. Cut through dough from each corner of square to within 1/2 in. of center. Fold alternating points of square to center to form a pinwheel; pinch gently at center to seal. Repeat with remaining dough.

❈ Bake at 350° for 7-9 minutes or until set. Remove to wire racks to cool. Combine the confectioners' sugar and milk. Pipe 1/2 teaspoon frosting in center of each cookie; top with a red-hot candy. YIELD: 5 dozen.

POINSETTIA COOKIES

preventing sticking

Lightly dust the rolling pin and work surface with flour to help prevent sticking. Working too much extra flour into the dough will result in tough cookies.

BEST❈LOVED
COOKIES
& BARS

rolling dough

Roll out a portion of the dough at a time and keep the remaining dough in the refrigerator. Roll out from the center to the edge, keeping a uniform thickness and checking the thickness with a ruler. If the thickness of the dough is uneven, the cookies will bake unevenly. Thinner cookies will be crisp and may burn, while thicker cookies will be chewy.

RASPBERRY TREASURES

TASTE OF HOME TEST KITCHEN

Light and flaky, these delicate fruit-filled cookies have the look of petite and elegant pastries. We like them with a spot of raspberry or apricot filling and a cup of Christmas tea.

- **½ cup butter, softened**
- **1 package (3 ounces) cream cheese, softened**
- **1 teaspoon vanilla extract**
- **1 cup all-purpose flour**
- **⅛ teaspoon salt**
- **½ cup raspberry filling**
- **1 egg**
- **1 teaspoon water**

In a mixing bowl, cream butter and cream cheese. Beat in vanilla. Combine flour and salt; add to the creamed mixture. Divide dough in half; wrap each in plastic wrap. Refrigerate for 1 hour or until dough is easy to handle.

On a lightly floured surface, roll out dough to ⅛-in. thickness. Cut with a 3-in. round cookie cutter dipped in flour. Place 1 teaspoon raspberry filling in the center of each. Bring three edges together over filling, overlapping slightly (a small amount of filling will show); pinch edges gently. In a small bowl, beat egg and water; brush over dough.

Place 1 in. apart on ungreased baking sheets. Bake at 375° for 10-12 minutes or until golden brown. Cool for 1 minute before removing to wire racks. YIELD: 2 dozen.

RASPBERRY TREASURES

GRANDMA'S OATMEAL COOKIES

MARY ANN KONECHNE
KIMBALL, SOUTH DAKOTA

This recipe—a favorite of my husband's—goes back to my great-grandmother. At Christmastime, we use colored sugar for a festive touch.

- **1½ cups shortening**
- **2 cups sugar**
- **2 teaspoons baking soda**
- **4 teaspoons warm water**
- **4 eggs**
- **4 cups all-purpose flour**
- **½ teaspoon salt**
- **2 teaspoons ground cinnamon**
- **4 cups quick-cooking oats**
- **2 cups chopped raisins**
- **1 cup chopped walnuts**

Additional granulated sugar *or* colored sugar

In a large mixing bowl, cream shortenir and sugar. Dissolve baking soda in w ter; add to creamed mixture. Add egg one at a time, beating well after each a dition. Add remaining ingredients e cept additional sugar; mix well.

Roll out dough; sprinkle with sugar or cc ored sugar. Cut with desired cutters. Pla on greased baking sheets. Bake at 35 for 12-15 minutes. Remove to wire rac to cool. YIELD: 12 dozen.

CINNAMON STARS

JEAN JONES, PEACHTREE CITY, GEORGIA

These cookies fill your home with an irresistible aroma as they bake. My grandmother made them every Christmas when I was a child.

- **1 cup butter, softened**
- **2 cups sugar**
- **2 eggs**
- **2¾ cups all-purpose flour**
- **⅓ cup ground cinnamon**

In a mixing bowl, cream butter and su ar. Add eggs, one at a time, beating w after each addition. Combine flour ar cinnamon; gradually add to creamed mi

ture. Cover and refrigerate for 1 hour or until easy to handle.

On a lightly floured surface, roll out dough to ¼-in. thickness. Cut with a 2½-in. star-shaped cookie cutter dipped in flour. Place 1 in. apart on ungreased baking sheets.

Bake at 350° for 15-18 minutes or until edges are firm and bottom of cookies are lightly browned. Remove to wire racks to cool. YIELD: 5 dozen.

PICED CUTOUTS
LISA NARR, WEST BEND, WISCONSIN
ese tasty cookies have a wonderful ice flavor that also smells great.

- 1 **cup butter, softened**
- ½ **cups sugar**
- 1 **tablespoon molasses**
- 1 **egg**
- ¼ **cups all-purpose flour**
- 1 **tablespoon ground cinnamon**
- 1 **tablespoon ground ginger**
- 2 **teaspoons ground cardamom**
- 2 **teaspoons ground cloves**
- 2 **teaspoons baking soda**
- ¼ **cup orange juice**
- 1 **tablespoon grated orange peel**

In a mixing bowl, cream butter and sugar; beat in molasses and egg. Combine flour, spices and baking soda; add to creamed mixture alternately with orange juice. Stir in peel.

On a floured surface, roll the dough to ¹⁄₁₆-in. thickness. Cut with a 2½-in. cookie cutter dipped in flour; place on ungreased baking sheets.

Bake at 350° for 6-8 minutes or until edges are lightly browned. Remove to wire racks to cool. YIELD: about 9 dozen.

OLIDAY BISCOTTI
IA FOGLESONG, SAN BRUNO, CALIFORNIA
twice-baked Italian cookie, biscotti akes a wonderful "dunker." A pretty ay to present a batch is on a hristmasy plate arranged in wagon-heel fashion.

HOLIDAY BISCOTTI

- ½ **cup butter, softened**
- 1 **cup sugar**
- 3 **eggs**
- 2 **teaspoons vanilla extract**
- 1 **teaspoon orange extract**
- 3 **cups all-purpose flour**
- 2 **teaspoons baking powder**
- ½ **teaspoon salt**
- ⅔ **cup dried cranberries, coarsely chopped**
- ⅔ **cup pistachios, coarsely chopped**
- 2 **tablespoons grated orange peel**

❄ In a mixing bowl, cream butter and sugar. Add eggs, one at a time, beating well after each addition. Stir in the extracts. Combine flour, baking powder and salt; gradually add to creamed mixture and mix well (dough will be sticky). Stir in cranberries, pistachios and orange peel. Chill for 30 minutes.

❄ Divide dough in half. On a floured surface, shape each half into a loaf 1½ to 2 in. in diameter. Place on an ungreased baking sheet. Bake at 350° for 30-35 minutes.

❄ Cool for 5 minutes. Cut diagonally into ¾-in.-thick slices. Place slices, cut side down, on an ungreased baking sheet. Bake for 9-10 minutes. Turn slices over. Bake 10 minutes more or until golden brown. Cool on wire rack. Store in an airtight container. YIELD: 2 dozen.

SOUR CREAM CUTOUT COOKIES

SOUR CREAM CUTOUT COOKIES

MARLENE JACKSON, KINGSBURG, CALIFORNIA
These soft cookies make a comforting evening snack.

- 1 cup butter, softened
- 1½ cups sugar
- 3 eggs
- 1 cup (8 ounces) sour cream
- 2 teaspoons vanilla extract
- 3½ cups all-purpose flour
- 2 teaspoons baking powder
- 1 teaspoon baking soda

FROSTING
- ⅓ cup butter, softened
- 2 cups confectioners' sugar
- 2 to 3 tablespoons milk
- 1½ teaspoons vanilla extract
- ¼ teaspoon salt

✳ In a mixing bowl, cream butter and sugar. Beat in eggs. Add sour cream and vanilla; mix well. Combine flour, baking powder and baking soda; add to the creamed mixture and mix well. Chill dough at least 2 hours or overnight.

✳ On a heavily floured surface, roll the dough to ¼-in. thickness. Cut with a 3-in. cookie cutter dipped in flour. Place on lightly greased baking sheets. Bake at 350° for 10-12 minutes or until cookies spring back when lightly touched. Remove to wire racks to cool. Mix all frosting ingredients until smooth; spread over cookies. YIELD: about 3½ dozen.

MOLASSES CUTOUTS

DEB ANDERSON, JOPLIN, MISSOURI
You'll have fun decorating these spicy cutouts. They really stand out.

- ⅔ cup shortening
- 1¼ cups sugar
- 2 eggs
- 2 tablespoons buttermilk
- 2 tablespoons molasses
- 3½ cups all-purpose flour
- 1 teaspoon baking soda
- 1 teaspoon baking powder
- 1 teaspoon salt
- 1 teaspoon ground ginger
- ½ teaspoon ground cloves

Confectioners' sugar icing and miniature chocolate chips and M&Ms, optional

✳ In a mixing bowl, cream shortening and sugar. Add eggs, one at a time, beating well after each addition. Beat in buttermilk and molasses. Combine dry ingredients; gradually add to the creamed mixture and mix well. Chill for several hours.

✳ On a lightly floured surface, roll dough to ⅛-in. thickness. Cut with 5-in. cookie cutters dipped in flour. Place 2 in. apart on greased baking sheets. Bake at 375° for 8-10 minutes or until edges just begin to brown. Remove to wire racks to cool. Decorate as desired. YIELD: about dozen.

MOLASSES CUTOUTS

cookie cutter clue

To prevent the dough from sticking to the cookie cutter, dip the cutter in flour or spray it with nonstick cooking spray.

AVORITE SUGAR COOKIES

DITH SCHOLOVICH, WAUKESHA, WISCONSIN

e been delighting my children and andchildren for years with this ecial recipe. These cookies can suit y holiday or occasion throughout e year. The dough is very nice to ork with.

- 1 cup butter, softened
- 1 cup confectioners' sugar
- 1 egg, beaten
- /2 teaspoons almond extract
- 1 teaspoon vanilla extract
- /2 cups all-purpose flour
- 1 teaspoon salt

OSTING

- 3 cups confectioners' sugar
- 6 tablespoons butter, softened
- 1 teaspoon vanilla extract
- 2 to 4 tablespoons milk
- od coloring, optional
- lored sugar, optional

In a mixing bowl, cram butter and sugar. Add egg and extracts; beat until light and fluffy. Combine flour and salt; add to creamed mixture and mix well. Chill for 1-2 hours.

On a lightly floured surface, roll dough to ⅛-in. thickness. Cut with 2½-in. cookie cutters dipped in flour. Place on greased baking sheets.

Bake at 375° for 7-9 minutes or until lightly browned. Remove to wire racks to cool.

For frosting, in a mixing bowl, beat sugar, butter, vanilla and milk until creamy. Add a few drops of food coloring if desired. Frost cookies; decorate with colored sugar if desired. YIELD: 7 dozen.

ALLY ANN COOKIES

RAH JANE HAYES, DILWORTH, MINNESOTA

ese soft, cake-like cookies are pecially satisfying because they're ry low in fat.

- /2 cups sugar
- 1 cup molasses
- /2 cup brewed coffee, room temperature

SALLY ANN COOKIES

- 5 cups all-purpose flour
- 2 teaspoons baking soda
- ¾ teaspoon salt
- ½ teaspoon ground nutmeg
- ¼ teaspoon ground cloves
- ¼ teaspoon ground ginger

FROSTING

- 1½ cups sugar
- ½ cup water
- 1 teaspoon white vinegar
- 1 cup miniature marshmallows
- 2 egg whites

❈ In a mixing bowl, combine sugar, molasses and coffee. Combine dry ingredients; add to sugar mixture and mix well. Refrigerate for 2 hours.

❈ On a floured surface, roll out dough to about ¼-in. thickness. Cut with 3-in. to 4-in. cookie cutters dipped in flour. Place on baking sheets that have been coated with nonstick cooking spray. Bake at 350° for 8-10 minutes or until set. Remove to wire racks to cool.

❈ Meanwhile, for frosting, combine sugar, water and vinegar in a heavy saucepan. Cover and bring to a boil. Uncover and cook over medium-high heat until a candy thermometer reads 234°-240° (softball stage), about 5-10 minutes. Remove from the heat; stir in marshmallows until smooth.

❈ In a mixing bowl, beat egg whites until frothy. Gradually beat in sugar mixture; beat on high for 7-8 minutes or until stiff peaks form. Frost the cookies. YIELD: about 6 dozen.

cutting down on scraps

After the dough is rolled out, position the shapes from the cookie cutters close together to avoid having too many scraps. Save all the scraps and reroll them just once to prevent tough cookies.

CHRISTMAS SHORTBREAD WREATHS

CHRISTMAS SHORTBREAD WREATHS

DONNA GENDRE, STETTLER, ALBERTA

I adapted this recipe from plain shortbread to use for a cookie exchange. The wreaths are big sellers at bake sales. Since they're so quick and easy to prepare, I'm happy to share them at the holidays with teachers, friends and neighbors.

> 1 cup all-purpose flour
> 1/2 cup cornstarch
> 1/2 cup confectioners' sugar
> 3/4 cup butter, softened
> **Red and green sprinkles**

❄ In a bowl, combine flour, cornstarch and sugar. Blend in butter with a wooden spoon until the dough is smooth. Form into two balls. Chill for 30 minutes or until firm.

❄ On a floured surface, roll one ball into a 9-in. circle; transfer to a greased baking sheet. Cut out center with a small round cookie cutter. If desired, scallop outer and inner edges of wreath with the edge of a cookie cutter or a knife. Cut the wreath into 12 wedges. Separate the wedges, leaving 1/8 in. between. Decorate outer and inner edges with sprinkles. Repeat for remaining dough.

❄ Bake at 300° for 18-22 minutes or u[ntil] golden brown. Cool on pan for 5 minut[es.] Recut wreath into wedges. Remove t[o] wire rack to cool completely. To ser[ve,] arrange as a wreath on a large flat servi[ng] plate. **YIELD:** 2 dozen (2 wreaths).

FROSTED NUTMEG LOGS

SARAH MILLER, WAUCONDA, WASHINGTON

Every bite of these cookies tastes like [a] sip of eggnog, so it's no wonder we make them each Christmas. Other cookie recipes come and go, but this [is] a timeless classic.

> 1 cup butter, softened
> 3/4 cup sugar
> 1 egg
> 2 teaspoons vanilla extract
> 1/2 to 1 teaspoon rum extract
> 3 cups all-purpose flour
> 1 teaspoon ground nutmeg
> 1/4 teaspoon salt

FROSTING

> 1/3 cup butter, softened
> 2 cups confectioners' sugar
> 1 teaspoon vanilla extract
> 1/2 to 1 teaspoon rum extract
> 1 to 2 tablespoons half-and-half cream

❄ In a large mixing bowl, cream butter a[nd] sugar. Add egg and extracts; mix we[ll.] Combine the flour, nutmeg and salt; grad[-] ually add to the creamed mixture.

❄ On a lightly floured surface, shape dou[gh] into 1/2-in.-wide logs. Cut into 2-in. piec[es.] Place 2 in. apart on ungreased baki[ng] sheets. Bake at 350° for 11-14 minut[es] or until center is set and edges are lig[ht-] ly browned. Cool for 2 minutes befo[re] removing from pans to wire racks.

❄ For frosting, in a mixing bowl, combi[ne] the butter, confectioners' sugar, extra[cts] and enough cream to achieve a spreadi[ng] consistency. Frost cooled cookies. **YIE[LD:]** 4 1/2 dozen.

CHRISTMAS SUGAR COOKIES

PAULA MACLEAN, WINSLOW, ARIZONA

Sour cream keeps my favorite sugar cookies extra moist. You can dress them up even more with a drizzle of melted white chocolate or dip them in white chocolate, then sprinkle with crushed candy canes if you'd like.

1 cup butter, softened
2 cups confectioners' sugar
1 egg
¼ cup sour cream
¼ cup honey
2 teaspoons vanilla extract
4½ cups all-purpose flour
1 teaspoon baking soda
1 teaspoon cream of tartar
½ teaspoon ground mace
⅛ teaspoon salt
White candy coating
Green paste food coloring

❄ In a mixing bowl, cream butter and sugar. Beat in the egg, sour cream, honey and vanilla. Combine the dry ingredients; gradually add to creamed mixture. Cover and chill for 2 hours or until dough is easy to handle.

❄ On a lightly floured surface, roll out dough to ⅛-in. thickness. Cut with 3-in. cookie cutters dipped in flour. Place 1 in. apart on ungreased baking sheets.

❄ Bake at 325° for 8-10 minutes or until lightly browned. Remove to wire racks to cool. Melt candy coating; stir in food coloring. Drizzle over cookies. YIELD: about 8 dozen.

CHRISTMAS SUGAR COOKIES

GINGERBREAD CUTOUTS

GINGERBREAD CUTOUTS

VIRGINIA WATSON, KIRKSVILLE, MISSOURI
Baking gingerbread cookies was a Christmas tradition when our three sons were at home. Now, our granddaughter loves to help!

- ½ cup butter, softened
- ½ cup packed brown sugar
- ½ cup molasses
- 1 egg
- 3 cups all-purpose flour
- 1 teaspoon baking soda
- 1 teaspoon ground ginger
- ½ teaspoon salt
- ¼ teaspoon ground cinnamon
- ⅛ teaspoon ground cloves
- 1 to 2 tablespoons cold water

❋ In a mixing bowl, cream the butter and brown sugar. Beat in molasses and egg. Combine the flour, baking soda, ginger, salt, cinnamon and cloves; add to the creamed mixture alternately with water. Mix well. Cover and refrigerate for 1 hour or until easy to handle.

❋ On a well-floured surface, roll out dough to ¼-in. thickness. Cut with a rocking horse cookie cutter or cutter of your choice dipped in flour. Place 2 in. apart ⌐ greased baking sheets.

❋ Bake at 350° for 9-11 minutes or un edges are firm. Remove to wire racks cool. YIELD: about 2 dozen.

FIG-FILLED COOKIES

LINDA KAPPELT, LINESVILLE, PENNSYLVANIA
Family and friends know I have a fondness for Christmas cookies. Each year after Thanksgiving, they begin asking when the cookies will be ready

- ½ cup butter, softened
- ¼ cup sugar
- ¼ cup packed brown sugar
- 1 egg
- 1 teaspoon vanilla extract
- 1¾ cups all-purpose flour
- ½ teaspoon baking soda
- ¼ teaspoon salt

FILLING
- ⅔ cup finely chopped raisins
- ½ cup finely chopped dates
- ½ cup finely chopped dried figs
- ½ cup orange juice
- ⅓ cup finely chopped dried cherries *or* cranberries

FIG-FILLED COOKIE

2 teaspoons sugar

1 teaspoon grated lemon peel

1/4 teaspoon ground cinnamon

1/2 cup finely chopped pecans

GLAZE

3/4 cup confectioners' sugar

2 to 3 teaspoons lemon juice

In a large mixing bowl, cream butter and sugars. Beat in egg and vanilla. Combine the flour, baking soda and salt; stir into the creamed mixture. Divide dough in half; cover and refrigerate for at least 3 hours.

In a saucepan, combine the first eight filling ingredients. Bring to a boil. Reduce heat; simmer, uncovered, for 4-6 minutes or until the fruit is tender and liquid is absorbed, stirring occasionally. Remove from the heat; stir in pecans. Cool to room temperature.

Roll out each portion of dough between two pieces of waxed paper into a 10-in. x 8-in. rectangle. Cut each into two 10-in. x 4-in. rectangles. Spread 1/2 cup filling down the center of each rectangle. Starting at a long side, fold dough over filling; fold other side over top. Pinch to seal seams and edges. Place seam side down on parchment paper-lined baking sheets.

Bake at 375° for 10-15 minutes or until lightly browned. Cut each rectangle diagonally into 1-in. strips. Remove to wire racks to cool. Combine glaze ingredients; drizzle over cookies. YIELD: about 2 1/2 dozen.

FROSTED SPICE COOKIES

DEBBIE HURLBERT, HOWARD, OHIO

This recipe has been handed down through many generations of my husband's family. These cookies were always in his grandmother's cookie jar when he'd visit. Today, he enjoys them more than ever—and so do I.

1 cup butter, softened

1 cup sugar

1 cup molasses

1 egg

1 cup buttermilk

FROSTED SPICE COOKIES

6 cups all-purpose flour

1 tablespoon baking powder

1 teaspoon baking soda

1 teaspoon ground cinnamon

1 teaspoon ground ginger

1/2 teaspoon salt

1 cup chopped walnuts

1 cup golden raisins

1 cup chopped dates

FROSTING

3 3/4 cups confectioners' sugar

1/3 cup orange juice

2 tablespoons butter, melted

❋ In a large mixing bowl, cream butter and sugar. Add molasses, egg and buttermilk; mix well. Combine the flour, baking powder, baking soda, cinnamon, ginger and salt; gradually add to creamed mixture. Stir in walnuts, raisins and dates. Chill for 2 hours or until easy to handle.

❋ On a floured surface, roll out dough to 1/4-in. thickness. Cut with a 2 1/2-in. round cookie cutter dipped in flour. Place on greased baking sheets. Bake at 350° for 12-15 minutes. Remove to wire racks to cool.

❋ For frosting, beat all ingredients in a small bowl until smooth. Frost cookies. YIELD: 5-6 dozen.

transferring cutouts

To keep the cutouts intact before and after baking, transfer them to and from the baking sheet with a large metal spatula or pancake turner that supports the entire cutout.

APRICOT-FILLED TRIANGLES

MILDRED LORENCE, CARLISLE, PENNSYLVANIA

It's a good thing this recipe makes a big batch because no one can stop eating just one! These crisp buttery cookies truly do melt in your mouth.

- 1 **pound dried apricots (2½ cups)**
- 1½ **cups water**
- ½ **cup sugar**

DOUGH

- ⅔ **cup shortening**
- 3 **tablespoons milk**
- 1⅓ **cups sugar**
- 2 **eggs**
- 1 **teaspoon lemon extract**
- 4 **cups cake flour**
- 2 **teaspoons baking powder**
- 1 **teaspoon salt**

✳ In a small saucepan, cook apricots and water over low heat for 45 minutes or until the water is absorbed and apricots are soft. Cool sightly; transfer to a blender or food processor. Cover and process until smooth. Add the sugar; cover and process until blended. Set aside.

✳ In a large saucepan over low heat, m▮ shortening and milk. Remove from t▮ heat; stir in sugar. Add eggs, one at ▮ time, whisking well after each additio▮ Stir in extract. Combine the flour, baki▮ powder and salt; gradually add to t▮ saucepan. Cover and refrigerate for ▮ hours or until easy to handle.

✳ On a lightly floured surface, roll o▮ dough to ⅛-in. thickness. Cut with a ▮ in. round cookie cutter dipped in flo▮ Place 1 teaspoon apricot filling in the ce▮ ter of each. Bring three edges togeth▮ over filling, overlapping slightly (a sm▮ portion of filling will show in the cente▮ pinch edges gently. Place 1 in. apart ▮ ungreased baking sheets.

✳ Bake at 400° for 8-10 minutes or un▮ golden brown. Remove to wire racks ▮ cool. YIELD: 6 dozen.

FINNISH BUTTER COOKIE▮

AUDREY THIBODEAU, MESA, ARIZONA

These crispy Finnish cookies have a delicate texture and wonderful almon▮ flavor!

- ¾ **cup butter, softened**
- ¼ **cup sugar**
- 1 **teaspoon almond extract**
- 2 **cups all-purpose flour**
- 1 **egg white**
- 2 **tablespoons sugar**
- ⅓ **cup ground almonds**

✳ In a mixing bowl, cream butter and su▮ ar. Stir in extract. Add 1¼ cups flour; m▮ well. Knead in remaining flour. Cov▮ and chill at least 2 hours.

✳ On a lightly floured surface, roll o▮ dough to ¼-in. thickness. Cut with a sm▮ 1½- to 2-in. cookie cutter dipped in flou▮ place on ungreased baking sheets. Be▮ egg white until foamy; brush over coo▮ ies. Sprinkle with sugar and almonds.

✳ Bake at 350° for 7-8 minutes or until ligh▮ ly browned. Remove to wire racks to co▮ YIELD: 4 dozen.

APRICOT-FILLED TRIANGLES

DRIED CHERRY BISCOTTI

cutting biscotti

- The rectangular biscotti dough is baked, cut into slices, and then will be baked longer.
- With a serrated knife, cut the rectangular cookie diagonally into 1/2- or 3/4-in.-thick slices. Place the sliced cookies cut side down on a baking sheet and bake again as directed.

DRIED CHERRY BISCOTTI

SHARON MARTIN, MANISTEE, MICHIGAN

Need a holiday treat that's not overly sweet? I have an answer with this biscotti. The cherries and almonds add color and texture, and a dusting of powdered sugar dress them up.

- **2 tablespoons butter, softened**
- **1/2 cup sugar**
- **4 egg whites**
- **2 teaspoons almond extract**
- **2 cups all-purpose flour**
- **2 teaspoons baking powder**
- **1/4 teaspoon salt**
- **1/2 cup dried cherries**
- **1/4 cup chopped almonds, toasted**
- **2 teaspoons confectioners' sugar**

✻ In a small mixing bowl, beat butter and sugar for 2 minutes or until crumbly. Beat in egg whites and extract. Combine the flour, baking powder and salt; gradually add to sugar mixture. Stir in cherries and almonds (dough will be stiff).

✻ Press into an 8-in. square baking dish coated with nonstick cooking spray. Bake at 375° for 15-20 minutes or until lightly browned. Cool for 5 minutes. Remove from pan to a cutting board; cut biscotti in half with a serrated knife. Cut each half into 1/2-in. slices.

✻ Place slices cut side down on baking sheets coated with nonstick cooking spray. Bake for 8-10 minutes or until light golden brown, turning once. Remove to wire racks to cool. Sprinkle with confectioners' sugar. YIELD: 2 1/2 dozen.

ORANGE-CINNAMON CHOCOLATE CHIP COOKIES

DANIEL KAEPP, COLDWATER, MICHIGAN

I developed this recipe after years of searching for a chocolate chip cookie that would stand out from all others. Orange and cinnamon are tasty additions.

- 1 **cup butter, softened**
- ¾ **cup sugar**
- ¾ **cup packed brown sugar**
- 2 **eggs**
- 1 **tablespoon grated orange peel**
- 1 **teaspoon vanilla extract**
- 3½ **cups all-purpose flour**
- 1½ **teaspoons baking soda**
- 1¼ **teaspoons ground cinnamon**
- ¾ **teaspoon salt**
- 2 **cups (12 ounces) semisweet chocolate chips**
- 1 **cup chopped walnuts**

❈ In a large mixing bowl, cream butter and sugars. Beat in the eggs, orange peel and vanilla. Combine the flour, baking soda, cinnamon and salt; gradually add to the creamed mixture. Stir in the chips and walnuts. Cover and chill for 2 hours or until easy to handle.

❈ On lightly floured surface, roll out doug to ½-in. thickness. Cut with a 3-in. rou cookie cutter dipped in flour. Place 1 apart on greased baking sheets.

❈ Bake at 375° for 12-14 minutes or un lightly browned. Remove to wire racks cool. YIELD: about 3 dozen.

GINGER DIAMONDS

FRAN WILLIAMSON, WASHINGTON, INDIANA

These soft delicious cookies were a favorite of my son, who passed away years ago. I think of him each time I make them and know your family will enjoy them, too.

- 1 **cup shortening**
- 1½ **cups sugar**
- ½ **cup molasses**
- 2 **eggs**
- 3½ **cups all-purpose flour**
- 1 **teaspoon baking soda**
- 1 **teaspoon ground cinnamon**
- 1 **teaspoon ground cloves**
- ½ **teaspoon salt**
- ½ **teaspoon ground ginger**

Additional sugar

❈ In a large mixing bowl, cream shortenir and sugar. Beat in molasses. Add egg one at a time, beating well after each a dition. Combine the flour, baking sod cinnamon, cloves, salt and ginger; gra ually add to the creamed mixture. Cov and refrigerate for 30 minutes or un easy to handle.

❈ Divide dough in half. On a lightly floure surface, roll out each portion to ¼-i thickness. With a sharp knife, make cu 1½ in. apart in one direction, then mal diagonal cuts 1½ in. apart in the opposi direction. Generously sprinkle with add tional sugar.

❈ Place 1 in. apart on ungreased bakir sheets. Bake at 350° for 10-11 minute or until edges are golden brown. Remov to wire racks to cool. YIELD: 7 dozen.

ORANGE-CINNAMON CHOCOLATE CHIP COOKIES

ANISE BUTTER COOKIES

ANISE BUTTER COOKIES

KARI LYNN VAN GINKLE
CANDIA PARK, NEW MEXICO

Here in New Mexico, these cookies are known as "bizcochitos," which means "small biscuit." There are many variations of the recipe, which has been passed down through the generations. The cookies are enjoyed during the Christmas holidays and at wedding receptions and other celebrations.

- 2 cups butter, softened
- 1¾ cups sugar, *divided*
- 4 teaspoons aniseed, crushed
- 2 eggs
- ¼ cup orange juice concentrate
- 6 cups all-purpose flour
- 3 teaspoons baking powder
- ½ teaspoon salt
- 1 teaspoon ground cinnamon

In a large mixing bowl, cream the butter, 1½ cups sugar and aniseed. Add eggs, one at a time, beating well after each addition. Beat in orange juice concentrate. Combine the flour, baking powder and salt; gradually add to creamed mixture.

On a lightly floured surface, roll out dough to ¼-in. thickness. Cut with a 2½-in. round cookie cutter dipped in flour. Place 1 in. apart on ungreased baking sheets.

Combine the cinnamon and remaining sugar; sprinkle over cookies. Bake at 350° for 12-15 minutes or until golden brown. Remove to wire racks to cool. YIELD: 5 dozen.

BROWN SUGAR CUTOUTS

NORMA MUELLER, WAUWATOSA, WISCONSIN
I bake so many cookies for the holidays that I have one recipe box just for cookies alone! But of all of them, these simple cutouts are among my husband's favorites.

- 1 cup butter, softened
- 2 cups packed brown sugar
- 3 eggs
- 2 teaspoons grated lemon peel
- 3 cups all-purpose flour
- 1 teaspoon baking soda
- 1 teaspoon ground ginger

FROSTING
- 1½ cups confectioners' sugar
- ½ teaspoon vanilla extract
- 2 to 3 tablespoons half-and-half cream

Green food coloring, optional

❄ In a large mixing bowl, cream butter and brown sugar. Add the eggs and lemon peel; beat well. Combine the flour, baking soda and ginger; gradually add to creamed mixture and mix well. Cover and refrigerate for 2 hours or until easy to handle.

❄ On a floured surface, roll out dough to ⅛-in. thickness. Cut with 2-in. cookie cutters dipped in flour. Place 2 in. apart on ungreased baking sheets. Bake at 350° for 8-10 minutes or until golden brown. Remove to wire racks to cool.

❄ For frosting, in a bowl, combine confectioners' sugar, vanilla and enough cream to achieve spreading consistency. Add food coloring if desired to some or all of the frosting. Decorate cookies. YIELD: about 6 dozen.

BROWN SUGAR CUTOUTS

BEST LOVED
cookies
& BARS

SPICED CHERRY BELLS

PEGGY GRAVING, BUTTE, MONTANA

I always bake up a batch of these cookies for the dessert buffet I host on Christmas Eve. They're a hit!

1 cup butter, softened
1¼ cups packed brown sugar
¼ cup dark corn syrup
1 egg
1 tablespoon heavy whipping cream
3¼ cups all-purpose flour
1 teaspoon ground ginger
½ teaspoon instant coffee granules
½ teaspoon baking soda
½ teaspoon salt

FILLING
⅓ cup packed brown sugar
3 tablespoons maraschino cherry juice
1 tablespoon butter, softened
1½ cups finely chopped pecans
14 maraschino cherries, quartered

❉ In a mixing bowl, cream butter and brown sugar. Beat in corn syrup, egg and cream. Combine dry ingredients; gradually add to the creamed mixture and mix well. Cover and refrigerate dough for 2-4 hours or overnight.

❉ On a lightly floured surface, roll out dough to ⅛-in. thickness. Cut with a 2½-in. cookie cutter dipped in flour. Place 2 in. apart on ungreased baking sheets.

SPICED CHERRY BELLS

❉ In a bowl, combine the first three filling [in]gredients; mix well. Stir in pecans. Pla[ce] ½ teaspoon of filling in the center of ea[ch] cookie. Shape into a cone by foldi[ng] edges of dough to meet over filling; pin[ch] edges together. Place a piece of cherry [at] open end of each bell for clapper.

❉ Bake at 350° for 12-15 minutes or un[til] golden brown. Immediately remove to w[ire] racks to cool. YIELD: about 4½ dozen.

ENVELOPES OF FUDGE

DONNA NOWICKI, CENTER CITY, MINNESOTA

Sealed inside a golden crust is a delicious special delivery—a fudgy walnut filling that's almost like a brownie. These cookies are like two treats in one.

½ cup butter, softened
1 package (3 ounces) cream cheese, softened
1¼ cups all-purpose flour

FILLING
½ cup sugar
⅓ cup baking cocoa
¼ cup butter, softened
1 egg yolk
½ teaspoon vanilla extract
⅛ teaspoon salt
½ cup finely chopped walnuts

❉ In a mixing bowl, cream butter and crea[m] cheese. Gradually add the flour. On [a] lightly floured surface, knead un[til] smooth, about 3 minutes. Cover and r[e]frigerate for 1-2 hours or until dough [is] easy to handle.

❉ For filling, combine the sugar, cocoa, bu[t]ter, yolk, vanilla and salt. Stir in walnu[ts]; set aside. On a lightly floured surfac[e,] roll into a 12½-in. square; cut into 2½[-] in. squares. Place a rounded teaspoonf[ul] of filling in center of each square. Brin[g] two opposite corners to center. Moiste[n] edges with water and pinch togethe[r.] Place 1 in. apart on lightly greased bakin[g] sheets.

❉ Bake at 350° for 18-22 minutes or un[til] lightly browned. Remove to wire racks [to] cool. YIELD: 25 cookies.

PEANUT BUTTER CUTOUT COOKIES

EANUT BUTTER UTOUT COOKIES

NDI BAUER, MARSHFIELD, WISCONSIN

ere's a nice change of pace from the ore traditional sugar cutouts. And ildren will find that these peanut utter versions are just as much fun to ecorate with frosting, sprinkles and a ash of Yuletide imagination.

- **1 cup creamy peanut butter**
- **/4 cup sugar**
- **/4 cup packed brown sugar**
- **2 eggs**
- **/3 cup milk**
- **1 teaspoon vanilla extract**
- **/2 cups all-purpose flour**
- **/2 teaspoon baking powder**
- **/2 teaspoon baking soda**
- **anilla frosting**
- **ed, green, yellow and blue gel food coloring**
- **ssorted colored sprinkles**

In a large mixing bowl, cream peanut butter and sugars. Beat in the eggs, milk and vanilla. Combine the flour, baking powder and baking soda; add to creamed mixture and mix well. Cover and refrigerate for 2 hours or until easy to handle.

On a lightly floured surface, roll out dough to 1/4-in. thickness. Cut with 2-in. to 4-in. cookie cutters dipped in flour. Place 2 in. apart in ungreased baking sheets.

Bake at 375° for 7-9 minutes or until the edges are browned. Cool for 1 minute

before removing from pans to wire racks to cool completely. Frost and decorate as desired. YIELD: about 4 1/2 dozen.

EASY GINGERBREAD CUTOUTS

SANDY MCKENZIE, BRAHAM, MINNESOTA

I rely on this tried-and-true recipe during the holidays. The cream cheese frosting complements the cookies' gingery flavor and sets up nicely for easy packaging and stacking.

- **1 package (18 1/4 ounces) spice cake mix**
- **3/4 cup all-purpose flour**
- **2 eggs**
- **1/3 cup vegetable oil**
- **1/3 cup molasses**
- **2 teaspoons ground ginger**
- **3/4 cup canned cream cheese frosting, warmed slightly**

Red-hot candies

❋ In a mixing bowl, combine dry cake mix, flour, eggs, oil, molasses and ginger; mix well. Refrigerate for 30 minutes or until easy to handle.

❋ On a floured surface, roll out dough to 1/8-in. thickness. Cut with 5-in. cookie cutters dipped in flour. Place 3 in. apart on ungreased baking sheets.

❋ Bake at 375° for 7-10 minutes or until edges are firm and bottom is lightly browned. Remove to wire racks to cool. Decorate with cream cheese frosting as desired. Use red-hots for eyes, nose and buttons. YIELD: 2 1/2 dozen.

EASY GINGERBREAD CUTOUTS

cookie cutter suggestions

The cookie cutter sizes and shapes indicated in these recipes are only suggestions. Feel free to use whatever size and shape you like, but remember that the size or shape may affect the yield.

CHRISTMAS COOKIE ORNAMENTS

CHRISTMAS COOKIE ORNAMENTS

TASTE OF HOME TEST KITCHEN

The nice thing about these cookies is that you can bake them and freeze them undecorated. So on a leisurely autumn weekend, bake up as many batches as you need, cool and freeze. Then when Christmas comes around, just defrost them and decorate.

- ½ **cup butter, softened**
- ⅓ **cup shortening**
- 1 **cup sugar**
- ¼ **cup honey**
- 1 **egg**
- ½ **teaspoon vanilla extract**
- 3 **cups all-purpose flour**
- ¼ **teaspoon salt**

FROSTING

- 6⅔ **cups confectioners' sugar**
- ½ **cup water**
- 1 **tablespoon light corn syrup**
- 1 **teaspoon vanilla extract**

Assorted liquid *or* paste food coloring

- ❋ In a mixing bowl, cream the butter, shortening and sugar. Beat in the honey, egg and vanilla. Gradually add the flour and salt.

- ❋ Turn the dough onto a floured surface and roll to an ⅛-in. thickness. Cut into shapes using cookie cutters dipped in flour. Transfer cutouts to ungreased baking sheets.

- ❋ Using a straw, make a hole in the top of each cookie. Remove the center circle of dough. Bake the cookies at 350° for 6 minutes or until the edges are lightly

browned. Remove the cookies to w racks to cool.

- ❋ For frosting, combine the confectione sugar, water, corn syrup and vanilla. Be until smooth. Tint the frosting with liqu or paste food coloring in desired color

- ❋ Place each color of frosting in a pastry plastic bag. Cut a small hole in the tip each bag. Spread and pipe frosting on cookies as desired.

- ❋ If desired, create stitch marks on a stoc ing or veins on holly leaves by dipping toothpick in food coloring and painti on the lines.

- ❋ For hanging loops, cut forty 8-in. stri of ⅛-in.-wide ribbon. Thread a ribbo strip through the hole in each cookie a tie the ends into a bow. YIELD: 40 (3-i cookies.

SHORTBREAD CUTOUTS

CAROLE VOGEL, ALLISON PARK, PENNSYLVAN

Almonds give these cookies a special flavor. Use your favorite cookie cutter: to make different shapes. Then let the kids have a hand in adding the finishing touches.

- 1 **cup all-purpose flour**
- ½ **cup blanched almonds**
- ¼ **cup sugar**
- ¼ **teaspoon salt**
- ½ **cup cold butter**
- 1 **egg yolk**
- 2 **teaspoons cold water**
- ¼ **teaspoon almond extract**

- ❋ In a food processor, combine flour, a monds, sugar and salt; process until a monds are finely ground. Cut butter in cubes; add to processor. Pulse on ar off until mixture resembles coarse crumb

- ❋ Combine yolk, water and almond e tract. With the processor running, grad ally add yolk mixture; process until doug forms a ball. Wrap in plastic wrap and ch at least 30 minutes.

- ❋ On a lightly floured surface, roll out half the dough to ¼-in. thickness. Cut into d sired shapes; place on ungreased bakir sheets. Repeat with remaining dough.

Bake at 325° for 12-14 minutes or until edges are lightly browned. Cool 1 minute before removing to wire racks; cool completely. YIELD: about 3 dozen.

UTTERSCOTCH INGERBREAD COOKIES

RA COOK, ELK RIDGE, UTAH

ery time I make these wonderful okies, the spicy aroma takes me ck to my childhood. I helped Mom ake them and delivered them to ighbors.

1 **cup butter, softened**
1 **cup packed brown sugar**
2 **eggs**
3 **cups all-purpose flour**
2 **packages (3½ ounces** *each***) cook-and-serve butterscotch pudding mix**
3 **teaspoons ground ginger**
1 **teaspoon baking powder**
1 **teaspoon ground cinnamon**

In a large mixing bowl, cream the butter and brown sugar. Beat in the eggs. Combine the flour, pudding mixes, ginger, baking powder and cinnamon; gradually add to creamed mixture. Cover and refrigerate for 1 hour or until easy to handle.

On a lightly floured surface, roll out dough to ¼-in. thickness. Cut with cookie cutters dipped in flour. Place 1 in. apart on ungreased baking sheets. Bake at 350° for 6-8 minutes or until firm. Remove to wire racks to cool. Decorate as desired. YIELD: about 3 dozen.

UTTERSCOTCH GINGERBREAD COOKIES

VANILLA BUTTER ROLLOUTS

VANILLA BUTTER ROLLOUTS

COLLEEN SICKMAN, CHARLES CITY, IOWA

Even cooks who normally shy away from rolled cookies can make these with confidence. The dough is so easy to work with after a mere 30 minutes of chilling. They can be decorated in a variety of ways.

1½ **cups butter, softened**
1½ **cups sugar**
2 **eggs**
1 **tablespoon vanilla extract**
4 **cups all-purpose flour**
1 **teaspoon baking soda**
1 **teaspoon cream of tartar**
1 **teaspoon salt**

❋ In a large mixing bowl, cream butter and sugar. Add eggs, one at a time, beating well after each addition. Beat in vanilla. Combine the flour, baking soda, cream of tartar and salt; gradually add to the creamed mixture. Cover and refrigerate for 30 minutes or until easy to handle.

❋ On a lightly floured surface, roll out dough to ¼-in. thickness. Cut with 2½-in. cookie cutters dipped in flour. Place 2 in. apart on ungreased baking sheets.

❋ Bake at 350° for 8-10 minutes or until edges are lightly browned. Cool for 1 minute before removing to wire racks to cool completely. Decorate as desired. YIELD: about 7 dozen.

BEST☀LOVED
COOKIES
& BARS

SANTA SUGAR COOKIE

SANTA SUGAR COOKIES

TASTE OF HOME TEST KITCHEN AND
JILL BORUFF, SOAP LAKE, WASHINGTON

Ho ho ho! St. Nick can drop in any time at all when you bake these cute-as-can-be treats. We followed Jill's cookie recipe and formed Santas with heart-shaped cookie cutters.

1½ cups butter, softened
1½ cups shortening
1½ cups sugar
1½ cups confectioners' sugar
 3 eggs
4½ teaspoons vanilla extract
6¾ cups all-purpose flour
1½ teaspoons baking soda
1½ teaspoons cream of tartar
1½ teaspoons salt

FROSTING
 ¼ cup semisweet chocolate chips

Brown and red miniature M&M's
 1 carton (12 ounces) soft whipped frosting
 1 tablespoon butter, softened
 1 cup confectioners' sugar

Red colored sugar

Red jimmies

❉ In a mixing bowl, cream the butter, short-ening and sugars. Add eggs, one a time, beating well after each additic Beat in vanilla. Combine the flour, baki soda, cream of tartar and salt; gradua add to creamed mixture. Refrigerate 1-2 hours or until easy to handle.

❉ On a lightly floured surface, roll c dough to ¼-in. thickness. Cut with a 3 in. heart-shaped cookie cutter dipped flour. Place 1 in. apart on ungreased b ing sheets. Bake at 375° for 8-10 minu or until firm (do not overbake). Remove wire racks to cool.

❉ In a microwave or heavy saucepan, m chocolate chips. Cut a small hole in t corner of a pastry or plastic bag; insert round pastry tip. Add melted chocola For eyes, pipe two dots in the center each cookie; attach brown M&M's. Pip small dot of chocolate below eyes; atta a red M&M for nose. Pipe eyelashes.

❉ In a bowl, combine the frosting, butt and sugar; mix well. For hat, frost t top 1 in. of the pointed end of cook Sprinkle with red sugar. Frost the sid and rounded ends for beard. Place tw jimmies for the mouth. Cut a hole in t corner of a small plastic or pastry bag; sert #16 star tip. Fill with remaining fro ing. Pipe a zigzag boarder under hat fur hatband. Pipe a pom-pom on top hat. YIELD: about 8 dozen.

UT-FILLED HORNS

NNY FIELD, WAYNESBORO, VIRGINIA

imply the best" is what most folks
y after sampling these rich, flaky
okies. It's a thrill to share them with
ends and family.

- 2 cups butter, softened
- 2 packages (8 ounces *each*) cream cheese, softened
- 2 egg yolks
- /2 cups all-purpose flour
- 2 teaspoons baking powder

LING

- 4 cups finely chopped walnuts
- /2 to 2 cups sugar
- 6 tablespoons evaporated milk
- /2 teaspoons vanilla extract

In a large mixing bowl, cream the butter
and cream cheese. Add the egg yolks.
Combine flour and baking powder; gradually add to the creamed mixture. Cover
and chill overnight.

Combine filling ingredients in a bowl (mixture will be thick). Divide dough into
fourths (dough will be sticky). On a well-
sugared surface, roll out each portion into a 12-in. x 10-in. rectangle. Cut into 2-
in. squares. Place about 1 teaspoon filling
in the center of each square. Fold over
two opposite corners; seal tightly.

Place 2 in. apart on ungreased baking
sheets. Bake at 350° for 15-18 minutes
or until lightly browned. Remove to wire
racks to cool. YIELD: 10 dozen.

HITE VELVET CUTOUTS

M HINKLE, WAUSEON, OHIO

e make these cutouts every
hristmas and give lots of them as
fts. One year, we baked a batch a
eek all through December to be sure
e'd have plenty for ourselves, too.
ese rich cookies melt in your mouth!

- 2 cups butter, softened
- 1 package (8 ounces) cream cheese, softened
- 2 cups sugar
- 2 egg yolks
- 1 teaspoon vanilla extract
- 4½ cups all-purpose flour

BUTTER CREAM FROSTING

- 3½ cups confectioners' sugar, *divided*
- 3 tablespoons butter, softened
- 1 tablespoon shortening
- ½ teaspoon vanilla extract
- 3 to 4 tablespoons milk, *divided*

Red *and/or* green food coloring, optional

❉ In a mixing bowl, cream butter and cream cheese until light and fluffy. Add sugar, egg yolks and vanilla; mix well. Gradually add flour. Cover and chill 2 hours or until firm.

❉ On a floured surface, roll out dough to ¼-in. thickness. Cut into 3-in. shapes; place 1 in. apart on greased baking sheets. Bake at 350° for 10-12 minutes or until set (not browned). Cool 5 minutes; remove to wire racks to cool completely.

❉ For frosting, combine 1½ cups sugar, but-ter, shortening, vanilla and 3 tablespoons milk in a mixing bowl; beat until smooth. Gradually add remaining sugar; beat until light and fluffy, about 3 minutes. Add enough remaining milk and food coloring if desired until frosting reaches desired consistency. Frost cookies. YIELD: about 7 dozen.

WHITE VELVET CUTOUTS

SANDWICH cookies

RASPBERRY SANDWICH SPRITZ

JOAN O'BRIEN, PUNTA GORDA, FLORIDA

I started baking these Christmas classics when I was a sophomore in high school...and I am still making them now for my grown children and grandkids. The combination of jam, buttery shortbread, chocolate and sprinkles adds up to a fancy and festive treat.

- 1 cup butter, softened
- ¾ cup sugar
- 1 egg
- 1 teaspoon vanilla extract
- 2¼ cups all-purpose flour
- ½ teaspoon salt
- ¼ teaspoon baking powder
- 1 cup seedless raspberry jam
- 1 cup (6 ounces) semisweet chocolate chips

Chocolate sprinkles

❈ In a large mixing bowl, cream butter and sugar. Beat in egg and vanilla. Combine the flour, salt and baking powder; gradually add to creamed mixture.

❈ Using a cookie press fitted with a ribbon disk, form dough into long strips on un-greased baking sheets. Cut each strip to 2-in. pieces (do not separate). Bake 375° for 8-10 minutes or until edges golden brown. Cut again if necessa Remove to wire racks to cool.

❈ Spread the bottom of half of the cook with jam; top with remaining cookies a microwave, melt chocolate chips; until smooth. Place chocolate sprink in a bowl. Dip each end of cookies in me ed chocolate, then in sprinkles. Place waxed paper; let stand until firm. YIE about 4½ dozen.

DUTCH ALMOND COOKIE

LINDA DEJONG, LYNDEN, WASHINGTON

This recipe comes from ladies of Dut descent at my sister's church. The pleasant almond flavor pairs well with a cup of coffee.

- 1 cup butter, softened
- 2 cups sugar
- 2 eggs
- 1 teaspoon almond extract
- 3½ cups all-purpose flour
- 1 teaspoon baking powder
- 1 teaspoon baking soda
- ½ teaspoon salt
- 6 tablespoons almond paste
- 1 egg white, lightly beaten
- 3 dozen whole almonds

❈ In a large mixing bowl, cream butter a sugar. Beat in eggs and extract. Comb the flour, baking powder, baking soda a salt; gradually add to the creamed m ture and mix well. Cover and refriger for 1 hour or until easy to handle.

❈ On a lightly floured surface, roll dough to ¼-in. thickness; cut with a 2 round cookie cutter dipped in flour. Pl half of the circles 2 in. apart on ungreas baking sheets. Crumble ½ teaspoon mond paste over each; top with rema ing circles. Pinch edges to seal.

❈ Cut a small slit in top of each cook Brush with egg white. Press an almon each slit. Bake at 350° for 10-12 minu or until lightly browned. Remove to v racks to cool. YIELD: 3 dozen.

RASPBERRY SANDWICH SPRITZ

PAINTED HOLIDAY DELIGHTS

PAINTED HOLIDAY DELIGHTS

JUDY DEGENSTEIN, OTTAWA, KANSAS

These soft sandwich cookies are eye-catching, thanks to the holiday designs you paint on with food coloring. Orange juice in the dough and strawberry preserves in the filling add a light fruity flavor. I make them for special occasions.

- **2 cups all-purpose flour**
- **1/2 cup sugar**
- **1/2 cup confectioners' sugar**
- **2 teaspoons ground cinnamon**
- **1/4 teaspoon baking powder**
- **1/4 teaspoon salt**
- **1/2 cup cold butter**
- **1 egg**
- **1/4 cup orange juice**

FILLING

- **1 package (8 ounces) cream cheese, softened**
- **3 tablespoons confectioners' sugar**
- **3 tablespoons strawberry preserves**

GLAZE

- **1 cup confectioners' sugar**
- **1/4 teaspoon vanilla extract**
- **1 to 2 tablespoons milk**

Assorted food coloring

❄ In a bowl, combine the first six ingredients. Cut in butter until mixture resembles coarse crumbs. Combine egg and orange juice; stir into crumb mixture just until moistened. Shape into a ball; cover and chill for 1-2 hours or until easy to handle.

❄ On a floured surface, roll out dough to 1/8-in. thickness. Cut with a 2-in. round cookie cutter dipped in flour. Place 1 in. apart on ungreased baking sheets. Bake at 375° for 8-10 minutes or until lightly browned. Remove to wire racks to cool.

❄ Combine filling ingredients; spread on the bottom of half of the cookies. Top with remaining cookies.

❄ For glaze, combine sugar, vanilla and enough milk to achieve desired consistency. Spread over tops of cookies; dry. Using a small new paintbrush and food coloring, paint holiday designs on cookie tops. Store in the refrigerator. YIELD: about 2 dozen.

CHOCOLATE MINT WHOOPIE PIES

CHOCOLATE MINT WHOOPIE PIES

TASTE OF HOME TEST KITCHEN

These cute, cake-like sandwich cookies would be a pretty addition to any holiday goodie tray. The recipe may be lightened up a bit, but the cookies are still full of chocolate mint flavor.

- ½ **cup sugar**
- 3 **tablespoons canola oil**
- 1 **egg**
- 1 **cup all-purpose flour**
- ¼ **cup baking cocoa**
- ½ **teaspoon baking soda**
- ¼ **teaspoon salt**
- 4 **tablespoons fat-free milk,** *divided*
- 2 **tablespoons butter, softened**
- 1⅓ **cups confectioners' sugar**
- ⅛ **teaspoon mint extract**
- 4 **drops green food coloring, optional**

❋ In a bowl, beat sugar and oil until crumbly. Add egg; beat for 1 minute. Combine the flour, cocoa, baking soda and salt. Gradually beat into sugar mixture. Add 2 tablespoons milk; mix well. With lightly floured hands, roll dough into 36 balls.

❋ Place 2 in. apart on baking sheets coated with nonstick cooking spray. Flatten slightly with a glass coated with cooki spray. Bake at 425° for 5-6 minutes until edges are set and tops are cracke Cool for 2 minutes before removing wire racks to cool.

❋ In a mixing bowl, combine butter a confectioners' sugar until crumbly. Beat extract, food coloring if desired and maining milk. Spread on the bottom half of the cookies; top with remaini cookies. YIELD: 1½ dozen.

CHRISTMAS SANDWICH CREMES

JANICE POECHMAN, WALKERTON, ONTARIO

These melt-in-your-mouth sandwich cookies have a scrumptious filling. I helped my sister make these in high school when she needed a project in her home economics class. She got a A+ on them!

- 1 **cup butter, softened**
- ⅓ **cup heavy whipping cream**
- 2 **cups all-purpose flour**

Sugar

FILLING

- ½ **cup butter, softened**
- 1½ **cups confectioners' sugar**
- 2 **teaspoons vanilla extract**

Food coloring

CHRISTMAS SANDWICH CREMES

BEST❋LOVED
COOKIES
&BARS

In a mixing bowl, combine butter, cream and flour; mix well. Cover and refrigerate for 2 hours or until the dough is easy to handle.

Divide into thirds; let one portion stand at room temperature for 15 minutes (keep remaining dough refrigerated until ready to roll out). On a floured surface, roll out dough to 1/8-in. thickness. Cut with a 1 1/2-in. round cookie cutter dipped in flour. Place cutouts in a shallow dish filled with sugar; turn to coat. Place on ungreased baking sheets. Prick with a fork several times. Bake at 375° for 7-9 minutes or until set. Remove to wire racks to cool.

For filling, in a mixing bowl, cream butter and sugar. Add vanilla. Tint with food coloring. Spread about 1 teaspoon of filling over half of the cookies; top with remaining cookies. YIELD: 4 dozen.

AINBOW COOKIES

ARY ANN LEE, MARCO ISLAND, FLORIDA

lways bake my Rainbow Cookies 2
eeks ahead. That allows them enough
ne to "mellow," leaving them moist
d full of almond flavor!

1 can (8 ounces) almond paste
1 cup butter, softened
1 cup sugar
4 eggs, *separated*
2 cups all-purpose flour
6 to 8 drops red food coloring
6 to 8 drops green food coloring
1/4 cup seedless red raspberry jam
1/4 cup apricot jam
1 cup (6 ounces) semisweet chocolate chips

Grease the bottoms of three matching 13-in. x 9-in. x 2-in. baking pans (or reuse one pan). Line the pans with waxed paper; grease the paper.

Place almond paste in a large mixing bowl; break up with a fork. Cream with butter, sugar and egg yolks until light, fluffy and smooth. Stir in flour. In another mixing bowl, beat egg whites until soft peaks form. Fold into dough, mixing until thoroughly blended.

RAINBOW COOKIES

❋ Divide dough into three portions (about 1 1/3 cups each). Color one portion with red food coloring and one with green; leave the remaining portion uncolored. Spread each portion into the prepared pans. Bake at 350° for 10-12 minutes or until edges are light golden brown.

❋ Invert onto wire racks; remove waxed paper. Place another wire rack on top and turn over. Cool completely.

❋ Place green layer on a large piece of plastic wrap. Spread evenly with raspberry jam. Top with uncolored layer and spread with apricot jam. Top with pink layer. Bring plastic wrap over layers. Slide onto a baking sheet and set a cutting board or heavy, flat pan on top to compress layers. Refrigerate overnight.

❋ The next day, melt chocolate in a double boiler. Spread over top layer; allow to harden. With a sharp knife, trim edges. Cut into 1/2-in. strips across the width; then cut each strip into 4-5 pieces. Store in airtight containers. YIELD: about 8 dozen.

read the
recipe first
Read the entire recipe before you begin. Make sure you understand the cooking techniques and directions.

EVERGREEN SANDWICH COOKIES

EVERGREEN SANDWICH COOKIES

EVELYN MOLL, TULSA, OKLAHOMA

A fluffy vanilla filling makes these cookies a big holiday favorite at our house. My family also likes their rich shortbread flavor.

　1　**cup butter, softened**
　2　**cups all-purpose flour**
　$1/3$　**cup milk**
　$1/4$　**teaspoon salt**

FILLING
　$1/4$　**cup shortening**
　$1/4$　**cup butter, softened**
　2　**cups confectioners' sugar**
　$4\frac{1}{2}$　**teaspoons milk**
　$1/2$　**teaspoon vanilla extract**
Green paste food coloring

GLAZE
　$1\frac{1}{3}$　**cups confectioners' sugar**
　4　**teaspoons milk**
Green paste food coloring
Green colored sugar

✳ In a mixing bowl, combine butter, flo milk and salt; mix well. Cover; refrigera for $1\frac{1}{2}$ hours or until easy to handle.

✳ Divide dough into thirds. On a floured s face, roll out each portion to $1/8$-in. thic ness. Cut with a $3\frac{3}{4}$-in. Christmas tr cookie cutter dipped in flour. Place on u greased baking sheets. Prick each with fork several times. Bake at 375° for 8- minutes or until set. Remove to wire rac to cool.

✳ For filling, in a mixing bowl, cream sho ening, butter and confectioners' sug Add milk and vanilla. Tint with food col ing. Spread about a tablespoon each ov half of the cookies; top with remainir cookies.

✳ For glaze, combine confectioners' sug and milk until smooth; set aside $1/4$ cu Stir food coloring into remaining glaz spread a thin layer over cooled cookie If desired, sprinkle tops of half of t cookies with colored sugar. Let stand u til set. Pipe garland onto half of the coc ies with reserved glaze. Let stand until s YIELD: about 2 dozen.

EANUT BUTTER 'N' ELLY COOKIES

ARGARET WILSON, HEMET, CALIFORNIA

is classic combination makes a great
ndwich cookie. I know you'll enjoy
em as much as I do!

/2 cup shortening
/2 cup peanut butter
/2 cup sugar
/2 cup packed brown sugar
1 egg
/4 cups all-purpose flour
/4 teaspoon baking soda
/2 teaspoon baking powder
/4 teaspoon salt
m or jelly

In a mixing bowl, cream shortening,
peanut butter and sugars. Beat in egg.
Combine dry ingredients; gradually add
to the creamed mixture. Cover and chill
for 1 hour. Roll into 1-in. balls; place 2 in.
apart on greased baking sheets. Flatten
balls slightly.

Bake at 375° for 10 minutes or until gold-
en brown. Remove to wire racks to cool.
Spread jam on the bottom of half of the
cookies; top with remaining cookies.
YIELD: about 4½ dozen.

HERRY-FILLED EART COOKIES

JDREY GROE, LAKE MILLS, IOWA

nese crisp, flaky cookies are a
onderful way to show you care. They
ke a little effort, but the smiles of
tisfaction make it worthwhile.

½ cup butter, softened
½ cup shortening
1 cup sugar
1 egg
½ cup milk
1 teaspoon vanilla extract
½ cups all-purpose flour
2 teaspoons baking powder
1 teaspoon baking soda
½ teaspoon salt

FILLING
½ cup sugar
4½ teaspoons cornstarch
½ cup orange juice
¼ cup red maraschino cherry juice
12 red maraschino cherries, chopped
1 tablespoon butter
Additional sugar

✳ In a mixing bowl, cream the butter and
shortening; gradually add sugar. Add egg,
milk and vanilla. Combine dry ingredients;
gradually add to creamed mixture. Mix
well. Cover and refrigerate for at least 2
hours.

✳ Meanwhile, for filling, combine sugar
and cornstarch in small saucepan. Add
juices, cherries and butter. Bring to a boil;
boil and stir for 1 minute. Chill.

✳ On a lightly floured surface, roll out
dough to ⅛-in. thickness; cut with a 2½-
in. heart-shaped cookie cutter dipped in
flour.

✳ Place half of the cookies on greased baking sheets; spoon ½ teaspoon filling in
the center of each. Use a 1½-in. heart-
shaped cutter to cut small hearts out of
the other half of the cookies. (Bake small
heart cutouts separately.) Place the remaining hearts over filled cookies; press
edges together gently. Fill centers with
additional filling if needed. Sprinkle with
sugar.

✳ Bake at 375° for 8-10 minutes or until lightly browned. Remove to wire racks to cool.
YIELD: about 4½ dozen filled cookies.

CHERRY-FILLED HEART COOKIES

FRUIT-FILLED SPRITZ COOKIES

INGEBORG KEITH, NEWARK, DELAWARE
From the first time I baked these cookies, they've been a lip-smacking success. Old-fashioned and attractive, they make a perfect holiday pastry.

- 1½ cups chopped dates
- 1 cup water
- ½ cup sugar
- 2 teaspoons orange juice
- 2 teaspoons grated orange peel
- 1 cup maraschino cherries, chopped
- ½ cup flaked coconut
- ½ cup ground nuts

DOUGH

- 1 cup butter, softened
- 1 cup sugar
- ½ cup packed brown sugar
- 3 eggs
- ½ teaspoon almond extract
- ½ teaspoon vanilla extract
- 4 cups all-purpose flour
- ½ teaspoon baking soda
- ½ teaspoon salt

Confectioners' sugar

✳ In a saucepan, combine the first five ingredients; bring to a boil, stirring constantly. Reduce heat; cook and stir for 8 minutes

FRUIT-FILLED SPRITZ COOKIES

or until thickened. Cool completely. Stir cherries, coconut and nuts; set aside.

✳ In a mixing bowl, cream butter and sugars. Beat in eggs and extracts. Combine the flour, baking soda and salt; gradually add to creamed mixture.

✳ Using a cookie press fitted with a bar die, press a 12-in.-long strip of dough on an ungreased baking sheet. Spread fruit filling over dough. Press another strip over filling. Cut into 1-in. pieces (there no need to separate the pieces). Repeat with remaining dough and filling.

✳ Bake at 375° for 12-15 minutes or until edges are golden. Recut into pieces if necessary. Remove to wire racks to cool. Dust with confectioners' sugar. YIELD about 7½ dozen.

CRANBERRY LEMON SANDWICHES

PATRICIA MICHALSKI, OSWEGO, NEW YORK
I bake cookies all year long, so my friends and family call me the "Cookie Lady!" Whenever I bake these for Christmas, I make three batches…one to keep at home for my husband and two to give as gifts.

- 1 cup butter, softened
- 1 cup shortening
- 1 cup sugar
- 1 cup confectioners' sugar
- 2 eggs
- 2 teaspoons vanilla extract
- 4 cups all-purpose flour
- 1 teaspoon cream of tartar
- 1 teaspoon grated lemon peel
- ½ teaspoon salt
- ¾ cup dried cranberries

FILLING:

- ⅔ cup butter, softened
- 2¾ cups confectioners' sugar
- ¼ cup milk
- 1¼ teaspoons grated lemon peel

✳ In a mixing bowl, cream butter, shortening and sugars. Add eggs, one at a time, beating well after each addition. Beat in vanilla. Combine flour, cream of tartar

IPPED PEANUT BUTTER SANDWICH COOKIES

lemon peel and salt; gradually add to the creamed mixture. Stir in cranberries. Cover and refrigerate for 2 hours or until easy to handle.

Roll into 1-in. balls. Place 2 in. apart on ungreased baking sheets. Flatten with a glass dipped in sugar. Bake at 350° for 12-14 minutes or until edges are lightly browned. Remove to wire racks to cool.

Combine filling ingredients in a mixing bowl; beat until smooth. Spread on the bottom of half of the cookies; top with remaining cookies. YIELD: about 4½ dozen.

IPPED PEANUT BUTTER ANDWICH COOKIES

CKIE HOWELL, GORDO, ALABAMA
his is a tempting treat you'll love to ve. The recipe is almost too simple to elieve!

- ½ cup creamy peanut butter
- 1 sleeve (4 ounces) round butter-flavored crackers
- 1 cup white, semisweet, *or* milk chocolate chips
- 1 tablespoon shortening

Spread peanut butter on half of the crackers; top with remaining crackers to make sandwiches. Refrigerate.

In a double boiler over simmering water, melt chocolate chips and shortening, stirring until smooth. Dip sandwiches and place on waxed paper until chocolate hardens. YIELD: 9 servings.

ALMOND RASPBERRY STARS

DARLENE WEAVER, LEBANON, PENNSYLVANIA
The first Christmas that I baked these, I ended up quickly making a second batch! The whole family enjoyed them.

- ¾ cup butter
- ½ cup confectioners' sugar
- 1 teaspoon vanilla extract
- ½ teaspoon almond extract
- 1¾ cups plus 2 tablespoons all-purpose flour
- 2 tablespoons finely chopped almonds
- 1 tablespoon sugar
- ½ teaspoon ground cinnamon
- 1 egg white, lightly beaten
- ⅓ cup raspberry jam

✳ In a mixing bowl, cream the butter and confectioners' sugar until light and fluffy. Add extracts and beat until well mixed. Stir in flour. Shape into a ball; cover and chill for 15 minutes. On a slightly floured surface, roll dough to a ¼-in. thickness. Cut into about 72 stars, half 2½ in. and half 1½ in.

✳ Combine almonds, sugar and cinnamon. Brush small stars with egg white and immediately sprinkle with cinnamon-sugar mixture. Leave large stars plain. Bake on ungreased baking sheets at 350° for 10 minutes (small stars) to 12 minutes (large stars) or until the tips just begin to brown. Remove to wire racks to cool.

✳ To assemble, spread enough jam over large star to cover the center. Top with a small star. Press lightly; jam should show around edge of small star. Let jam set before storing. YIELD: about 3 dozen.

ALMOND RASPBERRY STARS

BEST★LOVED
cookies
&BARS

AUSTRIAN NUT COOKIES

AUSTRIAN NUT COOKIES

MARIANNE WEBER, SOUTH BEACH, OREGON

These are my family's favorite Christmas cookies. If you arrange the slivered almonds in pinwheel fashion, the cookie looks like a poinsettia.

- **1 cup all-purpose flour**
- **2/3 cup finely chopped almonds**
- **1/3 cup sugar**
- **1/2 cup cold butter**
- **1/2 cup raspberry jam**

FROSTING

- **1 square (1 ounce) unsweetened chocolate, melted and cooled**
- **1/3 cup confectioners' sugar**
- **2 tablespoons butter, softened**

Slivered almonds

In a bowl, combine flour, chopped almonds and sugar. Cut in butter until mixture resembles coarse crumbs. Form into a ball; cover and refrigerate for 1 hour.

On a floured surface, roll the dough to 1/8-in. thickness. Cut with a 2-in. round cutter dipped in flour; place 1 in. apart on greased baking sheets. Bake at 375° for 7-10 minutes or until the edges are lightly browned. Remove to wire racks to cool completely. Spread 1/2 teaspoon jam on half of the cookies; top with another cookie.

For frosting, combine chocolate, confectioners' sugar and butter. Spread on tops of cookies. Decorate with slivered almonds. YIELD: 20 sandwich cookies.

LEMON-CREAM SANDWICH COOKIES

CAROL STEINER, ARROWWOOD, ALBERTA

A light lemon filling sandwiched between flaky butter cookies makes these a perfect accompaniment to ho tea or coffee. They're a great treat at Christmas time and a nice change of pace from more typical chocolate or nut cookies.

- **3/4 cup butter, softened**
- **1/2 cup confectioners' sugar**
- **2 teaspoons lemon extract**
- **1 1/2 cups all-purpose flour**
- **1/4 cup cornstarch**

LEMON FILLING

- **1/4 cup butter, softened**
- **1 1/2 cups confectioners' sugar**
- **2 tablespoons lemon juice**
- **2 teaspoons grated lemon peel**

In a mixing bowl, cream butter and co fectioners' sugar. Beat in the extrac Combine flour and cornstarch; beat in creamed mixture. Divide into two bal wrap in plastic wrap and refrigerate for hour.

On a lightly floured surface, roll ea portion of dough to 1/8-in. thickness. C into 2-in. rounds. Place on ungreased ba ing sheets. Bake at 350° for 10-12 minut or until the edges are lightly browne Remove to wire racks to cool.

For filling, in a small mixing bowl, crea butter and confectioners' sugar. Beat lemon juice and peel. Spread over th bottoms of half of the cookies; top wi remaining cookies. YIELD: 2 dozen.

EDITOR'S NOTE: This recipe does not u eggs.

JAM-FILLED WREATHS

MONICA WILSON, POMONA, NEW YORK

I make these beautiful, wreath-shaped cookies with jewel-red centers every Christmas. The dusting of powdered sugar gives them a snowy winter look. I'm always grateful my mother cut this recipe out of a newspaper some 30 years ago.

/4 cup butter, softened

1 cup sugar

2 eggs

/2 cups all-purpose flour

1 teaspoon baking powder

1 teaspoon ground cinnamon

/2 teaspoon ground allspice

1 cup quick-cooking oats

/4 cup finely chopped nuts

1 jar (18 ounces) seedless raspberry jam

onfectioners' sugar

In a mixing bowl, cream butter and sugar. Add the eggs, one at a time, beating well after each addition. Combine flour, baking powder, cinnamon and allspice; add to the creamed mixture. Stir in oats and nuts; mix well. Refrigerate for 3 hours or until dough is easy to handle.

On a floured surface, roll out half of the dough to ⅛-in. thickness. Cut with a 2½-in round cookie cutter dipped in flour. Repeat with remaining dough, using a 2½-in. doughnut cutter, so the center is cut out of each cookie. Place on lightly greased baking sheets. Bake at 400° for 6-8 minutes or until lightly browned. Remove to wire racks to cool.

Spread 1 teaspoon jam over solid cookies. Place cookies with centers cut out over jam, forming a sandwich. Dust with confectioners' sugar. Fill centers with additional jam if desired. YIELD: 2½ dozen.

JAM-FILLED WREATHS

MINT SANDWICH COOKIES

MINT SANDWICH COOKIES

TASTE OF HOME TEST KITCHEN

Chocolate-covered mint candies are the "filling" in these doctored-up sugar cookies. You can use colored sugar to suit the season.

1 tube (18 ounces) refrigerated sugar cookie dough, softened

¼ cup all-purpose flour

⅛ teaspoon peppermint extract

Coarse sugar

40 chocolate-covered thin mints

- In a large mixing bowl, beat the cookie dough, flour and extract until blended. Roll into ½-in. balls.

- Place 2 in. apart on greased baking sheets. Coat the bottom of a glass with nonstick cooking spray, then dip in coarse sugar. Flatten balls with prepared glass to ¼-in. thickness, dipping in additional sugar as needed.

- Bake at 350° for 7-9 minutes or until set. Carefully remove one cookie from baking sheet and immediately place a mint on the bottom of the cookie; top with another cookie, pressing lightly. Repeat with remaining cookies and mints. Cool on wire racks. YIELD: 40 cookies.

cooling baked goods

Cool baked goods on a wire rack to allow air to circulate around the food.

HOLLY BERRY COOKIES

HOLLY BERRY COOKIES

AUDREY THIBODEAU, MESA, ARIZONA

What would Christmas be without overflowing tins of cookies? These festive filled cookies are the all-time favorites of my family. Back when our children were small, we began baking them the day after Halloween and put them away in the freezer.

- 2 cups all-purpose flour
- 1 cup sugar
- 1 teaspoon ground cinnamon
- 3/4 teaspoon baking powder
- 1/4 teaspoon salt
- 1/2 cup cold butter
- 1 egg
- 1/4 cup milk
- 2/3 cup seedless raspberry jam

GLAZE

- 2 cups confectioners' sugar
- 2 tablespoons milk
- 1/2 teaspoon vanilla extract

Red-hot candies

Green food coloring

❅ In a large bowl, combine the first five ingredients. Cut in butter until mixture resembles coarse crumbs. In a small bowl, beat egg and milk. Add to crumb mixture just until moistened. Cover and refrigerate for 1 hour or until dough is easy to handle.

❅ On a lightly floured surface, roll o dough to 1/8-in. thickness. Cut with a in. round cookie cutter dipped in flo Place on ungreased baking sheets. Ba at 375° for 8-10 minutes or until edges a lightly browned. Remove to wire racks cool. Spread jam on half of the cooki top each with another cookie.

❅ In a small mixing bowl, combine sug milk and vanilla until smooth; spre over cookies. Decorate with red-hots b fore glaze is set. Let dry. Using a small ne paintbrush and green food coloring, pa holly leaves on cookies. YIELD: 2 dozen

CHOCOLATE-FILLED SPRITZ

THERESA RYAN

WHITE RIVER JUNCTION, VERMONT

I found this delicious cookie recipe years ago. Over time, I decided to liv them up with a creamy chocolate filling. They're fabulous!

- 1 cup butter, softened
- 2/3 cup sugar
- 1 egg
- 1/2 teaspoon vanilla extract
- 1/2 teaspoon lemon *or* orange extract
- 2 1/4 cups all-purpose flour
- 1/4 teaspoon baking powder
- 1/4 teaspoon salt

Red and green colored sugar

- 4 squares (1 ounce *each*) semisweet chocolate

❅ In a large mixing bowl, cream butter a sugar. Beat in egg and extracts. Combi the dry ingredients; gradually add to t creamed mixture.

❅ Using a cookie press fitted with the di of your choice, press dough 2 in. apart o to ungreased baking sheets. Sprink half of cookies with colored sugars. Ba at 350° for 10-12 minutes or until set (c not brown). Remove to wire racks to co

❅ In a microwave, melt the chocolat spread over the bottom of the plain coo ies; top with sugared cookies. YIELD: abo 3 dozen.

ANTA CLAUS COOKIES

ARY KAUFENBERG, SHAKOPEE, MINNESOTA

eed just six ingredients to create
ese cute Kris Kringle confections.
ore-bought peanut butter sandwich
okies turn jolly with white chocolate,
lored sugar, mini chips and red-hots.

2 packages (6 ounces *each*) white baking chocolate, chopped

1 package (1 pound) Nutter Butter sandwich cookies

d colored sugar

2 vanilla *or* white chips

4 miniature semisweet chocolate chips

2 red-hot candies

❄ In a heavy saucepan over low heat, melt white chocolate, stirring occasionally. Dip one end of each cookie into the melted chocolate. Place on wire racks. For Santa's hat, sprinkle red sugar on top part of chocolate. Press one vanilla chip off-center on hat for pom-pom; let stand until set.

❄ Dip other end of each cookie into melted chocolate for beard, leaving center of cookie uncovered. Place on wire racks. With a dab of melted chocolate, attach semisweet chips for eyes and a red-hot candy for nose. Place on waxed paper until chocolate sets. YIELD: 32 cookies.

ANTA CLAUS COOKIES

BEST☀LOVED
cookies
&BARS

packing and shipping cookies

Here are some pointers to ensure that cookies arrive at their destination as delicious and attractive as when you baked them.

- First, select cookies that are sturdy and will travel well, such as bars and brownies, drop, icebox and sandwich cookies. Cutouts and other thin cookies might break or crumble during shipping. Cookies requiring refrigeration are a poor choice for shipping because they'll spoil.

- Bake and completely cool cookies just before packing and shipping so they arrive as fresh as possible.

- Wrap them in bundles of two (for drop cookies, place their bottoms together) with plastic wrap. Wrap bars individually. Pack crisp and soft cookies in separate tins and pack any strong-flavored cookies, such as gingersnaps, separate from mild-flavored cookies.

CHOCOLATE SANDWICH COOKIES

CHOCOLATE SANDWICH COOKIES

KAREN BOURNE, MAGRATH, ALBERTA
These are my family's very favorite cookies. They're soft, chewy and totally delicious.

- 2 **packages (18¼ ounces *each*) devil's food cake mix**
- 4 **eggs, lightly beaten**
- ⅔ **cup vegetable oil**
- 1 **package (8 ounces) cream cheese, softened**
- 3 **to 4 cups confectioners' sugar**
- ½ **teaspoon vanilla extract**

Red *and/or* green food coloring, optional

✳ In a mixing bowl, beat cake mixes, eggs and oil (batter will be very stiff). Roll into 1-in. balls; place on ungreased baking sheets and flatten slightly. Bake at 350° for 8-10 minutes or until a slight indentation remains when lightly touched. Remove to wire racks to cool.

✳ In another mixing bowl, beat cream cheese and butter. Add sugar and vanilla; mix until smooth. If desired, tint with food coloring. Spread on bottom of half of the cookies. Top with remaining cookies. YIELD: 4 dozen.

CHRISTMAS SANDWICH COOKIES

ELIZABETH KLAGER, ST. CATHARINES, ONTAR
My mother-in-law gave me the recipe for these lovely melt-in-your-mouth cookies. They're a Christmas tradition at our house.

- 1 **cup butter, softened**
- ½ **cup confectioners' sugar**
- 2 **teaspoon milk**
- 2 **cups all-purpose flour**
- ½ **cup cornstarch**
- ⅛ **teaspoon salt**

FILLING
- 5 **tablespoons raspberry jam**

FROSTING
- ¼ **cup butter, softened**
- 1 **cup confectioners' sugar**
- 1 **teaspoon vanilla extract**

Green food coloring

Red candied cherries and colored sprinkl

✳ In a mixing bowl, cream butter, confe
tioners' sugar and milk. Combine flo
cornstarch and salt; add to the cream
mixture, beating just until dough form
ball.

✳ On a lightly floured surface, knead
times. Roll out to ⅜-in. thickness. Cut w
a 2-in. round cookie cutter dipped in flo
Place 1 in. apart on ungreased baki
sheets.

CHRISTMAS SANDWICH COOKIES

Bake at 350° for 12-13 minutes or until edges are lightly browned. Remove to wire racks to cool. Spread jam over the bottom of half of the cookies; top with remaining cookies.

In a mixing bowl, cream butter, confectioners' sugar, vanilla and food coloring. Pipe frosting in tree shapes or other decorations on cookies. Garnish with candied cherries and sprinkles. YIELD: 2 dozen.

HOCOLATE MINT ANDWICH COOKIES

RTHA BRATT, LYNDEN, WASHINGTON

e minty filling sandwiched between o chocolaty cookies is a real treat for mily, friends and you!

- **6 tablespoons butter**
- **/2 cups packed brown sugar**
- **2 tablespoons water**
- **2 cups (12 ounces) semisweet chocolate chips**
- **2 eggs**
- **1 teaspoon vanilla extract**
- **/2 cups all-purpose flour**
- **/2 teaspoons baking soda**
- **1 teaspoon salt**

LING

- **/2 cups confectioners' sugar**
- **/4 cup butter**
- **3 tablespoons milk**
- **/2 teaspoon peppermint extract**
- **3 drops green food coloring, optional**

sh salt

In a saucepan, combine the butter, brown sugar, water and chocolate chips. Cook and stir over low heat until chips are melted. Cool. Beat in eggs and vanilla. Combine the flour, baking soda and salt; gradually add to the chocolate mixture.

Drop by rounded teaspoonfuls 2 in. apart onto ungreased baking sheets. Bake at 350° for 10-12 minutes or until firm. Remove to wire racks to cool.

In a large mixing bowl, combine filling ingredients until smooth. Spread on the bottom of half of the cookies; top with remaining cookies. YIELD: about 2½ dozen sandwich cookies.

SNOWMEN COOKIES

![Snowmen cookies photograph]

SNOWMEN COOKIES

SHERRI JOHNSON, BURNS, TENNESSEE

These cute snowmen cookies make great treats for children's parties. Kids are always willing to chip in and help decorate them.

- **1 package (16 ounces) Nutter Butter cookies**
- **1¼ pounds white candy coating, melted**
- **Miniature chocolate chips**
- **M&M miniature baking bits**
- **Pretzel sticks, halved**
- **Orange and red decorating gel *or* frosting**

❄ Using tongs, dip cookies in candy coating; shake off excess. Place on waxed paper.

❄ Place two chocolate chips on one end of cookies for eyes. Place baking bits down middle for buttons. For arms, dip ends of two pretzel stick halves into coating; attach one to each side. Let stand until hardened. Pipe nose and scarf with gel or frosting. YIELD: 32 cookies.

packing and shipping cookies
(continued)

- Line a tin or box with crumpled waxed paper to cushion the cookies. Snugly pack the cookies to within 1 inch of the top. Use crumpled waxed paper or bubble wrap to fill in any gaps between cookies and side of container and to cover tops of the cookies. Close box or tin.

- Wrap the cookie container in a slightly larger cardboard box and cushion with bubble wrap, crumpled paper or shipping peanuts. Seal the box and label it as "Fragile and Perishable."

FROSTED MAPLE PYRAMIDS

WANDA GOODELL, KENT, WASHINGTON

The cute shape of these cookies makes them a splendid sight on a Christmas cookie tray. You could use star-shaped cookie cutters in place of the round ones.

- ½ **cup shortening**
- ⅓ **cup packed brown sugar**
- 1 **egg**
- 1 **teaspoon vanilla extract**
- ¼ **teaspoon maple flavoring**
- 1¼ **cups all-purpose flour**
- ¼ **teaspoon salt**
- ¼ **teaspoon baking powder**

FROSTING
- ¼ **cup butter, softened**
- ¾ **cup confectioners' sugar**
- 1 **teaspoon vanilla extract**

Red candied cherries, halved

❋ In a mixing bowl, cream shortening a brown sugar. Beat in the egg, vanilla a maple flavoring. Combine the flour, s and baking powder; gradually add to t creamed mixture. Cover and refrigera for 2 hours or until easy to handle.

❋ On a lightly floured surface, roll o dough to ⅛-in. thickness. With 2- round cookie cutters dipped in flour, out 18 circles. Repeat with 1½-in. and in. round cookie cutters. Place 1 in. ap on greased baking sheets. Bake at 37 for 7-9 minutes or until lightly browne Remove to wire racks to cool.

❋ In a small mixing bowl, cream butter a confectioners' sugar. Beat in vanilla. To semble cookies, place a 2-in. cookie waxed paper. Spread with 1 teaspo frosting. Top with a 1½-in. cookie; fro Top with a 1-in. cookie; frost. Garnish w candied cherries. YIELD: 1½ dozen.

FROSTED MAPLE PYRAMIDS

TAR SANDWICH COOKIES

TI SCHMIDT, CANTON, OHIO

aked these treats for a church tea. he night before, I gave a sample to e folks setting up. They like the okies so much, they saved the rest to sure they'd get some the next day!

- **1 cup butter, softened**
- **2 cups all-purpose flour**
- **/3 cup heavy whipping cream**

gar

LING

- **/2 cup butter, softened**
- **/2 cups confectioners' sugar**
- **2 teaspoons vanilla extract**
- **4 to 8 teaspoons heavy whipping cream**

quid _or_ paste food coloring, optional

In a mixing bowl, beat the butter, flour and cream. Cover and refrigerate for 1 hour or until easy to handle.

On a lightly floured surface, roll out dough to ⅛-in. thickness. Cut with a 2-in. star cookie cutter dipped in flour. Sprinkle tops of cookies with sugar; place on ungreased baking sheets. Prick each cookie 3-4 times with a fork. Bake at 375° for 7-9 minutes or until set. Remove to wire racks to cool.

For filling, combine the butter, confectioners' sugar, vanilla and enough cream to achieve desired spreading consistency. Tint with food coloring if desired. Carefully spread filling on the bottom of half of the cookies; top with remaining cookies. YIELD: about 5 dozen.

'MORE SANDWICH OOKIES

BY METZGER, LARCHWOOD, IOWA

apture the taste of campfire s'mores your kitchen. Graham cracker crumbs ded to chocolate chip cookie dough ing out the flavor of the fireside vorite. Melting the cookies' arshmallow centers in the microwave akes them simple to assemble.

- **¾ cup butter, softened**
- **½ cup sugar**

STAR SANDWICH COOKIES

- **½ cup packed brown sugar**
- **1 egg**
- **2 tablespoons milk**
- **1 teaspoon vanilla extract**
- **1¼ cups all-purpose flour**
- **1¼ cups graham cracker crumbs (about 20 squares)**
- **½ teaspoon baking soda**
- **¼ teaspoon salt**
- **⅛ teaspoon ground cinnamon**
- **2 cups (12 ounces) semisweet chocolate chips**
- **24 to 28 large marshmallows**

❈ In a mixing bowl, cream butter and sugars. Beat in the egg, milk and vanilla. Combine the flour, graham cracker crumbs, baking soda, salt and cinnamon; gradually add to creamed mixture. Stir in chocolate chips.

❈ Drop by tablespoonfuls 2 in. apart onto ungreased baking sheets. Bake at 375° for 8-10 minutes or until golden brown. Remove to wire racks to cool.

❈ Place four cookies bottom side up on a microwave-safe plate; top each with a marshmallow. Microwave, uncovered, on high for 16-20 seconds or until marshmallows begin to puff (do not overcook). Top each with another cookie. Repeat. YIELD: 2 dozen.

BEST✷LOVED
cookies
&BARS

REFRIGERATOR cookies

PEPPERMINT PINWHEELS
PAGE 142

CHOCOLATE-DIPPED COOKIES
PAGE 151

SPICED ALMOND COOKIES
PAGE 167

JEWELED COOKIE SLICES

ROSELLA PETERS
GULL LAKE, SASKATCHEWAN

I often mark recipes with "G" for good, "VG" for very good; this seasonal favorite is marked "VVG"! I usually double the recipe.

- ⅓ cup butter, melted
- ⅓ cup sugar
- ¼ cup packed brown sugar
- 1 egg
- ½ teaspoon vanilla extract
- ½ cup chopped candied pineapple *or* red and green candies cherries
- 2 tablespoons chopped blanched almonds
- 1½ cups all-purpose flour
- 1 teaspoon baking powder
- ⅛ teaspoon baking soda
- ⅛ teaspoon ground nutmeg

❉ In a mixing bowl, beat butter and sugars. Add egg and vanilla mix well. Stir in pineapple and almonds. Combine dry ingredients; add to butter mixture. Spread evenly into a foil-lined 8-in. x 4-in. x 2-in. loaf pan. Cover and refrigerate for at least 2 hours.

❉ Invert dough onto a cutting board; remove foil. Cut into ¼-in. slices; place on greased baking sheets. Bake at 350°for

JEWELED COOKIE SLICES

10-12 minutes or until lightly browne[d] Remove to wire racks to cool. YIELD: ab[out] 2½ dozen.

LEMON PECAN SLICES

MELISSA BRANNING, FONTANA, WISCONSIN

These attractive morsels are my daughter's favorite. The lemon glaze pairs well with the delicate nut-toppe[d] cookie.

- 1 cup butter, softened
- ¾ cup packed brown sugar
- ½ cup sugar
- 2 eggs
- 1½ teaspoons vanilla extract
- 1 tablespoon grated lemon peel
- 3 cups all-purpose flour
- 1½ teaspoons baking powder
- ¾ teaspoon salt

TOPPING
- ¾ cup finely chopped pecans
- ¼ cup sugar

LEMON GLAZE
- 1¼ cups confectioners' sugar
- 5 teaspoons lemon juice
- 1 drop yellow food coloring, option[al]

❉ In a mixing bowl, cream the butter an[d] sugars. Separate one egg; refrigerate eg[g] white. Add the egg yolk, second egg[,] vanilla and lemon peel to creamed mi[x]ture; mix well. Combine the flour, bakin[g] powder and salt; gradually beat int[o] creamed mixture. Shape into thre[e] 7-in. rolls; wrap each in plastic wra[p.] Refrigerate for 2 hours or until firm.

❉ Unwrap logs. Lightly beat reserved eg[g] white. Combine pecans and sugar. Brus[h] each log with egg white, then roll in peca[n] mixture, pressing firmly into dough.

❉ Cut into ¼-in. slices. Place 2 in. apart o[n] ungreased baking sheets. Bake at 400° f[or] 6-7 minutes or until very lightly browne[d.] Remove to wire racks to cool. Combin[e] glaze ingredients; drizzle over cookie[s.] YIELD: about 7 dozen.

PINWHEELS AND CHECKERBOARDS

PINWHEELS AND CHECKERBOARDS

ILL HEATWOLE PITTSVILLE, MARYLAND

My mom used to make these cookies
very Christmas, and I still love them.
They are so colorful...and you can get
two kinds of cookies from one dough!
They're perfect for including in gift
boxes or bags.

- ¼ cups butter, softened
- 1 cup packed brown sugar
- ½ cup sugar
- 2 eggs
- ¼ teaspoon vanilla extract
- 4 cups all-purpose flour
- 1 teaspoon baking powder
- 1 teaspoon salt
- ¼ teaspoon baking soda

Red and green gel food coloring

- 1 square (1 ounce) unsweetened
  chocolate, melted and cooled

In a large mixing bowl, cream butter and
sugars. Beat in eggs and vanilla. Combine
flour, baking powder, salt and baking soda; gradually add to creamed mixture.
Divide dough into fourths. Tint one portion red and one portion green. Stir
chocolate into another portion. Wrap
chocolate and plain portions in plastic
wrap; chill for 1 hour or until dough is easy
to handle.

❄ For pinwheel cookies, divide red and
green portions in half. Roll out each portion between waxed paper into a 9-in. x
6-in. rectangle. Refrigerate for 30 minutes. Remove waxed paper. Place one
green rectangle over a red rectangle. Roll
up tightly jelly-roll style, starting with a
long side; wrap in plastic wrap. Repeat.
Chill for 2 hours or until firm.

❄ For checkerboard cookies, divide plain
and chocolate portions in half. Roll out
each portion between waxed paper into
a 6-in. x 4-in. rectangle. Cut each rectangle lengthwise into eight ½-in. strips.
Stack the strips in groups of four, alternating plain and chocolate strips and forming
eight separate stacks. Form a four-stack
block by alternating chocolate-topped
and plain-topped stacks. Repeat. Press
together gently. Wrap in plastic. Chill for
at least 2 hours.

❄ Unwrap and cut pinwheel and checkerboard dough into ¼-in. slices. Place 1 in.
apart on ungreased baking sheets. Bake
at 375° for 9-11 minutes or until set.
Remove to wire racks to cool. YIELD: 6
dozen pinwheel and 4 dozen checkerboard cookies.

PEPPERMINT
PINWHEELS

CARAMEL DATE PINWHEELS

DORIS BARB, EL DORADO, KANSAS
When I want to make a cookie with fruit in it, this recipe is my first choice. It turns out well each time and has earned plenty of praise, including ribbons at our state fair.

- ⅔ **cup butter, softened**
- 1 **cup packed brown sugar**
- 1 **egg**
- 1 **teaspoon vanilla extract**
- 1¾ **cups all-purpose flour**
- ½ **teaspoon baking soda**
- ¼ **teaspoon salt**

FILLING
- 1 **package (8 ounces) chopped dates**
- ⅓ **cup sugar**
- ½ **cup water**
- ½ **cup finely chopped walnuts**
- 2 **tablespoons chopped red candied cherries**

※ In a mixing bowl, cream butter and brow sugar. Beat in egg and vanilla. Combin flour, baking soda and salt; gradually ad to the creamed mixture. Refrigerate for : least 2 hours.

※ Meanwhile, in a saucepan, combine th dates, sugar and water. Cook and stir ove medium heat until thickened, about minutes. Stir in walnuts and cherries. Co completely.

※ Divide dough in half; roll one portion be tween two sheets of waxed paper into 12-in. x 10-in. rectangle. Spread with ha of the filling. Roll up tightly jelly-roll styl starting with a long side; wrap in waxe paper. Repeat with remaining dough an filling. Cover and refrigerate for 2 hours until firm.

※ Cut into ⅜-in. slices with a sharp knife place 1 in. apart on greased bakin sheets. Bake at 375° for 8-10 minutes until lightly browned. Remove to wir racks to cool. YIELD: 7-8 dozen.

PEPPERMINT PINWHEELS

MARCIA HOSTETTER, CANTON, NEW YORK
Put a spin on your holidays with these bright swirls! This recipe makes rich-tasting cookies with a minty flavor that is a pleasant surprise.

- ¾ **cup butter, softened**
- ¾ **cup sugar**
- 1 **egg yolk**
- 1 **teaspoon vanilla extract**
- 2 **cups all-purpose flour**
- ½ **teaspoon baking powder**
- ½ **teaspoon salt**
- ½ **teaspoon peppermint extract**
- ¼ **teaspoon red liquid food coloring**

※ In a large mixing bowl, cream butter and sugar. Beat in egg yolk and vanilla. Combine the flour, baking powder and salt; gradually add to creamed mixture and mix well. Divide dough in half and add extract and red food coloring to one portion.

※ On a work surface, roll out each portion of dough between waxed paper into a 16-in. x 10-in. rectangle. Remove waxed paper. Place red rectangle over plain rectangle; roll up tightly jelly-roll style, starting with a long side. Wrap in plastic wrap. Refrigerate overnight or until firm.

※ Unwrap the dough and cut into ¼-in. slices. Place 2 in. apart on lightly greased baking sheets. Bake at 350° for 12-14 minutes or until set. Cool for 2 minutes before removing to wire racks to cool completely. YIELD: about 4 dozen.

BEST LOVED
cookies
& BARS

CEBOX HONEY COOKIES

RISTI GLEASON, FLOWER MOUND, TEXAS

randma Wruble always had a batch of
ese cookies in the cookie jar and
other roll in the refrigerator ready to
ice and bake. Their honey and lemon
avor is delicious.

- ½ cups shortening
- 2 cups packed brown sugar
- 2 eggs
- ½ cup honey
- 1 teaspoon lemon extract
- ½ cups all-purpose flour
- 2 teaspoons baking soda
- 2 teaspoons baking powder
- 1 teaspoon salt
- 1 teaspoon ground cinnamon

In a mixing bowl, cream shortening and
brown sugar. Add eggs, one at a time,
beating well after each addition. Add
honey and extract; mix well. Combine the
remaining ingredients; gradually add to
creamed mixture.

Shape into two 12-in. rolls; wrap each in
plastic wrap. Refrigerate for 2 hours or until firm. Unwrap and cut into ¼-in. slices.
Place 1 in. apart on ungreased baking
sheets.

Bake at 325° for 12-14 minutes or until
golden brown. Remove to wire racks to
cool. YIELD: 8 dozen.

JEWELED COOKIES

JEWELED COOKIES

RUTH ANN STELFOX, RAYMOND, ALBERTA

Candied fruits give a stained-glass
look to these cookies. They're like
shortbread, but dressed up.

- 1 pound butter, softened
- 2½ cups sugar
- 3 eggs
- 5 cups all-purpose flour
- 1 teaspoon baking soda
- 1½ cups raisins
- 1 cup coarsely chopped walnuts
- ½ cup *each* chopped red and green candied cherries
- ½ cup chopped candied pineapple

❊ In a mixing bowl, cream butter and sugar. Add eggs, one at a time, beating well
after each. Combine flour and baking soda; add to creamed mixture. Stir in raisins,
nuts, cherries and pineapple; mix well.
Shape into 2-in. rolls; wrap in waxed paper or foil. Freeze at least 2 hours.

❊ Cut into ¼-in. slices; place on greased
baking sheets. Bake at 350° for 8-10 minutes or until lightly browned. Remove to
wire racks to cool. YIELD: 12-14 dozen.

CEBOX HONEY COOKIES

STRIPED ICEBOX COOKIES

PATRICIA REESE, PEWAUKEE, WISCONSIN

I've been using this recipe ever since I was a little girl. I like it because it's easier than making cutout cookies. You can easily mix-and-match your favorite ingredients to create different looks.

- 1 **cup butter, softened**
- 1½ **cups sugar**
- 1 **egg**
- 2½ **cups all-purpose flour**
- 1½ **teaspoons baking powder**
- ¼ **teaspoon salt**
- ¼ **cup chopped maraschino cherries, drained**
- 2 **drops red food coloring**
- 1 **square (1 ounce) semisweet chocolate, melted**
- 1 **tablespoon nonpareils**

✳ In a mixing bowl, cream butter and sugar. Beat in egg. Combine the flour, baking powder and salt; gradually add to the creamed mixture. Divide into thirds; place in three bowls. Add cherries and food coloring to one portion, chocolate to another portion and nonpareils to remaining portion.

✳ Line a 9-in. x 5-in. x 3-in. loaf pan with waxed paper. Spread cherry dough over bottom. Cover with chocolate dough, then remaining dough. Cover with plastic wrap and refrigerate for 2 hours or until firm.

✳ Remove dough from pan; cut in ha lengthwise. Cut each portion into ¼-i slices. Place 1 in. apart on lightly grease baking sheets. Bake at 375° for 10-1 minutes or until edges begin to brow Remove to wire racks to cool. YIELD: dozen.

TWO-TONE CHRISTMAS COOKIES

MARIE CAPOBIANCO
PORTSMOUTH, RHODE ISLAND

I dreamed up this recipe using two of my favorite flavors—pistachio and raspberry. These pink and green cookies are tasty and eye-catching, too. They're perfect for formal or informal gatherings, and everybody likes them and asks for the recipe.

- 1 **cup butter, softened**
- 1½ **cups sugar**
- 2 **egg yolks**
- 2 **teaspoons vanilla extract**
- 1 **teaspoon almond extract**
- 3½ **cups all-purpose flour**
- 1 **teaspoon salt**
- 1 **teaspoon baking powder**
- ½ **teaspoon baking soda**
- 9 **drops green food coloring**
- 1 **tablespoon milk**
- ⅓ **cup chopped pistachios**
- 9 **drops red food coloring**
- 3 **tablespoons seedless raspberry preserves**
- 2 **cups (12 ounces) semisweet chocolate chips, melted**

Additional chopped pistachios

✳ In a mixing bowl, cream butter and sug ar. Beat in the egg yolks and extract Combine the flour, salt, baking powde and baking soda; gradually add t creamed mixture. Divide dough in hal Stir green food coloring, milk and nut into one portion; mix well. Add red foo coloring and jam to the other half.

✳ Shape each portion between two piece of waxed paper into an 8-in. x 6-in. recta gle. Cut in half lengthwise. Place on green rectangle on a piece of plasti

STRIPED ICEBOX COOKIES

wrap. Top with pink rectangle; press together lightly. Repeat. Wrap each in plastic wrap and refrigerate overnight.

Unwrap the dough and cut in half lengthwise. Return one of the rectangles to the refrigerator. Cut the remaining rectangle into 1/8-in. slices. Place 1 in. apart on ungreased baking sheets. Bake at 375° for 7-9 minutes or until set. Remove to wire racks to cool. Repeat with the remaining dough. Drizzle cooled cookies with melted chocolate. Sprinkle with additional pistachios. **YIELD:** 6½ dozen.

RISP PECAN ROUNDS

NISE DEJONG
TSBURGH, PENNSYLVANIA

dapted an old recipe to produce
ese lightly sweet cookies. They have
wonderful cinnamon and nutmeg
vor that makes them most-requested
our house for the holidays.

- /2 **cups all-purpose flour**
- /4 **cup packed brown sugar**
- 2 **tablespoons sugar**
- /2 **teaspoon salt**
- /4 **teaspoon ground cinnamon**
- /4 **teaspoon ground nutmeg**
- /3 **cup cold butter**
- 2 **tablespoons maple syrup**
- /2 **cup chopped pecans**

AZE
- 1 **egg yolk**
- 1 **teaspoon water**

PPING
- /2 **teaspoons sugar**
- /2 **teaspoon ground cinnamon**

In a bowl, combine the first six ingredients. Cut in butter until mixture resembles coarse crumbs. Stir in syrup. Add pecans. Shape into a 12-in. roll; wrap in plastic wrap. Refrigerate for 4 hours or until firm. Unwrap and cut into 1/4-in. slices. Place 1 in. apart on ungreased baking sheets.

For glaze, beat egg yolk and water. For topping, combine sugar and cinnamon. Brush glaze over cookies and sprinkle with cinnamon-sugar. Bake at 325° for 20-25 minutes or until golden brown. Remove to wire racks to cool. **YIELD:** about 3½ dozen.

GRANDPA'S COOKIES

GRANDPA'S COOKIES

KAREN BAKER, DOVER, OHIO

My grandpa, a widower, raised his three sons on his own and did all the cooking and lots of baking. I can still picture him making these tasty old-fashioned cookies.

- 2 **cups butter, softened**
- 4 **cups packed brown sugar**
- 4 **eggs**
- ½ **cup water**
- 1 **teaspoon vanilla extract**
- 7 **cups all-purpose flour**
- 1 **tablespoon cream of tartar**
- 1 **tablespoon baking soda**

❉ In a large mixing bowl, cream butter and brown sugar. Add eggs, water and vanilla; mix well. Combine remaining ingredients; add to the creamed mixture and mix well.

❉ Shape into three rolls; wrap in plastic wrap. Chill 4 hours or overnight. Cut rolls into 1/4-in. slices; place 2 in. apart on greased baking sheets. Bake at 375° for 8-10 minutes or until lightly browned. Remove to wire racks to cool. **YIELD:** about 10 dozen.

refrigerating dough

Wrap dough tightly to prevent it from drying out while in the fridge. Refrigerate dough until firm. Generally, the dough can be refrigerated up to 1 week or frozen for up to 6 months.

keeping rolls of dough round

To keep a nice round shape for refrigerated cookie dough, place each roll inside a tall glass and place the glass on its side in the refrigerator. The rounded glass will prevent the bottom of the roll from flattening out.

SPUMONI SLICE

SPUMONI SLICES

MARY CHUPP, CHATTANOOGA, TENNESSEE
My sweet rectangles get their name from the old-fashioned tri-colored ice cream. Our whole family loves them.

- **1 cup butter, softened**
- **1½ cups confectioners' sugar**
- **1 egg**
- **1 teaspoon vanilla extract**
- **2½ cups all-purpose flour**
- **2 squares (1 ounce *each*) semisweet chocolate, melted**
- **½ cup chopped pecans**
- **3 to 5 drops green food coloring**
- **¼ cup finely chopped candied red cherries**
- **½ teaspoon almond extract**
- **3 to 5 drops red food coloring**

✳ In a mixing bowl, cream butter and sugar. Beat in egg and vanilla. Gradually add flour and mix well. Divide dough in thr portions. Stir chocolate into one portic mix well. Add pecans and green food c oring to the second portion. Add cherri almond extract and red food coloring the third.

✳ Roll each portion between two pieces waxed paper into an 8-in. x 6-in. recta gle. Remove waxed paper. Place choc late rectangle on a piece of plastic wra Top with the green and pink rectangle press together lightly. Wrap with plast wrap and chill overnight.

✳ Cut chilled dough in half lengthwis Return one rectangle to the refrigerat Cut remaining rectangle into ⅛-in. slice Place 1 in. apart on ungreased bakir sheets.

✳ Bake at 375° for 5-7 minutes or until se Cool for 2 minutes before removing wire racks. Repeat with remaining doug
YIELD: about 7 dozen.

RAINBOW BUTTER COOKIES

ANNETTE TATE, SANDY, UTAH

Our family can't get through the holidays without these fun, colorful cookies. They come out of my oven by the dozens!

- 1/2 cup plus 2 tablespoons butter, softened
- 1/2 cup packed brown sugar
- 1/4 cup sugar
- 1 egg
- 1 teaspoon vanilla extract
- 2 cups all-purpose flour
- 1/2 teaspoon baking powder
- 1/2 teaspoon salt
- 1/8 teaspoon baking soda

Green, red and yellow food coloring

Milk

In a mixing bowl, cream butter and sugars. Add the egg and vanilla; mix well. Combine dry ingredients; gradually add to creamed mixture. Divide dough into three portions; tint each a different color.

Roll each portion of dough on waxed paper into a 9-in. x 5-in. rectangle. Freeze for 10 minutes. Cut each rectangle in half lengthwise. Lightly brush top of one rectangle with milk. Top with another colored dough. Remove waxed paper; brush top with milk. Repeat with remaining dough, alternating colors, to make six layers. Press together lightly; cut in half lengthwise.

Wrap each with plastic wrap. Chill several hours or overnight. Unwrap dough; cut into 1/8-in. slices. Place 2 in. apart on ungreased baking sheets.

Bake at 350° for 8-10 minutes. Cool for 1-2 minutes; remove from pans to wire racks. YIELD: about 4 dozen.

CHOCOLATE MINT CREAMS

BEVERLY FEHNER, GLADSTONE, MISSOURI

This recipe came from an old family friend and is always high on everyone's cookie request list. I make at least six batches for nibbling and to give as gifts.

- 1 cup butter, softened
- 1 1/2 cups confectioners' sugar
- 2 squares (1 ounce each) unsweetened chocolate, melted and cooled
- 1 egg
- 1 teaspoon vanilla extract
- 2 1/2 cups all-purpose flour
- 1 teaspoon baking soda
- 1 teaspoon cream of tartar
- 1/4 teaspoon salt

FROSTING

- 1/4 cup butter, softened
- 2 cups confectioners' sugar
- 2 tablespoons milk
- 1/2 teaspoon peppermint extract

Green food coloring, optional

❊ In a large mixing bowl, cream butter and confectioners' sugar. Add the chocolate, egg and vanilla; mix well. Combine the dry ingredients; gradually add to creamed mixture, beating well. Shape dough into a 2-in.-diameter roll; wrap in plastic wrap. Refrigerate for 1 hour or until firm.

❊ Unwrap dough and cut into 1/8-in. slices. Place 2 in. apart on ungreased baking sheets. Bake at 400° for 7-8 minutes or until edges are firm. Remove to wire racks to cool.

❊ In a small mixing bowl, combine frosting ingredients. Frost cookies. Store in airtight containers. YIELD: about 6 dozen.

CHOCOLATE MINT CREAMS

CRANBERRY NUT SWIRLS

CRANBERRY NUT SWIRLS

CARLA HODENFIELD
MANDAN, NORTH DAKOTA

This recipe originated with my sister-in-law. It gets used a lot over the holidays when we want to "pull a fast one" on the guys in our family—they claim they don't like cranberries in any shape or form, but everyone enjoys these.

- ½ **cup butter, softened**
- ¾ **cup sugar**
- 1 **egg**
- 1 **teaspoon vanilla extract**
- 1½ **cups all-purpose flour**
- ¼ **teaspoon baking powder**
- ¼ **teaspoon salt**
- ½ **cup finely ground cranberries**
- ½ **cup finely chopped walnuts**
- 1 **tablespoon grated orange peel**
- 3 **tablespoons brown sugar**
- 2 **teaspoons milk**

❄ In a mixing bowl, cream butter and sugar until light and fluffy; beat in egg and vanilla. Combine dry ingredients; add to the creamed mixture. Refrigerate at least 1 hour.

❄ In a small bowl, combine cranberries, walnuts and orange peel; set aside. On a lightly floured surface, roll dough into a 10-in. square. Combine brown sugar ar milk; spread over dough. Sprinkle with tcranberry mixture, leaving about a ½-iedge at both ends of dough; roll up tightly jelly-roll style. Wrap with waxed papchill several hours or overnight.

❄ Cut roll into ¼-in. slices and place on wgreased baking sheets. Bake at 375° f14-15 minutes or until edges are ligbrown Remove to wire racks to co
YIELD: about 3½ dozen.

JEWELED COCONUT CRISPS

EILEEN MILACEK, WAUKOMIS, OKLAHOMA

When I anticipate a busy day during the holiday season, I make this cookiedough the night before. The next day,just slice and bake!

- 1 **cup butter, softened**
- 1 **cup sugar**
- 2 **tablespoons milk**
- 1½ **teaspoons vanilla extract**
- 2½ **cups all-purpose flour**
- ¾ **cup finely chopped red and green candied cherries**
- ¾ **cup finely chopped pecans**
- 1 **cup flaked coconut**

❄ In a mixing bowl, cream butter and sugar. Beat in milk and vanilla. Stir in flocherries and pecans. Shape into two in. logs. Sprinkle the coconut over waxepaper; place each log on waxed pap

JEWELED COCONUT CRISPS

and roll in coconut. Wrap in plastic wrap. Refrigerate for 4 hours or until firm.

Unwrap dough and cut into ¼-in. slices. Place 2 in. apart on ungreased baking sheets. Bake at 375° for 10-12 minutes or until the edges are lightly browned. Remove to wire racks to cool. YIELD: about 5 dozen.

UTTERMILK PICE CRISPS

ARLA MASON, CEDAR RAPIDS, IOWA
hese cookies were a Christmas adition for one of the families in my ildhood church. I looked forward to roling at their house because we ere rewarded with one of these tasty orsels!

1 **cup butter, softened**
2 **cups sugar**
1 **egg**
⅓ **cup buttermilk**
⅔ **cups all-purpose flour**
2 **teaspoons baking soda**
2 **teaspoons ground cinnamon**
1 **teaspoon** *each* **ground allspice, ground cloves and ground nutmeg**

In a large mixing bowl, cream butter and sugar until light and fluffy. Beat in egg and buttermilk. Combine the flour, baking soda, cinnamon, allspice, cloves and nutmeg; gradually add to the creamed mixture. Shape into two 9-in. rolls; wrap each in plastic wrap. Refrigerate for 4 hours or until firm.

Unwrap and cut into ¼-in. slices. Place 2 in. apart on ungreased baking sheets. Bake at 350° for 10-12 minutes or until golden brown. Remove to wire racks to cool. YIELD: 6 dozen.

OUBLE BUTTERSCOTCH OOKIES

VERLY DUNCAN, BIG PRAIRIE, OHIO
e made this old-fashioned recipe for ars. It can also be made with iniature chocolate chips or coconut in ace of the toffee bits.

/2 **cup butter, softened**

DOUBLE BUTTERSCOTCH COOKIES

½ **cup shortening**
4 **cups packed brown sugar**
4 **eggs**
1 **tablespoon vanilla extract**
6 **cups all-purpose flour**
3 **teaspoons baking soda**
3 **teaspoons cream of tartar**
1 **teaspoon salt**
1 **package English toffee bits (10 ounces)** *or* **almond brickle chips (7½ ounces)**
1 **cup finely chopped pecans**

✻ In a large mixing bowl, cream the butter, shortening and brown sugar until light and fluffy. Add eggs, one at a time, beating well after each addition. Beat in vanilla. Combine the flour, baking soda, cream of tartar and salt; gradually add to the creamed mixture and mix well. Stir in toffee bits and pecans. Shape into three 14-in. rolls; wrap each in plastic wrap. Refrigerate for 4 hours or until firm.

✻ Unwrap and cut into ½-in. slices. Place 2 in. apart on greased baking sheets. Bake at 375° for 9-11 minutes or until lightly browned. Cool for 1-2 minutes before removing from pans to wire racks to cool completely. YIELD: about 7 dozen.

slicing cookie dough

Use a thin, sharp knife to slice through the dough. Cut one roll at a time, keeping additional rolls refrigerated until ready to use. After each slice, rotate the roll to avoid having one side that's flat.

LEMON TEA COOKIES

LEMON TEA COOKIES

PHYLLIS DIETZ, WESTLAND, MICHIGAN
These cookies taste rich and buttery and have a lovely lemon filling. The recipe has been in our family since the 1950s, when my mother got it from a French friend in her club. Mom always made them at Christmas, and now my sister and I do the same.

- ¾ **cup butter, softened**
- ½ **cup sugar**
- 1 **egg yolk**
- ½ **teaspoon vanilla extract**
- 2 **cups all-purpose flour**
- ¼ **cup finely chopped walnuts**

FILLING

- 3 **tablespoons butter, softened**
- 4½ **teaspoons lemon juice**
- ¾ **teaspoon grated orange peel**
- 1½ **cups confectioners' sugar**
- 2 **drops yellow food coloring, optional**

✳ In a large mixing bowl, cream butter and sugar until light and fluffy. Beat in the egg yolk and vanilla. Gradually add flour. Shape into two 14-in. rolls; reshape each roll into a 14-in. x 1⅛-in. x 1⅛-in. block.

Wrap each in plastic wrap. Refrigera[te] overnight.

✳ Unwrap and cut into ¼-in. slices. Place [ ] in. apart on ungreased baking shee[t.] Sprinkle half of the cookies with nuts, ge[n]tly pressing into dough. Bake at 400° f[or] 8-10 minutes or until golden brow[n] around the edges. Remove to wire rac[k] to cool.

✳ In a small mixing bowl, cream butte[r,] lemon juice and orange peel. Gradua[lly] add confectioners' sugar. Tint yellow if d[e]sired. Spread about 1 teaspoon on bo[t]tom of the plain cookies; place the n[ut]topped cookies over filling. YIELD: abo[ut] 4½ dozen.

ORANGE PECAN COOKIES

ELEANOR HENRY, DERRY, NEW HAMPSHIRE
This cookie is pure heaven with a glas[s] of milk. It has a subtle orange flavor and just a sprinkling of chopped pecans throughout.

- 1 **cup butter, softened**
- ½ **cup sugar**
- ½ **cup packed brown sugar**
- 1 **egg**
- 2 **tablespoons orange juice**
- 1 **tablespoon grated orange peel**
- 2½ **cups all-purpose flour**
- ½ **teaspoon baking soda**
- ½ **teaspoon salt**
- ½ **cup chopped pecans**

✳ In a mixing bowl, cream butter and su[g]ars. Beat in egg, orange juice and pe[el.] Combine flour, baking soda and sa[lt;] gradually add to creamed mixture. Stir [in] pecans. Shape dough into two 11½-i[n.] rolls; wrap in plastic wrap. Chill for 4 hou[rs] or overnight.

✳ Unwrap and cut into ¼-in. slices. Pla[ce] 2 in. apart on lightly greased bakin[g] sheets. Bake at 400° for 7-8 minutes [or] until golden brown. Remove to wire rac[k] to cool. YIELD: 6 dozen.

CHOCOLATE-DIPPED COOKIES

TASTE OF HOME TEST KITCHEN

This tender, flavorful cookie is made even better by being dipped in chocolate. The contrasting drizzle is a fancy finishing touch.

1/2 cup butter, softened
3/4 cup sugar
1 egg
1 teaspoon vanilla extract
1 cup all-purpose flour
1/3 cup baking cocoa
1/2 teaspoon baking soda
1/4 teaspoon salt
1/2 cup chopped almonds
1/2 cup miniature semisweet chocolate chips
2 ounces white candy coating, melted
2 ounces dark chocolate candy coating, melted
2 ounces milk chocolate candy coating, melted

✳ In a large mixing bowl, cream butter and sugar. Beat egg and vanilla. Combine the flour, cocoa, baking soda and salt; gradually add to the creamed mixture. Stir in almonds and chocolate chips. Cover and refrigerate for 2 hours. Divide dough in half. Shape into two 8-in. rolls; wrap each in plastic wrap. Refrigerate for 3 hours or until firm.

✳ Unwrap and cut into 1/4-in. slices. Place 2 in. apart on greased baking sheets. Bake at 350° for 8-10 minutes or until set. Remove to wire racks to cool.

✳ Dip half of the cookies in white coating; place on waxed paper. Dip remaining cookies in dark chocolate coating; place on waxed paper. Place milk chocolate coating in a resealable plastic bag; cut a small hole in one corner of the bag. Pipe designs on cookies. Let stand for 30 minutes or until set. YIELD: 4 1/2 dozen.

CHOCOLATE-DIPPED COOKIES

NEAPOLITAN COOKIES

JAN MALLO, WHITE PIGEON, MICHIGAN

My sister shared the recipe for these thin, tri-color treats several years ago. The crisp cookies are fun to eat—one section at a time or with all three in one bite.

      1 cup butter, softened
   1½ cups sugar
      1 egg
      1 teaspoon vanilla extract
   2½ cups all-purpose flour
   1½ teaspoon baking powder
     ½ teaspoon salt
     ½ teaspoon almond extract
      6 drops red liquid food coloring
     ½ cup chopped walnuts
      1 square (1 ounce) unsweetened chocolate, melted

✳ Line a 9-in. x 5-in. x 3-in. loaf pan with waxed paper; set aside. In a mixing bowl, cream butter and sugar. Beat in egg and vanilla. Combine flour, baking powder and salt; gradually add to the creamed mixture.

✳ Divide the dough into thirds. Add almo[nd] extract and food coloring to one p[or]tion; spread evenly into prepared pa[n.] Add nuts to second portion; spread eve[n]ly over first layer. Add melted chocola[te] to third portion; spread over second la[y]er. Cover with waxed paper; refrigera[te] overnight.

✳ Unwrap and cut loaf in half lengthwi[se.] Cut each portion into ⅛-in. slices. Plac[e] in. apart on ungreased baking shee[t.] Bake at 350° for 10-12 minutes or u[ntil] edges are firm. Remove to wire racks [to] cool. YIELD: 12 dozen.

CHERRY ICEBOX COOKIE[S]

PATTY COURTNEY, JONESBORO, TEXAS

The maraschino cherries add colorful flecks to these cookies.

      1 cup butter, softened
      1 cup sugar
     ¼ cup packed brown sugar
      1 egg
      1 teaspoon vanilla extract
   3¼ cups all-purpose flour
     ½ teaspoon baking soda
     ½ teaspoon ground cinnamon
     ¼ teaspoon cream of tartar
     ¼ cup maraschino cherry juice
   4½ teaspoons lemon juice
     ½ cup chopped walnuts
     ½ cup chopped maraschino cherries

✳ In a mixing bowl, cream butter and su[g]ars. Beat in egg and vanilla. Combine [dry] ingredients; gradually add to cream[ed] mixture. Add cherry and lemon juices. S[tir] in nuts and cherries. Shape into four [ ] in. rolls; wrap each in plastic wra[p.] Refrigerate for 4 hours or until firm.

✳ Unwrap and cut into ¼-in. slices. Plac[e] in. apart on ungreased baking shee[t.] Bake at 375° for 8-10 minutes or until t[he] edges begin to brown. Remove to w[ire] racks to cool. YIELD: about 6 dozen.

NEAPOLITAN COOKIES

ALMOND
ICEBOX COOKIES

ELIZABETH MONTGOMERY
TAYLORVILLE, ILLINOIS

With a roll of this cookie dough on hand, I can serve freshly-baked cookies in a snap.

- 1½ cups butter, softened
- 1 cup sugar
- 1 cup packed brown sugar
- 3 eggs
- 4 cups all-purpose flour
- 1 tablespoon ground cinnamon
- 1 teaspoon baking soda
- ½ cup finely chopped almonds
- 2 packages (2¼ ounces *each*) whole unblanched almonds

In a mixing bowl, cream butter and sugars. Add eggs, one at a time, beating well after each addition. Combine flour, cinnamon and baking soda; gradually add to the creamed mixture. Fold in chopped almonds. Shape into two 15-in. rolls; wrap each in plastic wrap. Refrigerate for 2 hours or overnight.

Unwrap and cut into ¼-in. slices. Place 2 in. apart on ungreased baking sheets; top each with a whole almond. Bake at 375° for 8-10 minutes or until edges begin to brown. Remove to wire racks to cool. YIELD: 10 dozen.

PINWHEEL COOKIES

PAULETTE MORGAN
MOORHEAD, MINNESOTA

These pretty pinwheel cookies have tempting swirly layers of orange and chocolate. I really mess up my kitchen whenever I bake a batch, but the smiles on the faces of family and friends enjoying them makes it all worthwhile.

- 1 cup butter, softened
- 1 package (3 ounces) cream cheese, softened
- 1 cup sugar
- 1 egg
- 1 tablespoon grated orange peel
- 1 teaspoon vanilla extract

PINWHEEL COOKIES

- 3½ cups all-purpose flour
- 1 teaspoon salt

FILLING

- 1 cup (6 ounces) semisweet chocolate chips
- 1 package (3 ounces) cream cheese, softened
- ½ cup confectioners' sugar
- ¼ cup orange juice

* In a mixing bowl, cream the butter, cream cheese and sugar. Add egg, orange peel and vanilla; mix well. Combine flour and salt; add to the creamed mixture and mix well. Cover and chill for 4 hours or until firm.

* Meanwhile, combine all filling ingredients in a small saucepan. Cook and stir over low heat until smooth; set aside to cool.

* On a floured surface, divide dough in half; roll each half into a 12-in. x 10-in. rectangle. Spread with filling. Carefully roll up tightly jelly-roll style and wrap in waxed paper. Chill overnight.

* Remove waxed paper; cut rolls into ¼-in. slices. Place on ungreased baking sheets. Bake at 375° for 8-10 minutes or until lightly browned. Remove to wire racks to cool. YIELD: about 8 dozen.

BEST LOVED
cookies
& BARS

CHERRY-PECAN ICEBOX COOKIES

CHERRY-PECAN ICEBOX COOKIES

BETYE DALTON, TUPELO, OKLAHOMA

During the holiday season, I keep a roll of dough for these crisp cookies in the freezer. It's nice to offer unexpected company a home-baked treat.

    1 cup butter, softened
1¼ cups sugar
    1 egg
2½ cups all-purpose flour
1½ teaspoons baking soda
⅛ teaspoon salt
    1 cup chopped pecans
¾ cup red *and/or* green candied cherries

❋ In a large mixing bowl, cream butter and sugar. Add egg; mix well. Combine the flour, baking soda and salt; add to the creamed mixture and mix well. Stir in pecans and candied cherries.

❋ Shape into four 8-in. rolls; wrap in plastic wrap. Refrigerate for at least 4 hours or until firm.

❋ Unwrap and cut into ⅛- to ¼-in. slices. Place 2 in. apart on ungreased bakir sheets. Bake at 350° for 7-8 minutes until lightly browned and edges are se Cool for 1-2 minutes before removing wire racks. YIELD: 13 dozen.

EDITOR'S NOTE: Dough may be frozen for u to 6 months. Remove from the freezer 1 hours hours before baking. Unwrap and c into ⅛- to ¼-in. slices. Place 2 in. apart ungreased baking sheets. Bake at 350° for 9 minutes or until lightly browned and edge are set. Cool for 1-2 minutes before remo ing to wire racks.

PEANUT BUTTER PINWHEELS

KANDY DICK, JUNCTION, TEXAS

Chocolate is swirled through these tasty peanut butter cookies.

½ cup shortening
½ cup creamy peanut butter
    1 cup sugar
    1 egg
    2 tablespoons milk
1¼ cups all-purpose flour
½ teaspoon baking soda

½ teaspoon salt

1 cup (6 ounces) semisweet chocolate chips

In a mixing bowl, cream shortening, peanut butter and sugar. Beat in egg and milk. Combine the flour, baking soda and salt; gradually add to the creamed mixture.

Roll out between waxed paper into a 12-in. x 10-in. rectangle. Melt chocolate chips; cool slightly. Spread over dough to within ½ in. of edges. Roll up tightly jelly-roll style, starting with a long side; wrap in plastic wrap. Refrigerate for 20-30 minutes or until easy to handle.

Unwrap dough and cut into ½-in. slices. Place 1 in. apart on greased baking sheets. Bake at 375° for 10-12 minutes or until the edges are lightly browned. Remove to wire racks to cool. YIELD: about 4 dozen.

OUBLE DELIGHTS

TH ANN STELFOX, RAYMOND, ALBERTA

ese treats are perfect for folks who e both chocolate and vanilla cookies ecause it gives them the best of both orlds! They're an appealing addition any cookie tray, and they're usually e first to disappear.

OCOLATE DOUGH

1 cup butter, softened

½ cups sugar

2 eggs

2 teaspoons vanilla extract

2 cups all-purpose flour

⅔ cup baking cocoa

¾ teaspoon baking soda

½ teaspoon salt

1 cup coarsely chopped pecans

5 squares (1 ounce *each*) white baking chocolate, cut into chunks

NILLA DOUGH

1 cup butter, softened

½ cups sugar

2 eggs

2 teaspoons vanilla extract

¾ cups all-purpose flour

2 teaspoons cream of tartar

1 teaspoon baking soda

½ teaspoon salt

1 cup coarsely chopped pecans

1 package (4 ounces) German sweet chocolate, cut into chunks

❈ For chocolate dough, in a large mixing bowl, cream butter and sugar. Beat in eggs and vanilla. Combine the flour, cocoa, baking soda and salt; gradually add to creamed mixture. Stir in pecans and white chocolate.

❈ For vanilla dough, in another large mixing bowl, cream butter and sugar. Beat in eggs and vanilla. Combine the flour, cream of tartar, baking soda and salt; gradually add to creamed mixture. Stir in pecans and German chocolate.

❈ Cover and refrigerate both doughs for 2 hours. Divide both doughs in half. Shape each portion into a 12-in. roll; wrap in plastic wrap. Refrigerate for 3 hours or until firm.

❈ Unwrap and cut each roll in half lengthwise. Place a chocolate half and vanilla half together, pressing to form a log; wrap in plastic wrap. Refrigerate for 1 hour or until the dough holds together when cut. Use a serrated knife to cut into ¼-in. slices.

❈ Place 2 in. apart on greased baking sheets. Bake at 350° for 8-10 minutes or until set. Remove to wire racks to cool. YIELD: about 15 dozen.

DOUBLE DELIGHTS

if cookies are not spreading enough...

- Add 1 to 2 tablespoons of milk or water to the remaining dough.
- Let the dough stand at room temperature before baking.
- Next time use butter, not margarine or shortening.

FRUIT 'N' NUT COOKIES

JENNIE LOFTUS, GASPORT, NEW YORK

Once after making a fruitcake, I had some fruit and nuts left over. I mixed them into a basic cookie dough along with pineapple and coconut. These soft, colorful cookies are a nice addition to a Christmas dessert tray.

- **3/4 cup butter, softened**
- **3/4 cup shortening**
- **1 1/4 cups packed brown sugar**
- **2 eggs**
- **1 teaspoon vanilla extract**
- **4 cups all-purpose flour**
- **2 teaspoons baking powder**
- **1/2 teaspoon salt**
- **1 can (8 ounces) crushed pineapple, drained**
- **1/2 cup chopped dates**
- **1/2 cup chopped red maraschino cherries**
- **1/2 cup chopped green maraschino cherries**
- **1/2 cup flaked coconut**
- **1/2 cup chopped pecans *or* walnuts**

In a large mixing bowl, cream the butt shortening and brown sugar. Add eg one at a time, beating well after each a dition. Beat in vanilla. Combine flour, ba ing powder and salt; gradually add the creamed mixture. Stir in remaini ingredients.

Shape into three 10-in. rolls; wrap ea in plastic wrap. Refrigerate for 2 hours until firm.

Unwrap and cut into 1/4-in. slices. Place in. apart on ungreased baking shee Bake at 375° for 8-10 minutes or un golden brown. Remove to wire racks cool. YIELD: 7 dozen.

FRUIT 'N' NUT COOKIES

ASPBERRY NUT PINWHEELS

ASPBERRY NUT
INWHEELS

T HABIGER, SPEARVILLE, KANSAS

won first prize in a recipe contest with
ese yummy swirl cookies a number of
ars ago. The taste of raspberries and
alnuts really comes through in each
te, and they're so much fun to make!

½ cup butter, softened

1 cup sugar

1 egg

1 teaspoon vanilla extract

2 cups all-purpose flour

1 teaspoon baking powder

¼ cup seedless raspberry jam

¾ cup finely chopped walnuts

In a large mixing bowl, cream butter and
sugar until light and fluffy. Beat in egg and
vanilla. Combine flour and baking powder; gradually add to creamed mixture
and mix well.

Roll out dough between waxed paper into a 12-in. square. Remove top piece of
waxed paper. Spread dough with jam and
sprinkle with nuts. Roll up tightly jelly-roll
style; wrap in plastic wrap. Refrigerate for
2 hours or until firm.

Unwrap dough and cut into ¼-in. slices.
Place 2 in. apart on ungreased baking
sheets. Bake at 375° for 9-12 minutes or
until edges are lightly browned. Remove
to wire racks to cool. YIELD: about 3½
dozen.

CRANBERRY SLICES

STACY DUFFY
AMERICAN DAIRY ASSOCIATION
CHICAGO, ILLINOIS

These festive cookies have flecks of
chewy cranberries and a pretty holiday
look. They're fun to share.

1 cup butter, softened

½ cup sugar

1 egg yolk

1 teaspoon vanilla extract

½ teaspoon salt

2¼ cups all-purpose flour

½ cup dried cranberries, chopped

6 tablespoons mined crystallized
ginger, optional

* In a mixing bowl, cream butter, sugar, egg
yolk, vanilla and salt until light and fluffy.
Gradually add flour. Stir in cranberries and
ginger if desired. Divide the dough in half;
form each half into a 6-in. x 3-in. x 1-in.
block. Wrap with plastic wrap and refrigerate for 3 hours or up to 2 days.

* To bake, cut the dough into ¼-in.-thick
slices; place on ungreased parchment-
lined baking sheets. Bake at 350° for
12-15 minutes or until edges are golden.
Remove to wire racks to cool. YIELD:
4 dozen.

EDITOR'S NOTE: Crystallized ginger is available in the spice section or the Oriental food
section in grocery stores.

CRANBERRY SLICES

For My Teacher

BEST LOVED
cookies
& BARS

PEPPERMINT CANDY COOKIES

PEPPERMINT CANDY COOKIES

MRS. ROBERT NELSON, DES MOINES, IOWA
The crushed peppermint candy adds a fun twist to these icebox sugar cookies.

- 1 cup shortening
- ½ cup sugar
- ½ cup packed brown sugar
- 2 eggs
- 1½ teaspoons vanilla extract
- 2¾ cups all-purpose flour
- 1 teaspoon salt
- ½ teaspoon baking soda
- ½ cup crushed peppermint candies

❋ In a mixing bowl, cream shortening and sugars. Add the eggs, one at a time, beating well after each addition. Beat in vanilla. Combine the dry ingredients; gradually add to the creamed mixture. Stir in crushed candies. Shape into a 15-in. roll; wrap in plastic wrap. Refrigerate for 4 hours or until firm.

❋ Unwrap and cut into ⅛-in. slices. Place 2 in. apart on ungreased baking sheets. Bake at 375° for 6-8 minutes or until edges begin to brown. Remove to wire racks to cool. YIELD: about 6 dozen.

SESAME COCONUT COOKIES

ROBERTA MYERS, ELWOOD, INDIANA
Even folks who normally pass on coconut treats can't resist these crisp cookies.

- 2 cups butter, softened
- 1½ cups sugar
- 1 teaspoon vanilla extract
- 3 cups all-purpose flour
- ½ teaspoon salt
- 2 cups flaked coconut
- 1 cup sesame seeds
- ½ cup finely chopped almonds

❋ In a mixing bowl, cream butter and sugar. Beat in vanilla. Combine flour and salt; gradually add to creamed mixtur[e]. Stir in the coconut, sesame seeds and [al]monds. Shape into three 10-in. rolls; wr[ap] each in plastic wrap. Refrigerate for 1 hours or until firm.

❋ Unwrap dough and cut into ¼-in. slice[s]. Place 1 in. apart on ungreased baki[ng] sheets. Bake at 300° for 25-30 minut[es] or until lightly browned. Cool for 2 m[in]utes before removing to wire racks. YIEL[D:] 10 dozen.

ICEBOX SUGAR COOKIES

LOUISE WORSHAM, KALAMAZOO, MICHIGAN
I've been making light, buttery and easily portable Icebox Sugar Cookies since I was a girl.

- 1 cup butter, softened
- 2 cups sugar
- 2 eggs
- 1 teaspoon vanilla extract
- 3½ cups all-purpose flour
- 1 teaspoon baking soda
- ½ teaspoon salt

❋ In a mixing bowl, cream butter and sugar. Beat in eggs and vanilla. Combin[e] flour, baking soda and salt; gradually ad[d] to creamed mixture.

❋ On a lightly floured surface, shape doug[h] into three 10-in.-long rolls. Tightly wra[p] each roll in waxed paper. Chill for 1 ho[ur] or until firm.

❋ Unwrap dough and cut into ⅜-in. slice[s]; place on greased baking sheets. Sprink[le] with sugar. Bake at 375° for 8-10 minut[es] or until lightly browned. Remove to wi[re] rack to cool. YIELD: about 8 dozen.

CHOCOLATE PEPPERMINT PINWHEELS

ELLEN JOHNSON, HAMPTON, VIRGINIA

My cookie-loving family is never satisfied with just one batch of these minty pinwheels, so I double the recipe each time I bake them.

- 1/2 cup shortening
- 3/4 cup sugar
- 1 egg
- 1 tablespoon milk
- 1 teaspoon peppermint extract
- 1/4 cups all-purpose flour
- 1/4 teaspoon salt
- 1/4 teaspoon baking powder
- 1 square (1 ounce) unsweetened chocolate, melted

In a mixing bowl, cream shortening and sugar. Add egg, milk and extract; mix well. Combine the flour, salt and baking powder; gradually add to creamed mixture. Divide dough in half. Add chocolate to one portion; mix well.

Roll each portion between waxed paper into a rectangle about 1/2 in. thick. Remove top sheet of waxed paper; place plain dough over chocolate dough. Roll up tightly jelly-roll style, starting with a long side. Wrap in plastic warp; refrigerate for 2 hours or until firm.

Unwrap dough and cut into 1/4-in. slices. Place 2 in. apart on greased baking sheets. Bake at 375° for 8-10 minutes or until lightly browned. Remove to wire racks to cool. YIELD: about 3 dozen.

DATE SWIRL COOKIES

DONNA GRACE, CLANCY, MONTANA

My granddaughter nicknamed my mother "Cookie Grandma" because she made wonderful cookies. Mom made these crisp and chewy cookies every Christmas.

FILLING

- 2 cups chopped dates
- 1 cup water
- 1 cup sugar
- 1 cup chopped nuts
- 2 teaspoons lemon juice

DOUGH

- 1 cup butter
- 1 cup packed brown sugar
- 1 cup sugar
- 3 eggs
- 1 teaspoon lemon extract
- 4 cups all-purpose flour
- 1 teaspoon salt
- 3/4 teaspoon baking soda

In a saucepan, combine filling ingredients. Cook over medium-low heat, stirring constantly, until mixture becomes stiff, about 15-20 minutes. Chill.

For dough, cream butter and sugars in a mixing bowl. Add eggs, one at a time, beating well after each addition. Add extract. Combine flour, salt and baking soda; gradually add to creamed mixture and mix well. Chill for at least 1 hour.

On a lightly floured surface, roll out half of the dough to a 12-in. x 9-in. rectangle, about 1/4 in. thick. Spread with half of the filling. Roll up tightly jelly-roll style, starting with the long end. Repeat with remaining dough and filling. Wrap with plastic wrap; chill overnight.

Cut rolls into 1/4-in. slices. Place 2 in. apart on greased baking sheets. Bake at 375° for 8-10 minutes or until lightly browned. Remove to wire racks to cool. YIELD: 4 dozen.

DATE SWIRL COOKIES

CHEWY ALMOND COOKIES

BETTY SPETH, VINCENNES, INDIANA
These old-fashioned cookies are often requested by my children and grandchildren. The unbaked cookie dough can be frozen (well wrapped) for up to 1 year. When ready to bake, remove from the freezer and let stand at room temperature for 15-30 minutes. Then just slice and bake.

- 3 tablespoons butter
- 1 cup packed brown sugar
- 1 egg
- ¼ teaspoon vanilla extract
- ¼ teaspoon almond extract
- 1½ cups all-purpose flour
- ¼ teaspoon baking soda
- ¼ teaspoon ground cinnamon
- ½ cup sliced almonds

❋ In a mixing bowl, beat butter and brown sugar until crumbly. Add egg and extracts; mix well. Combine flour, baking soda and cinnamon; gradually add to the creamed mixture and mix well. Shape into two 6-in. rolls; wrap each in plastic wrap. Refrigerate overnight.

❋ Unwrap and cut into ¼-in. slices. Place 2 in. apart on greased baking sheets. Sprinkle with almonds. Bake at 350° for 7-10 minutes or until lightly browned. Cool for 2-3 minutes before removing to wire racks. YIELD: 4½ dozen.

SIMPLE SUGAR COOKIES

MAXINE GUIN, BARNHART, MISSOURI
Powdered sugar takes the place of granulated sugar in this sweet standby. I received the recipe for these tasty cookies from a cook I worked with at our local school.

- 1 cup butter, softened
- 1¼ cups confectioners' sugar
- 1 egg
- 1 teaspoon vanilla extract
- 2 cups all-purpose flour
- 1 teaspoon baking soda
- 1 teaspoon cream of tartar
- ⅛ teaspoon salt

❋ In a mixing bowl, cream butter and sugar. Beat in egg and vanilla. Combine the flour, baking soda, cream of tartar and salt; gradually add to the creamed mixture. Shape into two 5-in. rolls; wrap in plastic wrap. Refrigerate for 1 hour or until firm.

❋ Unwrap and cut into ¼-in. slices. Place in. apart on ungreased baking sheet. Bake at 350° for 8-10 minutes. Remove to wire racks to cool. YIELD: 3½ dozen.

REFRIGERATOR COOKIES

DOTTIE GRAY, BARTLETT, TENNESSEE
At holiday time, I usually keep at least two rolls of this cookie dough in my freezer in case I need something special in a hurry.

- 1 cup butter, softened
- 1 cup sugar
- 2 tablespoons milk
- 1 teaspoon vanilla extract
- 2½ cups all-purpose flour
- ¾ cup chopped red and green candied cherries
- ½ cup finely chopped pecans

❋ In a mixing bowl, cream butter and sugar until fluffy. Add milk and vanilla; mix well. Add flour. Fold in the cherries and pecans. Shape dough into two 8-in. x 2-in. rolls; wrap in waxed paper and freeze.

❋ To bake, unwrap and let stand at room temperature for about 10 minutes. Cut into ¼-in. slices. Place 2 in. apart on ungreased baking sheets. Bake at 375° for 10-12 minutes or until lightly browned. Remove to wire racks to cool. YIELD: about 7 dozen.

CHEWY ALMOND COOKIES

HOLIDAY SUGAR COOKIES

HOLIDAY SUGAR COOKIES

KATIE KOZIOLEK, HARTLAND, MINNESOTA

I add a hint of lemon to these delightful sugar cookies. For make-ahead convenience, freeze the dough up to 3 months, then thaw in the fridge before baking and decorating them.

2 **cups butter, softened**

2 **cups sugar**

3 **eggs**

1 **tablespoon grated lemon peel**

2 **teaspoons vanilla extract**

6 **cups all-purpose flour**

1 **teaspoon baking soda**

FROSTING

3 **cups confectioners' sugar**

3 **tablespoons butter, melted**

¼ **cup milk**

Green food coloring

Red-hot candies

✳ In a large mixing bowl, cream butter and sugar. Add eggs, one at a time, beating well after each addition. Beat in lemon peel and vanilla. Combine flour and baking soda; gradually add to creamed mixture. Shape into three 10-in. rolls; wrap each in plastic wrap. Refrigerate for 4 hours or until firm.

✳ Unwrap and cut into ¼-in. slices. Place 2 in. apart on ungreased baking sheets. Bake at 350° for 10-15 minutes or until edges are lightly browned. Remove to wire racks.

✳ In a bowl, combine confectioners' sugar, butter, milk and food coloring; transfer to a resealable plastic bag; drizzle over cookies in the shape of a Christmas tree. Place one red-hot candy at the top of each tree. YIELD: about 9½ dozen.

if cookies are tough...

- Too much flour was worked into the dough. Add 1 or 2 tablespoons of shortening, butter or sugar to the remaining dough.

- The dough was over-handled or over-mixed. Next time, use a lighter touch when mixing.

dipping cookies in chocolate

- Melt the chocolate chips, baking chocolate or candy coating according to recipe directions. If necessary, transfer chocolate to a narrow container.

- Dip cookie partway into chocolate and scrape bottom of the cookie across the edge of the container to remove excess chocolate. Place on a baking sheet lined with waxed paper and allow to set at room temperature.

- Toward the end of the process, when the chocolate is running low, it might be necessary to spoon the chocolate over the cookies.

- If chocolate cools too much to coat the cookies properly, rewarm before finishing dipping.

CHOCOLATE COCONUT NEAPOLITANS

CHOCOLATE COCONUT NEAPOLITANS

LENA MARIE BROWNELL
ROCKLAND, MASSACHUSETTS

These yummy striped cookies with a chocolaty twist are easy and fun to make, but they do need some time in the freezer.

  1 **cup butter, softened**
1½ **cups sugar**
  1 **egg**
  1 **teaspoon vanilla extract**
2½ **cups all-purpose flour**
1½ **teaspoons baking powder**
 ½ **teaspoon salt**
  1 **teaspoon almond extract**
  4 **drops red food coloring**
 ½ **cup flaked coconut, finely chopped**
4½ **teaspoons chocolate syrup**
 ½ **cup semisweet chocolate chips**
1½ **teaspoons shortening**

❊ Line a 9-in. x 5-in. x 3-in. loaf pan with waxed paper; set aside. In a mixing bowl, cream butter and sugar. Beat in egg and vanilla. Combine the flour, baking powder and salt; gradually add to creamed mixture and mix well.

❊ Divide dough into thirds. Add almond extract and red food coloring to one portion; spread evenly into prepared pan.

Add coconut to second portion; spre[ad] evenly over first layer. Add chocola[te] syrup to third portion; spread over seco[nd] layer. Cover with foil; freeze for 4 hours [or] overnight.

❊ Unwrap loaf and cut in half lengthwis[e.] Cut each portion widthwise into ¼-i[n.] slices. Place 2 in. apart on ungreased ba[k-] ing sheets. Bake at 350° for 12-14 minut[es] or until the edges are lightly browne[d.] Remove to wire racks to cool.

❊ In a microwave, melt chocolate chips a[nd] shortening; stir until blended and smoo[th.] Dip one end of each cookie into choc[o-] late. Place on wire racks until set. YIEL[D:] 5½ dozen.

GINGER POPPY SEED COOKIES

MARY PRIESGEN, THERESA, WISCONSIN

Poppy seeds and ginger pair up nicely in these popular treats. The refrigerated dough slices easily and bakes quickly. The recipe yields 17 dozen cookies so you'll have plenty to share!

  3 **cups butter, softened**
1½ **cups sugar**
1½ **cups packed brown sugar**
  3 **eggs**
  2 **teaspoons vanilla extract**
7½ **cups all-purpose flour**
 ½ **cup poppy seeds**
  4 **teaspoons ground cinnamon**
  2 **teaspoons ground ginger**
1½ **teaspoons baking soda**
 ¾ **teaspoon salt**

❊ In a large mixing bowl, cream the butt[er] and sugars. Add the eggs and vanill[a.] Combine the remaining ingredients; ad[d] to creamed mixture. Shape into four 1[?-] in. rolls. Wrap each in plastic wra[p.] Refrigerate for 2 hours or overnight.

❊ Unwrap dough and cut into ¼-in. slice[s.] Place 2 in. apart on ungreased bakin[g] sheets. Bake at 375° for 9-11 minutes [or] until edges are golden brown. Remove t[o] wire racks to cool. YIELD: about 17 doze[n.]

HERRY
HRISTMAS SLICES

TIE KOZIOLEK, HARTLAND, MINNESOTA
u'll especially appreciate this recipe
ound the hurried holidays because
e dough can be frozen for up to 2
onths. So when planning your holiday
okie baking spree, be sure to include
ese cookies.

- 1 **cup butter, softened**
- 1 **cup confectioners' sugar**
- 1 **egg**
- 1 **teaspoon vanilla extract**
- ⁄4 **cups all-purpose flour**
- 2 **cups red and green candied cherries, halved**
- 1 **cup pecan halves**

In a mixing bowl, cream the butter and
sugar. Add egg and vanilla; beat until
fluffy. Add flour; mix well. Stir in cherries
and pecans. Chill for 1 hour.

Shape dough into three 10-in. rolls; wrap
in plastic wrap and place in a freezer
bag. Freeze up to 2 months or until ready
to bake. To bake, cut frozen rolls into
⅛-in. slices.

Place on ungreased baking sheets. Bake
at 325° for 10-12 minutes or until edges
are golden brown. Remove to wire racks
to cool. YIELD: about 11 dozen.

CHERRY CHRISTMAS SLICES

PECAN SWIRLS

PECAN SWIRLS

WANDA RASCOE, SHREVEPORT, LOUISIANA
I often recommend these attractive,
nutty spirals. Cream cheese makes the
cookies rich and tender and the sweet
filling showcases pecans.

- 2 **cups butter, softened**
- 2 **packages (8 ounces *each*) cream cheese, softened**
- 2 **teaspoons vanilla extract**
- 4 **cups all-purpose flour**
- ½ **teaspoon salt**
- 2¼ **cups finely chopped pecans**
- 1⅓ **cups sugar**

✳ In a large mixing bowl, cream butter and
cream cheese until smooth. Beat in vanilla. Combine flour and salt; gradually add
to creamed mixture. Divide into three
portions. Wrap each in plastic wrap; refrigerate for 2 hours or until dough is easy
to handle.

✳ On a lightly floured surface, roll each
portion into a 16-in. x 9-in. rectangle.
Combine pecans and sugar; sprinkle over
dough to within ½ in. of edges. Roll up
each rectangle tightly jelly-roll style, starting with a long side. Wrap in plastic wrap;
refrigerate for 2 hours.

✳ Unwrap and cut into ⅜-in. slices. Place
2 in. apart on lightly greased baking
sheets. Bake at 400° for 12-14 minutes
or until lightly browned. Remove to wire
racks to cool. YIELD: 7 dozen.

COCONUT CHOCOLATE SLICES

COCONUT CHOCOLATE SLICES

CHERI BOOTH, GERING, NEBRASKA
These crispy cookies with a chewy coconut center travel really well. I send a box to our son in the Army, and they always arrive unbroken.

- 1 package (3 ounces) cream cheese, softened
- 1/3 cup sugar
- 1 teaspoon vanilla extract
- 1 cup flaked coconut
- 1/2 cup finely chopped nuts

COOKIE DOUGH

- 6 tablespoons butter, softened
- 1 cup confectioners' sugar
- 1 egg
- 2 squares (1 ounce *each*) semisweet chocolate, melted and cooled
- 1 teaspoon vanilla extract
- 1 1/2 cups all-purpose flour
- 1/2 teaspoon baking soda
- 1/2 teaspoon salt

✳ In a small mixing bowl, beat cream cheese, sugar and vanilla until smooth. Stir in coconut and nuts. Refrigerate until easy to handle. For dough, in a mixing bowl, cream butter and confectioners' sugar. Beat in egg, chocolate and vanilla.

Combine the flour, baking soda and sa gradually add to creamed mixtu Refrigerate for 30 minutes or until easy handle.

✳ Roll dough between waxed paper int 14-in. x 4 1/2-in. rectangle. Remove t piece of waxed paper. Shape cocor filling into a 14-in. roll; place on dough in. from a long side. Roll dough arou filling and seal edges. Wrap in plas wrap. Refrigerate for 2-3 hours overnight.

✳ Unwrap and cut into 1/4-in. slices. Place in. apart on greased baking sheets. Ba at 350° for 8-10 minutes or until set. Cc for 1 minute before removing to w racks. YIELD: about 4 dozen.

CAPPUCCINO FLATS

JACQUELINE CLINE, DRUMMOND, WISCONSI
These coffee-flavored cookies are so delicious most people can't believe they're made in my own kitchen instead of a gourmet bakery!

- 1/2 cup butter, softened
- 1/2 cup shortening
- 1/2 cup sugar
- 1/2 cup packed brown sugar
- 1 tablespoon instant coffee granules
- 1 teaspoon warm water
- 1 egg
- 2 squares (1 ounce *each*) unsweetened chocolate, melted and cooled
- 2 cups all-purpose flour
- 1 teaspoon ground cinnamon
- 1/4 teaspoon salt
- 1 1/2 cups semisweet chocolate chips
- 3 tablespoons shortening

✳ In a mixing bowl, cream butter, shorte ing and sugars. Dissolve coffee in wate add to creamed mixture with egg ar melted chocolate. Mix well. Combir flour, cinnamon and salt; gradually ac to creamed mixture (dough will be stick Shape into two 6 1/2-in. rolls; wrap each plastic wrap. Refrigerate for 4 hours or u til firm.

✳ Unwrap and cut into 1/4-in. slices. Place

in. apart on ungreased baking sheets. Bake at 350° for 10-12 minutes or until firm. Remove to wire racks to cool. In a small saucepan over low heat, melt chocolate chips and shortening. Dip each cookie halfway; shake off excess. Place on waxed paper to harden. YIELD: about 4½ dozen.

TRAWBERRY-NUT INWHEEL COOKIES

TH GILLMORE, ALDEN, NEW YORK

l the "cookie monsters" I know love ese treats. I enjoy the cookies cause they're easy to roll up, cut and ke. The strawberry-walnut filling is ry tasty!

2 cup butter, softened
1 cup sugar
1 egg
1 teaspoon vanilla extract
2 cups all-purpose flour
1 teaspoon baking powder
2 cup strawberry jam
1 cup chopped walnuts

In a mixing bowl, cream butter and sugar. Add the egg and vanilla; mix well. Combine flour and baking powder; gradually add to creamed mixture.

On a lightly floured surface, roll dough into a 14-in. x 10-in. rectangle. Spread jam to within ½ in. of edges. Sprinkle nuts over jam. Roll up tightly jelly-roll style, starting with a long side. Wrap in plastic wrap; refrigerate for at least 3 hours or overnight.

Unwrap and cut into ¼-in. slices. Place 1 in. apart on greased baking sheets. Bake at 375° for 10-12 minutes or until lightly browned. Remove to wire racks to cool. YIELD: 4 dozen.

HOCOLATE CHIP CEBOX COOKIES

TTY HOLZINGER, WEST OLIVE, MICHIGAN

tting chocolate chips in these frigerator cookies make them liciously different. This treat is ways welcome at my house.

3 tablespoons butter, softened
2 tablespoons shortening
¼ cup sugar
¼ cup packed brown sugar
1 egg yolk
½ teaspoon vanilla extract
⅔ cup all-purpose flour
¼ teaspoon baking soda
¼ teaspoon salt
¼ cup miniature semisweet chocolate chips
¼ cup finely chopped pecans

✳ In a small mixing bowl, cream the butter, shortening and sugars. Beat in egg yolk and vanilla; mix well. Combine the flour, baking soda and salt; gradually add to creamed mixture and mix well. Stir in chips and pecans. Shape into a 9-in. roll; wrap in plastic wrap and refrigerate overnight.

✳ Unwrap and cut into ¼-in. slices. Place 2 in. apart on ungreased baking sheets. Bake at 375° for 8-10 minutes or until edges are golden brown. Cool for 2 minutes before removing to wire racks to cool completely. YIELD: 20 cookies.

CHOCOLATE CHIP ICEBOX COOKIES

if cookies are too brown...

- Oven temperature is too high. Check with an oven thermometer.

- Use heavy-gauge dull aluminum baking sheets. Dark baking sheets will cause the cookies to become overly browned.

BEST ⁕ LOVED

cookies & BARS

if cookies are too pale...

- Oven temperature is too low. Check with an oven thermometer.
- Use heavy-gauged dull aluminum baking sheets. Insulated baking sheets cause cookies to be pale in color.
- Next time use butter, not margarine or shortening. Or substitute 1 to 2 tablespoons corn syrup for the sugar.

HOLIDAY PINWHEEL

HOLIDAY PINWHEELS

TEJAY KUECHENMEISTER
BROOKINGS, SOUTH DAKOTA

The first time I made these pretty cookies, my husband ate the whole batch in just a few days! The fun green swirls are also great for St. Patrick's Day or any time of the year. Just change the color of the food coloring.

1 cup butter, softened
1¼ cups sugar
2 eggs
¼ cup light corn syrup
1 tablespoon vanilla extract
3 cups all-purpose flour
¾ teaspoon baking powder
½ teaspoon baking soda
½ teaspoon salt
½ teaspoon peppermint extract
Green food coloring

- In a large mixing bowl, cream butter a sugar. Add eggs, one at a time, beati well after each addition. Beat in co syrup and vanilla. Combine the flo baking powder, baking soda and sa gradually add to creamed mixture.
- Divide dough in half. To one portic add peppermint extract and food colc ing. Wrap each portion in plastic wrap; r frigerate for 2 hours or until firm.
- On a baking sheet, roll out each porti of dough between two sheets of wax paper into a 14-in. x 9-in. rectang Refrigerate for 30 minutes. Remo waxed paper. Place plain rectangle ov green rectangle. Roll up tightly jelly-r style, starting with a long side; wrap plastic wrap. Refrigerate dough for hours or until firm.
- Unwrap and cut into ¼-in. slices. Place in. apart on greased baking sheets. Ba at 350° for 8-10 minutes or until set. Cc

for 2 minutes before removing to wire racks. YIELD: 4½ dozen.

ATE NUT PINWHEELS
EDA WHITELEY, LISBON, CONNECTICUT
is is a family favorite any time, but pecially at the holidays. Sometimes freeze the dough and then bake the okies when I have time.

- 4 cups all-purpose flour
- ½ teaspoon baking soda
- 1 cup butter
- 1 cup packed brown sugar
- 1 cup sugar
- 2 eggs

TE FILLING
- 1 package (16 ounces) whole pitted dates
- ½ cup sugar
- 1 cup water
- ½ cup chopped walnuts

Sift together flour and baking soda. In a mixing bowl, cream butter and sugars. Add eggs; blend well. Add the flour mixture and beat until well mixed. Chill for 1 hour or until dough is easy to handle.

Meanwhile, for filling, place dates, sugar and water in a saucepan. Bring to a boil. Reduce heat; cook until dates are tender and most of the water has evaporated. Stir in nuts; cool.

Divide the dough into three portions. Between pieces of waxed paper, roll each portion into a 12-in. x 10-in. rectangle. Spread ⅓ of the filling over each. Roll up from one of the long sides. Wrap in plastic wrap; chill. Repeat with remaining dough and filling. Dough may be kept in the refrigerator up to 3 days. Slice dough into ⅓-in. cookies.

Place on greased baking sheets and bake at 350° for 10-12 minutes. Remove to wire racks to cool. YIELD: 9 dozen.

SPICED ALMOND COOKIES
WANDA DAILY, MILWAUKIE, OREGON
These cookies are my all-time favorite! The recipe has won ribbons at fairs and applause from family and guests alike. One of the reasons I like it is that I can make the dough and freeze it. Then, when I need another batch of cookies, I take a "log" out of the freezer, thaw it and make fresh cookies in minutes.

- 1 cup butter, softened
- ½ cup shortening
- 1 cup packed brown sugar
- 1 cup sugar
- 2 eggs
- 4 cups all-purpose flour
- 2 teaspoons ground cinnamon
- 1 teaspoon baking soda
- 1 teaspoon salt
- 1 teaspoon ground cloves
- 1 teaspoon allspice
- 1 cup slivered almonds

✻ In a mixing bowl, cream butter, shortening and sugars until light and fluffy. Add eggs and beat well. Combine dry ingredients; stir into creamed mixture along with nuts. Shape into three 9-in. x 1½-in. rolls; wrap in plastic wrap. Refrigerate for 2-3 days for spices to blend.

✻ Unwrap and cut into ¼-in. slices. Place 2 in. apart on ungreased baking sheets. Bake at 350° for 12-14 minute or until set. Remove to wire racks to cool. YIELD: 7 dozen.

SPICED ALMOND COOKIES

bars & brownies

THREE-LAYER CHOCOLATE BROWNIES
PAGE 170

HOLIDAY SHORTBREAD
PAGE 178

STRAWBERRY OATMEAL BARS
PAGE 180

secrets for successful bars & brownies

- Use butter, stick margarine (with at least 80% oil) or shortening. Whipped, tub, soft, liquid or reduced-fat products contain air and water and will produce flat, tough bars or brownies.

- Measure ingredients accurately, using appropriate measuring tools and technique.

- Avoid overmixing the batter. If it's handled too much, the gluten in the flour will be developed and the bars or brownies will not be soft.

- Use dull aluminum baking pans or glass dishes. Dark-colored pans may cause over-browning.

- Grease the pan with shortening or coat with nonstick cooking spray.

- To easily remove bars and brownies from a pan, line the bottom of the pan with foil, then grease. Add the batter and bake as directed.

THREE-LAYER CHOCOLATE BROWNIES

BILLIE HOPKINS, ENTERPRISE, OREGON
I often serve these hearty, cake-like brownies with a fork for easier eating. The oatmeal crust, fudgy filling and chocolate frosting make them a hit wherever I take them.

  1   **cup quick-cooking oats**
 ½   **cup packed brown sugar**
 ⅓   **cup all-purpose flour**
 ¼   **teaspoon baking soda**
 ¼   **teaspoon salt**
 ¼   **cup butter, melted**

FILLING

 ½   **cup butter**
  2   **squares (1 ounce *each*) semisweet chocolate**
  1   **cup sugar**
  2   **eggs, beaten**
 ¼   **cup milk**
  2   **teaspoons vanilla extract**
 ⅔   **cup all-purpose flour**
 ¼   **teaspoon baking soda**
 ¼   **teaspoon salt**

FROSTING

  3   **tablespoons butter, softened**
  1   **square (1 ounce) unsweetened chocolate, melted**
  1   **cup confectioners' sugar**
  1   **tablespoon milk**
 ¾   **teaspoon vanilla extract**

THREE-LAYER CHOCOLATE BROWNIES

✻ In a small mixing bowl, combine the fi[r]st six ingredients; beat on low speed un[til] blended. Press into a greased 9-in. squa[re] baking pan. Bake at 350° for 10 minute[s].

✻ Meanwhile, in a saucepan over low hea[t,] melt butter and chocolate. Remove fro[m] the heat; stir in sugar, eggs, milk and van[il]la. Combine flour, baking soda and sa[lt;] gradually stir into the chocolate mixtu[re] until smooth. Pour over crust.

✻ Bake 35-40 minutes longer or until the to[p] springs back when lightly touched. Co[ol] on wire rack.

✻ In a mixing bowl, combine frosting ingre[re]dients; beat until smooth. Frost cool[ed] brownies; cut into bars. YIELD: 1½ doze[n.]

JEWEL NUT BARS

JOYCE FITT, LISTOWEL, ONTARIO
These colorful bars, with the eye-catching appeal of candied cherries and the crunchy goodness of mixed nuts, are certain to become a holiday standby year after year. I get lots of compliments on the rich, chewy crust and the combination of sweet and sal[t] flavors.

 1¼   **cups all-purpose flour**
  ⅔   **cup packed brown sugar, *divided***
  ¾   **cup cold butter**
   1   **egg**
  ½   **teaspoon salt**
 1½   **cups mixed nuts**
 1½   **cups green and red candied cherries, halved**
   1   **cup (6 ounces) semisweet chocola[te] chips**

✻ In a bowl, combine flour and ⅓ cu[p] brown sugar; cut in butter until mixture r[e]sembles coarse crumbs. Press into a ligh[t]ly greased 13-in. x 9-in. x 2-in. baking pa[n.] Bake at 350° for 15 minutes.

✻ Meanwhile, in a mixing bowl, beat eg[g.] Add salt and remaining brown sugar. S[tir] in the nuts, cherries and chocolate chip[s.] Spoon evenly over crust. Bake 20 minut[es] longer. Cool on a wire rack. Cut into ba[rs.] YIELD: 3 dozen.

Y CHEESECAKE BARS

- Preheat oven for 10 to 15 minutes before baking.

- It's very important to evenly spread batter in the pan. If one corner is thinner than another, it will bake faster and be overbaked when the rest of the pan is done.

- Center the pan in the middle of the oven.

- Use a kitchen timer. Check bars when the minimum baking time has been reached, baking bars longer if needed. Follow the doneness tests given in individual recipes.

- Generally, bars and brownies should cool completely on a wire rack before being cut. However, crisp bars should be cut while still slightly warm.

OLIDAY
HEESECAKE BARS

THY DORMAN, SNOVER, MICHIGAN

hristmas officially arrives at our house
hen I make these melt-in-your mouth
ars. Red and green maraschino
erries add a jolly finish to each light
d creamy morsel.

2 cups all-purpose flour
⅔ cup packed brown sugar
⅔ cup cold butter
1 cup chopped walnuts

LING

2 packages (8 ounces *each*) cream cheese, softened
½ cup sugar
2 eggs
¼ cup milk
2 tablespoons lemon juice
1 teaspoon vanilla extract
Sliced red and green maraschino cherries, optional

❊ In a bowl, combine flour and brown sugar; cut in butter until mixture resembles coarse crumbs. Stir in walnuts. Reserve 1 cup. Press remaining crumbs onto the bottom of an ungreased 13-in. x 9-in. x 2-in. baking pan. Bake at 350° for 12 minutes.

❊ Meanwhile, in a mixing bowl, beat cream cheese and sugar until light and fluffy. Add eggs, one at a time, beating well after each addition. Beat in milk, lemon juice and vanilla; pour over crust. Sprinkle with reserved crumbs.

❊ Bake 25-30 minutes longer or until edges are lightly browned and filling is almost set. Cool in pan on a wire rack. Cut into bars. Garnish with cherries if desired. Store in the refrigerator. YIELD: 2 dozen.

HOLIDAY BROWNIES

HOLIDAY BROWNIES

ERNA MADSEN, BOTHELL, WASHINGTON

Folks always ask for this recipe whenever I make these brownies. I make batches and batches of this tasty treat before the holidays and give them as gifts.

- ½ cup butter
- 4 squares (1 ounce *each*) unsweetened chocolate
- 2 cups sugar
- 1¼ cups all-purpose flour
- 2 teaspoons ground cinnamon
- ½ teaspoon salt
- 4 eggs, beaten
- 1 teaspoon vanilla extract
- 1½ cups halved red *and/or* green candied cherries, *divided*
- 1 cup chopped walnuts

✳ In a heavy saucepan, melt butter and chocolate over low heat. Cool for 10 minutes. In a bowl, combine the sugar, flour, cinnamon and salt. Stir in the cooled chocolate mixture, eggs and vanilla until smooth. Fold in 1¼ cups cherries and the walnuts.

✳ Transfer to a greased 13-in. x 9-in. x 2-in. baking pan. Arrange remaining cherries over top. Bake at 350° for 35 minutes or until a toothpick inserted near the center comes out clean. Cool on a wire rack. Cut into bars. YIELD: 2 dozen.

SUGAR DIAMONDS

GLADYS DE BOER, CASTLEFORD, IDAHO

I don't have patience for decorating, s⟨o⟩ I look for recipes with interesting shape⟨s⟩ and textures, like this bar cookie.

- 1 cup butter, softened
- 1 cup sugar
- 1 egg, *separated*
- ½ teaspoon vanilla extract
- 2 cups all-purpose flour
- ½ teaspoon ground cinnamon

Pinch salt

- ½ cup chopped pecans

✳ In a mixing bowl, cream butter and su⟨g⟩ar. Add egg yolk and vanilla. Combi⟨ne⟩ flour, cinnamon and salt; gradually a⟨dd⟩ to creamed mixture. Spoon into a grease⟨d⟩ 15-in. x 10-in. x 1-in. baking pan.

✳ Cover dough with plastic wrap and pre⟨ss⟩ evenly into pan; remove wrap. In anoth⟨er⟩ mixing bowl, beat egg white until foam⟨y;⟩ brush over dough. Sprinkle with pecan⟨s.⟩

✳ Bake at 300° for 30 minutes. Cut int⟨o⟩ 1½-in. diamond shapes while war⟨m.⟩ YIELD: about 6 dozen.

ONE-BOWL BROWNIES

CHERYL SMITH, HART, TEXAS

With just one bowl to clean up after mixing, these brownies are no fuss.

- 1 cup butter
- 2 cups sugar
- 4 eggs
- 1 teaspoon vanilla extract
- 6 tablespoons baking cocoa
- 2 cups all-purpose flour

Pinch salt

- ½ cup chopped nuts

✳ In a mixing bowl, cream butter and su⟨g⟩ar. Beat in eggs and vanilla. Combine c⟨o⟩coa, flour and salt; stir into creamed mi⟨x⟩ture. Add nuts.

✳ Pour into a greased 13-in. x 9-in. x 2-i⟨n.⟩ baking pan. Bake at 375° for 20-25 mi⟨n⟩utes or until a toothpick inserted near th⟨e⟩ center comes out clean. Cool on a wi⟨re⟩ rack. Cut into bars. YIELD: 2½ dozen.

CARAMEL HEAVENLIES

AWN BURNS, TROY, OHIO

My mom made these dressy, sweet cookies for cookie exchanges when I was a little girl, letting me sprinkle on the almonds and coconut. They're so easy to fix that sometimes I can't wait until Christmas to make a batch.

- 12 graham crackers (4¾ inches x 2½ inches)
- 2 cups miniature marshmallows
- ¾ cup butter
- ¾ cup packed brown sugar
- 1 teaspoon ground cinnamon
- 1 teaspoon vanilla extract
- 1 cup sliced almonds
- 1 cup flaked coconut

Line a 15-in. x 10-in. x 1-in. baking pan with foil. Place graham crackers in pan; cover with marshmallows. In a saucepan over medium heat, cook and stir butter, brown sugar and cinnamon until the butter is melted and sugar is dissolved. Remove from the heat; stir in vanilla.

Spoon over the marshmallows. Sprinkle with almonds and coconut. Bake at 350° for 14-16 minutes or until browned. Cool completely. Cut into 2-in. squares, then cut each square in half to form triangles. YIELD: about 6 dozen.

CARAMEL HEAVENLIES

CHOCOLATE-DRIZZLED CHERRY BARS

CHOCOLATE-DRIZZLED CHERRY BARS

JANICE HEIKKILA, DEER CREEK, MINNESOTA

I've been making bars since I was in third grade, but these are special. I bake them for the church Christmas party every year...and folks always rave about them and ask for a copy of the recipe.

- 2 cups all-purpose flour
- 2 cups quick-cooking oats
- 1½ cups sugar
- 1¼ cups butter, softened
- 1 can (21 ounces) cherry pie filling
- 1 teaspoon almond extract
- ¼ cup semisweet chocolate chips
- ¾ teaspoon shortening

✳ In a mixing bowl, combine flour, oats, sugar and butter until crumbly. Set aside 1½ cups for topping. Press remaining crumb mixture into an ungreased 13-in. x 9-in. x 2-in. baking dish. Bake at 350° for 15-18 minutes or until edges begin to brown.

✳ In a bowl, combine pie filling and extract; carefully spread over crust. Sprinkle with reserved crumb mixture.

✳ Bake 20-25 minutes longer or until edges and topping are lightly browned. In a microwave or heavy saucepan, melt chocolate chips and shortening; stir until smooth. Drizzle over warm bars. Cool completely on a wire rack. YIELD: 3 dozen.

drizzling chocolate over bars

- Melt chocolate according to recipe directions. Transfer to a resealable plastic bag and cut a small hole in one corner. While moving the bag back and forth over the bars, gently squeeze out the melted chocolate.

- You can also put the melted chocolate in a small bowl and use a spoon or fork to drizzle it.

BEST LOVED
cookies
& BARS

storing bars & brownies

- Cover a pan of uncut brownies or bars with foil—or put the pan in a large resealable plastic bag. If made with perishable ingredients, such as cream cheese, they should be covered and refrigerated. Once the bars are cut, store them in an airtight container.

- Most bars and brownies freeze well for up to 3 months. To freeze a pan of uncut bars, place in an airtight container or resealable plastic bag. Or wrap individual bars in plastic wrap and stack in an airtight container. Thaw at room temperature before serving them.

CHOCOLATE CREAM CHEESE BROWNIES

CHOCOLATE CREAM CHEESE BROWNIES

LISA GODFREY, TEMPLE, GEORGIA

Whenever I take these to a gathering, someone will usually announce, "Lisa brought those brownies"—and everyone knows exactly which ones they are!

- 1 package (4 ounces) German sweet chocolate
- 3 tablespoons butter
- 2 eggs
- ¾ cup sugar
- ½ cup all-purpose flour
- ½ teaspoon baking powder
- ¼ teaspoon salt
- 1 teaspoon vanilla extract
- ¼ teaspoon almond extract
- ½ cup chopped nuts

FILLING
- 2 tablespoons butter, softened
- 1 package (3 ounces) cream cheese, softened
- ¼ cup sugar
- 1 egg
- 1 tablespoon all-purpose flour
- ½ teaspoon vanilla extract

❋ In a saucepan, melt chocolate and butter over low heat, stirring until smooth. Remove from the heat; set aside.

❋ In a small mixing bowl, beat the egg. Gradually add sugar, beating until thi and pale yellow. Combine the flour, ba ing powder and salt; add to egg mixtu and mix well. Stir in the extracts and r served melted chocolate. Add the nu Pour half of the batter into a greased 8-i square baking dish; set aside.

❋ For filling, in another small mixing bov beat the butter, cream cheese and sug until light and fluffy. Add the egg, flo and vanilla; mix well. Pour over batter pan. Spoon remaining batter over fillin With a knife, cut through batter to crea a marbled effect.

❋ Bake at 325° for 35-40 minutes or a toot pick inserted near the center comes o clean. Cool on a wire rack. Cut into bar Store in the refrigerator. YIELD: about dozen.

CRANBERRY NUT BARS

KAREN JAROCKI, MONTE VISTA, COLORADO

My husband's aunt sent us these bars one Christmas. The fresh cranberry flavor was such a nice change from the usual cookies. I had to have the recipe and she was gracious enough to provide it.

- ½ cup butter, softened
- ¾ cup sugar
- ¾ cup packed brown sugar
- 2 eggs
- 1 teaspoon vanilla extract
- 1½ cups all-purpose flour
- 1 teaspoon baking powder
- ½ teaspoon salt
- 1 cup chopped fresh or frozen cranberries
- ½ cup chopped walnuts

❋ In a mixing bowl, cream butter and sug ars. Add the eggs, one at a time, beatin well after each addition. Beat in vanill Combine the flour, baking powder an salt; gradually add to creamed mixture Stir in cranberries and walnuts.

❋ Spread into a greased 13-in. x 9-in. x 2 in. baking pan. Bake at 350° for 20-2 minutes or until golden brown. Cool on wire rack. Cut into bars. YIELD: 3 dozen.

LACK FOREST ROWNIES

NI REEVES, MEDICINE HAT, ALBERTA

though I enjoy sweets, other recipes ve failed me. But not this one! It's asy, and the ingredients are always on nd. Even people who don't like most weets can't pass these up.

- 4 eggs, beaten
- 2 cups sugar
- 1 cup butter, melted
- ½ teaspoons vanilla extract
- 1 teaspoon almond extract
- ⅓ cups all-purpose flour
- 1 cup baking cocoa
- 1 teaspoon baking powder
- ½ teaspoon salt
- 1 cup maraschino cherries
- ½ cup chopped nuts

NG

- 2 cups confectioners' sugar
- 6 tablespoons baking cocoa
- ¼ cup milk
- ¼ cup butter, softened
- 1 teaspoon vanilla extract
- ¼ cup chopped nuts

In a large mixing bowl, beat the eggs, sugar, butter, vanilla and almond extract. Combine the flour, cocoa, baking powder and salt; stir into egg mixture until blended. Fold in cherries and nuts.

Pour into a greased 13-in. x 9-in. x 2-in. baking pan. Bake at 350° for 35 minutes or until a toothpick inserted near the center comes out clean.

Meanwhile, for icing, in a small mixing bowl, beat the confectioners' sugar, cocoa, milk, butter and vanilla until smooth. Frost cooled brownies. Sprinkle with nuts. Cut into bars. YIELD: 3 dozen.

FRUITCAKE BARS

TERRY MERCEDE, DANBURY, CONNECTICUT

This recipe has been a family favorite for years. People who declare they won't eat fruitcake love these bars! They're so easy to make and they're colorful, too—chock-full of candied pineapple and red and green cherries.

- ¾ cup butter, softened
- 1¾ cups packed brown sugar
- 3 eggs
- 1 tablespoon vanilla extract
- 1½ cups all-purpose flour
- 3 cups coarsely chopped walnuts
- 1½ cups coarsely chopped candied pineapple
- 1¾ cups red and green candied cherries, halved
- 2 cups pitted dates, halved

❋ In a mixing bowl, cream the butter and brown sugar. Add eggs, one at a time, beating well after each. Stir in vanilla. Add flour and walnuts; mix well.

❋ Spread evenly into a greased and floured 15-in. x 10-in. x 1-in. baking pan. Sprinkle with pineapple, cherries and dates; press lightly into dough.

❋ Bake at 325° for 45-50 minutes or until lightly browned. Cool before cutting. YIELD: 8 dozen.

FRUITCAKE BARS

cutting bars into diamond shapes

With a large knife, make a diagonal cut from one corner of the pan to the opposite corner; repeat, forming an "X." Make diagonal cuts at 1-1/2-in. intervals parallel to the lines of the "X," forming a diamond pattern.

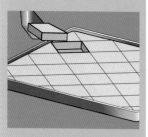

SUGARED RAISIN PEAR DIAMONDS

SUGARED RAISIN PEAR DIAMONDS

JEANNE ALLEN, RYE, COLORADO

With their tender golden crust and tempting pear and raisin filling, these fabulous bars stand out on any buffet table. Substitute apples for the pears, and you'll still get yummy results!

- 2½ cups plus 4½ teaspoons all-purpose flour, *divided*
- ¼ cup plus 6 tablespoons sugar, *divided*
- ½ teaspoon salt
- ¾ cup cold butter
- ½ teaspoon grated lemon peel
- ½ cup half-and-half cream
- 6 cups diced peeled ripe pears (about 7)
- 6 tablespoons golden raisins
- ¼ cup lemon juice
- ⅛ to ¼ teaspoon ground cinnamon
- 1 egg, lightly beaten

Additional sugar

✼ In a bowl, combine 2½ cups flour, ¼ cu[p] sugar and salt. Cut in butter and lemo[n] peel until the mixture resembles coars[e] crumbs. Gradually add cream, tossin[g] with a fork until dough forms a ball.

✼ Divide in half. Roll out one portion [of] dough onto lightly floured waxed pap[er] or pastry cloth into a 16-in. x 11½-i[n.] rectangle. Transfer to an ungreased 15-[in.] x 10-in. x 1-in. baking pan.

✼ Bake at 350° for 10-15 minutes or un[til] lightly browned. Cool on a wire rac[k.] Increase temperature to 400°.

✼ In a bowl, combine the pears, raisin[s,] lemon juice, cinnamon and remainin[g] flour and sugar. Spread over crust. Ro[ll] out remaining dough into a 16-in. x 1[?-] in. rectangle; place over filling. Trim a[nd] seal edges. Brush top with egg; sprink[le] with additional sugar.

✼ Bake for 30-34 minutes or until golde[n] brown. Cool on a wire rack. Cut into di[a-] mond-shaped bars. YIELD: about 2 doze[n.]

RISPY DATE BARS

NA SHEEHAN, SPOKANE, WASHINGTON

nake these chewy bars around the
lidays because they make a nice-size
tch for my family. Plus, they keep
ell in the refrigerator, so I can make
em when it's convenient.

- 1 cup all-purpose flour
- ½ cup packed brown sugar
- ½ cup cold butter

LLING

- 1 cup chopped dates
- ½ cup sugar
- ½ cup butter
- 1 egg, beaten
- 2 cups crisp rice cereal
- 1 cup chopped nuts
- 1 teaspoon vanilla extract

OSTING

- 1 package (3 ounces) cream cheese, softened
- 2 cups confectioners' sugar
- ½ teaspoon vanilla extract

In a bowl, combine the flour and sugar;
cut in butter until crumbly. Press into a
greased 9-in. square baking pan. Bake at
375° for 10-12 minutes or until golden
brown.

Meanwhile, in a heavy saucepan, combine
dates, sugar and butter; bring to a boil.
Reduce heat; cook and stir for 3 minutes.
Add ½ cup hot mixture to egg; return all
to pan. Bring to a boil. Remove from the
heat; stir in cereal, nuts and vanilla.
Spread over crust. Cool on a wire rack.

In a mixing bowl, combine frosting ingredients; beat until creamy. Frost cooled
bars; cut and store in the refrigerator.
YIELD: 2 dozen.

FUDGY CHERRY BROWNIES

JEANNE HARTMAN
LITTLESTOWN, PENNSYLVANIA

When I first saw this recipe in a local
newspaper years ago, I couldn't wait to
try it for our guests that very night. I
knew it was a winner from the first bite.
These rich, fudgy brownies have been
making friends merry ever since!

- 2 cups (12 ounces) semisweet chocolate chips, *divided*
- ¼ cup butter, softened
- 2 cups biscuit/baking mix
- 1 can (14 ounces) sweetened condensed milk
- 1 egg
- ½ teaspoon almond extract
- ½ cup chopped maraschino cherries
- ⅓ cup sliced almonds, toasted

✻ In a heavy saucepan or microwave, melt
1 cup chocolate chips and butter; stir until smooth. In a mixing bowl, combine biscuit mix, milk, egg and almond extract.
Stir in chocolate mixture; mix well. Fold in
cherries and remaining chocolate chips.

✻ Pour into a greased 13-in. x 9-in. x 2-in.
baking pan. Sprinkle with almonds. Bake
at 350° for 20-25 minutes or until a toothpick inserted near the center comes out
with moist crumbs and the edges pull
away from the sides. Cool on a wire rack.
Cut into bars. YIELD: 3 dozen.

FUDGY CHERRY BROWNIES

HOLIDAY SHORTBREAD

HOLIDAY SHORTBREAD

ERMA HILTPOLD, KERRVILLE, TEXAS

This special Christmas treat came to me from Scotland through a relative. I compared this recipe with one a friend makes, since her husband is of Scottish descent, and found this shortbread to be quite authentic.

- 5 **cups all-purpose flour**
- 1 **cup sugar**
- ½ **teaspoon salt**
- 2 **cups cold butter**

❅ In a large mixing bowl, combine flour, sugar and salt. Cut in butter until mixture resembles fine crumbs. Pat into an ungreased 15-in. x 10-in. x 1-in. baking pan. Prick all over with a fork.

❅ Bake at 325° for 35 minutes or until center is set. Cool for 10-15 minutes. Cut into small squares. Continue to cool to room temperature. YIELD: 5 dozen.

ORANGE BROWNIES

ROSELLA PETERS, GULL LAKE, SASKATCHEWA

Chocolate and orange go together deliciously in these moist, fudgy brownies. Pecans add crunch while orange peel sprinkled on the frosting lends the finishing touch.

- ½ **cup butter**
- ¼ **cup baking cocoa**
- 2 **eggs**
- 1 **cup sugar**
- ¾ **cup all-purpose flour**
- ½ **cup chopped pecans**
- 2 **tablespoons orange juice concentrate**
- 1 **tablespoon grated orange peel**
- ⅛ **teaspoon salt**

FROSTING

- 1½ **cups confectioners' sugar**
- 3 **tablespoons butter, softened**
- 2 **tablespoons orange juice concentrate**
- 1 **tablespoon grated orange peel, optional**

❅ In a small saucepan, melt butter. Stir in cocoa until smooth. Remove from the heat. a bowl, beat eggs until frothy. Witho stirring, add the sugar, flour, pecans, orang juice concentrate, peel and salt. Pour coc mixture over the top; mix well. Transfer a greased 8-in. square baking pan.

ORANGE BROWNIES

Bake at 350° for 28-32 minutes or until edges begin to pull away from sides of pan. Cool completely on a wire rack.

For frosting, combine confectioners' sugar, butter and orange juice concentrate; mix well. Spread over the brownies. Cut into bars; garnish with orange peel if desired. YIELD: 16 servings.

NOWY APRICOT BARS

AN MATHIS, HAYESVILLE, NORTH CAROLINA
dusting of confectioners' sugar adds the appeal of these soft and chewy ricot bars. A packaged baking mix akes them a snap to prepare.

1 package (7 ounces) dried apricots

1 cup water

/2 cups plus ⅔ cup biscuit/baking mix, *divided*

/2 cup sugar

/2 cup cold butter

2 cups packed brown sugar

4 eggs

1 cup chopped walnuts

1 teaspoon vanilla extract

nfectioners' sugar

In a saucepan, bring the apricots and water to a boil. Reduce heat; simmer, uncovered, for 10 minutes. Drain and cool. Chop apricots and set aside.

In a bowl, combine 2½ cups biscuit mix and sugar. Cut in butter until crumbly. Pat into an ungreased 15-in. x 10-in. x 1-in. baking pan. Bake at 350° for 10-12 minutes or until the edges are lightly browned. Cool on a wire rack.

In a large mixing bowl, beat brown sugar and eggs until blended. Stir in the apricots, walnuts, vanilla and remaining biscuit mix; spread over crust.

Bake 20-25 minutes longer or until golden brown. Cool on a wire rack. Cut into bars. Dust with confectioners' sugar. Store in the refrigerator. YIELD: 5 dozen.

COCONUT CRANBERRY BARS

COCONUT CRANBERRY BARS

DOLLY MCDONALD, EDMONTON, ALBERTA
I begged a neighbor for the recipe after tasting these yummy bars at a coffee she hosted. The colors make them real eye-pleasers, too!

1½ cups graham cracker crumbs (about 24 squares)

½ cup butter, melted

1½ cups vanilla *or* white chips

1½ cups dried cranberries

1 can (14 ounces) sweetened condensed milk

1 cup flaked coconut

1 cup pecan halves

❖ Combine cracker crumbs and butter; press into a greased 13-in. x 9-in. x 2-in. baking pan. In a bowl, combine the remaining ingredients; mix well. Gently spread over crust.

❖ Bake at 350° for 25-28 minutes or until edges are golden brown. Cool on a wire rack. Cut into bars. YIELD: 3 dozen.

patting a crust into a pan

Transfer the dough or crumb mixture to a greased pan and spread evenly. Press into the pan, using your fingers. Make sure to go into the corners and along the sides.

BEST★LOVED
cookies
& BARS

tips for cutting bars & brownies

- With a knife, use a gentle sawing motion. Remove the corner piece first. Then the rest will be easier to remove.

- For perfectly sized bars, lay a clean ruler on top of the bars and make cut marks with the point of a knife. Use the edge of the ruler as a cutting guide.

- For basic bars and brownies (those without soft fillings or toppings), line the pan with foil before baking. When cool, lift the foil from the pan. Trim the edges of the bars or brownies, then cut into bars, squares or diamonds. The scraps can be crumbled and used as a topping for ice cream or pudding.

- An 8-in. square pan will yield 16 (2-in.) squares or 64 (1-in.) squares. A 9-in. square pan will yield 54 (1½-in. x 1-in.) bars or 81 (1-in.) squares. A 13-in. x 9-in. x 2-in. pan will yield 78 (1½-in. x 1-in.) bars.

STRAWBERRY OATMEAL BARS

STRAWBERRY OATMEAL BARS

FLO BURTNETT, GAGE, OKLAHOMA
Their fruity filling and fluffy coconut topping make these bars truly one of a kind. They really dress up my trays of Christmas goodies.

1¼ cups all-purpose flour
1¼ cups quick-cooking oats
½ cup sugar
½ teaspoon baking powder
¼ teaspoon salt
¾ cup butter, melted
2 teaspoons vanilla extract
1 cup strawberry preserves
½ cup flaked coconut

❊ In a bowl, combine dry ingredients. Add butter and vanilla; stir until crumbly. Set aside 1 cup. Press remaining crumb mixture evenly into an ungreased 13-in. x 9-in. x 2-in. baking pan. Spread preserves over crust. Combine coconut and reserved crumb mixture; sprinkle over preserves.

❊ Bake at 350° for 25-30 minutes or until coconut is lightly browned. Cool on a wire rack. Cut into bars. YIELD: 3 dozen.

LEMON COCONUT BARS

DORIS JEAN ARMSTRONG
SANTA FE, NEW MEXICO
When I pull these bar cookies from the oven, everyone gathers to catch a citrusy whiff. The lemony filling, with its chewy coconut texture, squeezes a welcome hint of sunshine into each satisfying bite.

½ cup butter, softened
1 cup sugar
1 egg
¼ cup molasses
2¼ cups all-purpose flour
1 teaspoon cinnamon
½ teaspoon baking soda
¼ teaspoon salt

FILLING
½ cup sugar
¼ cup lemon juice
1 tablespoon grated lemon peel
1 tablespoon butter
2 eggs
⅛ teaspoon salt
1 cup flaked coconut

❊ In a mixing bowl, cream butter and sugar. Beat in egg and molasses. Combine flour, cinnamon, baking soda and salt; gradually add to creamed mixture and mix well. Refrigerate for 2 hours or overnight.

❊ For filling, in a saucepan, combine sugar, lemon juice, peel, butter, eggs and salt. Cook and stir over low heat until thickened, about 10 minutes. Remove from the heat; stir in coconut. Cool slightly; chill.

❊ Divide dough into fourths. Roll each portion into a 15-in. x 3½-in. rectangle. Spread ¼ cup filling off-center down each rectangle. Bring long edges together over filling; seal edges. Cut into 1½-in. bars; place on ungreased baking sheets.

❊ Bake at 350° for 12-15 minutes or until edges are lightly browned. Cool for 2 minutes; remove to a wire rack to cool completely. YIELD: about 3½ dozen.

IFT-WRAPPED ROWNIES

PRIS ROOTS, BIG TIMBER, MONTANA

th bright green and red frosting bbon" piped on top, these ocolaty "packages" are a pretty dition to any holiday gathering. ey'll make a sweet gift for everyone your Christmas list!

2 **cup shortening**

4 **squares (1 ounce *each*) semisweet baking chocolate**

3 **eggs**

1 **cup sugar**

2 **teaspoons vanilla extract, *divided***

2 **cup all-purpose flour**

2 **cup chopped nuts**

2 **teaspoon salt**

2 **teaspoon baking powder**

2 **cups confectioners' sugar**

4 **cup heavy whipping cream**

Red and green food coloring

✳ In a small saucepan over low heat, melt shortening and chocolate; set aside. In a mixing bowl, beat eggs, sugar and 1 teaspoon vanilla. Add the flour, nuts, salt, baking powder and chocolate mixture; mix well.

✳ Pour into a greased 8-in. square baking pan. Bake at 350° for 20-25 minutes or until a toothpick inserted near the center comes out clean. Cool on a wire rack. Cut into 2-in. x 1-in. rectangles; remove from pan.

✳ In a bowl, combine confectioners' sugar, cream and remaining vanilla; set half aside. Spread remaining frosting over top of brownies. Tint half of the reserved frosting red and half green.

✳ Cut a small hole in the corner of two plastic or pastry bags; fill one bag with red frosting and one with green. Insert pastry tip if desired. To decorate, pipe ribbon and bows on brownies or create designs of your choice. YIELD: 2½ dozen.

IFT-WRAPPED BROWNIES

ICE SKATE BROWNIES

KATHY KITTELL, LENEXA, KANSAS

Figure on these sweet treats winning lots of smiles! They're perfect for a wintertime bash, a classroom treat or any time you'd like to surprise your family.

- **16 squares (1 ounce *each*) white baking chocolate**
- **1 cup butter**
- **1 cup sugar**
- **4 eggs**
- **2 teaspoons vanilla extract**
- **1 teaspoon salt**
- **2 cups all-purpose flour**
- **2 cups (12 ounces) semisweet chocolate chips, *divided***
- **2 packages (10 to 12 ounces *each*) vanilla *or* white chips**
- **¼ cup plus ½ teaspoon shortening, *divided***
- **34 miniature candy canes**

Red and blue gel food coloring

❄ Chop half of the white baking chocolate squares. Set chopped chocolate aside.

❄ In a saucepan, combine the butter and remaining white chocolate squares. Cook and stir over low heat until melted. Stir until smooth and blended.

❄ In a mixing bowl, beat sugar and eggs until light and lemon-colored. Beat in the

melted white chocolate, vanilla and s. Stir in the flour. Fold in 1½ cups of cho late chips and reserved chopped wh chocolate.

❄ Spoon batter into a greased 15-in 10-in. x 1-in. baking pan. Bake at 35 for 25-30 minutes or until a toothpick serted near the center comes out cle Cool on a wire rack.

❄ Trace an ice skate pattern onto tracing per with pencil and cut out. Trace arou pattern onto cardboard and cut out template.

❄ Using the template and a sharp knife, out 34 skates from brownies, flipping template over as desired to cut sor skates in reverse. Place on a waxed pap lined baking sheet and freeze for 15- minutes or until set.

❄ Meanwhile, in a microwave-safe bo combine the vanilla chips and ¼ cup shortening. Microwave at 70% power 1 minute. Heat in 10- to 20-second int vals until chips are melted, stirring u smooth and blended.

❄ Using a two-pronged meat fork, dip ea brownie into melted vanilla chip mixtu Place on a waxed paper-lined baki sheet. Let stand until set.

❄ Combine the remaining chocolate ch and shortening in a microwave-safe bo Microwave on high for 1-2 minutes until melted. Stir until smooth and blen ed. Spread melted chocolate over t heel of each skate.

❄ For skate blades, use knife to trim t curved end of each candy cane. Referri to photo at left for position, use red gel pipe laces on skates. Use blue gel to p a snowflake on each. YIELD: 34 brownies

ICE SKATE BROWNIES

SPICE CAKE BARS

DENA HAYDEN, VASSAR, MICHIGAN

Whenever I went to Grandmother's, she served these flavorful bars, toppe with creamy frosting. Today, I do the same for our grandchildren, who like the little treats just as much.

- **1 cup butter, softened**
- **1 cup sugar**

1 cup molasses

1 cup hot water

1 egg

3 cups all-purpose flour

2 teaspoons ground ginger

2 teaspoons ground allspice

1 teaspoon baking soda

1 teaspoon ground cloves

OSTING

½ cup shortening

½ cup butter, softened

2 to 3 teaspoons lemon juice

4 cups confectioners' sugar

In a mixing bowl, cream butter and sugar. Beat in molasses, water and egg. Combine flour, ginger, allspice, baking soda and cloves; gradually add to the creamed mixture. Pour into a greased 15-in. x 10-in. x 1-in. baking pan.

Bake at 375° for 18-22 minutes or until a toothpick inserted near the center comes out clean. Cool on wire rack. In a mixing bowl, cream shortening, butter and lemon juice. Beat in sugar until fluffy. Frost bars. **YIELD:** about 2 dozen.

INGER
HORTBREAD WEDGES

NA HOFFMAN, HEBRON, INDIANA

h, buttery and lightly spiced with ger, this shortbread couldn't be tier. Plus, since it uses pantry ples, it's a handy last-minute gift.

½ cup butter, softened

⅓ cup sugar

1 teaspoon ground ginger

1 cup all-purpose flour

In a mixing bowl, cream the butter, sugar and ginger. Add flour; mix well (dough will be crumbly). Press dough into an ungreased 8-in. round baking pan. Using a fork, prick score lines to form eight wedges.

Bake at 325° for 32-35 minutes or until edges are golden brown. Immediately cut into wedges along score marks. Cool in pan on a wire rack. **YIELD:** 8 wedges.

FRUIT-AND-CHEESE BARS

FRUIT-AND-CHEESE BARS

TINA HAGEN, EMO, ONTARIO

One pan of these sweet, rich bars goes a long way. Colorful candied fruit makes it especially festive.

½ cup butter, softened

½ cup packed brown sugar

1 cup all-purpose flour

1 package (8 ounces) cream cheese, softened

¼ cup sugar

1 egg

1 tablespoon lemon juice

½ cup chopped mixed candied fruit

✱ In a small mixing bowl, cream butter and brown sugar. Add flour; beat until crumbly. Set aside ½ cup for topping. Press remaining crumb mixture into a greased 8-in. square baking dish. Bake at 350° for 10-12 minutes or until lightly browned.

✱ Meanwhile, in a mixing bowl, beat cream cheese and sugar until smooth. Beat in the egg and lemon juice. Stir in candied fruit. Spread over crust; sprinkle with reserved crumb mixture.

✱ Bake 18-20 minutes longer or until firm. Cool on a wire rack. Cut into bars. Store in the refrigerator. **YIELD:** about 2½ dozen.

lining a baking pan with foil

• To easily remove bars and brownies from the pan, first line it with foil. Cut a piece of foil that is larger than the pan. Turn the pan upside down and mold the foil around the bottom and sides of the pan. Remove the foil, turn the pan right side up and place the formed foil in the pan, allowing the foil to extend beyond the edges of the pan.

• Grease the foil, add the batter and bake as directed. After bars or brownies are completely cooled, simply lift the foil out of the pan.

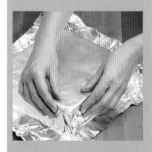

marbling batters

To give batters a marbled look, spoon one batter in a random pattern over the other batter. Cut through the batter with a knife. Be careful not to overdo it, or the two batters will blend together, and you'll lose the swirl effect.

MINT SWIRL BAR

MINT SWIRL BARS

DEBBIE DEVORE, FREMONT, NEBRASKA
My folks love these cake-like bars, so I always make them for the holidays. The chocolaty mint squares look simply scrumptious and taste even better.

- 1 **package (3 ounces) cream cheese, softened**
- ¼ **cup butter, softened**
- ¾ **cup sugar**
- 2 **eggs**
- ⅔ **cup all-purpose flour**
- ½ **teaspoon baking powder**
- ½ **teaspoon salt**
- ⅓ **cup chopped walnuts**
- 1 **square (1 ounce) semisweet chocolate, melted**
- ½ **teaspoon peppermint**
- 2 **to 3 drops green or red food coloring, optional**

GLAZE
- 1 **square (1 ounce) semisweet chocolate**
- 1 **tablespoon butter**
- 1 **cup confectioners' sugar**
- ½ **teaspoon vanilla extract**
- 2 **to 3 tablespoons boiling water**

❋ In a mixing bowl, beat cream cheese, butter and sugar. Add eggs, one at a time, beating well after each addition. Combine the flour, baking powder and salt; add creamed mixture and mix well. Trans half of the batter to another bowl; stir nuts and chocolate. Spread into a greas 9-in. square baking pan.

❋ Stir peppermint extract and food colori if desired into remaining batter. Spo over chocolate layer; cut through batt with a knife to swirl. Bake at 350° for 1 20 minutes or until a toothpick insert near the center comes out clean. Co on a wire rack.

❋ In a saucepan, melt chocolate and bu ter. Remove from the heat; stir in confe tioners' sugar, vanilla and enough wat to achieve glaze consistency. Pour ov brownies and spread evenly. Cut into ba when glaze is set. YIELD: 2 dozen.

ALMOND VENETIAN DESSERT

REVA BECKER, FARMINGTON HILLS, MICHIGA
These beautiful bars feature three colorful layers, an apricot filling and a chocolate topping.

- ½ **cup almond paste**
- ¾ **cup butter, softened**
- ½ **cup sugar**
- 2 **eggs, separated**
- ¼ **teaspoon almond extract**
- 1 **cup all-purpose flour**

⅛ teaspoon salt

5 drops green food coloring

4 drops red food coloring

⅓ cup apricot preserves

3 squares (1 ounce *each*) semisweet chocolate

Grease the bottoms of three 8-in. square baking dishes. Line with waxed paper and grease the paper; set aside.

Place almond paste in a large mixing bowl; break up with a fork. Add the butter, sugar, egg yolks and extract; beat until smooth and fluffy. Stir in flour and salt. In another mixing bowl, beat egg whites until soft peaks form. Stir a fourth of the whites into the dough, then fold in the remaining whites (dough will be stiff).

Divide dough evenly into three portions, about ⅔ cup each. Tint one portion green and one portion red; leave the remaining portion white. Spread each portion into a prepared pan. Bake at 350° for 13-15 minutes or until edges are golden brown. Immediately invert onto wire racks; remove waxed paper. Place another wire rack on top; turn over. Cool completely.

Place green layer on a large piece of plastic wrap. Spread evenly with ⅓ cup apricot preserves. Top with white layer and spread with remaining preserves. Top with red layer. Bring plastic over layers. Slide onto a baking sheet and set a cutting board on top to compress the layers. Refrigerate overnight.

In a microwave-safe bowl, melt chocolate. Remove the cutting board and unwrap dessert. Spread melted chocolate over top; let stand until set. With a sharp knife, trim edges. Cut into 2-in. x ⅝-in. bars. Store in an airtight container. YIELD: about 2 dozen.

UTTERSCOTCH ROWNIE PINWHEELS

RGINIA NICKY, BLOOMINGTON, ILLINOIS

neighbor gave the recipe for these
ch, chewy treats to my mother when I
as still in grade school, and I've been
eparing them each Christmas for
ver 30 years. The pinwheel effect
akes them extra special to share.

1 cup semisweet chocolate chips

4 tablespoons butter, *divided*

1 can (14 ounces) sweetened condensed milk

1 cup all-purpose flour

1 teaspoon vanilla extract

Confectioners' sugar

1 cup butterscotch chips

½ cup chopped walnuts

❊ Grease a 15-in. x 10-in. x 1-in. baking pan; line with waxed paper and spray the paper with nonstick cooking spray. Set aside.

❊ In a microwave or heavy saucepan, melt the chocolate chips and 2 tablespoons of butter; stir until smooth. Stir in milk, flour and vanilla; mix well. Spread into prepared pan.

❊ Bake at 325° for 8 minutes or until a toothpick inserted near the center comes out clean. Cool in pan on a wire rack for 5 minutes. Turn onto a kitchen towel dusted with confectioners' sugar. Gently peel off waxed paper. Roll up brownie in the towel, jelly-roll style, starting with a long side. Cool completely on a wire rack.

❊ Melt butterscotch chips and remaining butter. Unroll brownie; spread filling to within ½ in. of edges. Sprinkle with walnuts. Reroll; wrap in foil. Refrigerate for 2 hours or until firm. Unwrap and dust with confectioners' sugar. With a sharp thin knife, cut into ¼-in. slices. YIELD: 5 dozen.

BUTTERSCOTCH BROWNIE PINWHEELS

GENERAL RECIPE INDEX

This index lists recipes by major ingredient. For specific types of cookies, refer to individual chapters in the book.

BEST★LOVED

cookies
& BARS